THE POWER OF THE WORD

A Reading and Language Text

Evelyne S. Merrill

WINTHROP PUBLISHERS, INC.
Cambridge, Massachusetts

Library of Congress Cataloging in Publication Data

Merrill, Evelyne S.
 The power of the word.

 1. Reading (Higher education) 2. Reading (Secondary education) I. Title.
LB2395.M46   428.42   72-13795
ISBN 0-87626-685-5

Cover and Design by Joe Guertin

Illustrations by Daniel Thaxton

Copyright © 1973 by Winthrop Publishers, Inc.
 17 Dunster Street, Cambridge, Massachusetts 02138

All rights reserved. No part of this book may be reproduced in any form or by any means without permission in writing from the publisher. Printed in the United States of America. Current printing (last number): 10 9 8 7 6 5 4 3 2 1.

Contents

To the Student / viii
To the Instructor / ix

SECTION ONE
POWER THROUGH GROWTH AND ACCURACY / 1

Word Recognition Techniques / 2
ENGLISH SPELLING PATTERNS / 4
   Generalization 1: CVC Pattern
   Exercises
CVC PATTERN WITH AFFIXES / 7
   Generalization 2
   Exercises
CVC PLUS CVC / 9
   Generalization 3
   Exercises
CONTRASTING PATTERNS—*CVCe* PATTERN / 13
   Exercises
   Generalization 4
   Exercises
OTHER SPELLING PATTERNS / 17
   Exercise
   Generalization 5: CVVC Pattern
   Exercises
   Generalization 6: CVrC Pattern
   Exercises
SYLLABICATION / 22
   Exercise
   Generalization 7: CV Pattern
   Exercise
ACCENT / 25
   Exercise
THE REDUCED VOWEL / 26
   Exercise
   Generalization 8: The Reduced Vowel
   Exercises
FLEXIBILITY / 30
   Exercises
FINAL TEST / 35
   Exercises

Improving Comprehension / 37
PARAGRAPH ANALYSIS / 37
   Reading: "What Camper Fits Your Family?" / 38

—*Better Homes and Gardens*
Exercises

SECTION TWO
POWER FROM SIGNALS / 49

Affixes / 51
Prefixes / 51
    Exercises

Suffixes as Clues to Word Class and to Sentence Meaning / 55
   Noun Suffixes
    Exercises
   Verb Suffixes
    Exercises

Improving Comprehension / 64
Reading: "What You Can Do Now with Inflatable Boats"
   —*Family Weekly*
   Exercises

Punctuation / 67
Pairs of Commas / 67
Pairs of Dashes / 67
Parentheses / 68
Quotation Marks / 68
Ellipses / 68
Italics / 68
   Reading: "Craig's Message"
     —*Time, The Weekly Newsmagazine*
   Reading: "Mountain to Molehill"
     —*Time, The Weekly Newsmagazine*
   Exercise

Use of Context Clues to Increase Vocabulary / 73
Types of Context Clues / 74
Getting Word Meanings from Context / 74
   Exercises
   Reading: "The Population Bomb"
     —*Paul Ehrlich*
   Exercise

SECTION THREE
POWER THROUGH SEEING RELATIONSHIPS / 83

Sentences / 84
   Exercises
   Reading: "They Never Shout 'Mush'"
     —*Yankee*
   Exercise

Paragraphs / 90
    Exercises

SECTION FOUR
POWER THROUGH REFERENCE / 105

The Dictionary / 107
USE OF THE DICTIONARY—PRONUNCIATION / 107
    Exercise
INTERPRETATION OF DIACRITICAL MARKS / 108
    Exercises
THE DICTIONARY ENTRY / 113
    Exercises

The Newspaper / 115
THE FEATURE ARTICLE / 115
   Reading: "Butch Cassidy's Sister Tells All"
     —Charles Hillinger, L.A. Times
    Exercise
THE EDITORIAL / 118
   Reading: "Equal Rights for 18-Year-Olds
     —L.A. Times
    Exercise

The Encyclopedia / 121
   Reading: "Johnny Appleseed"
     —The World Book Encyclopedia
    Exercise
   Reading: "Stans Will Urge Timetable to Put U.S. on Metric Track"
     —Victor Cohn, The Washington Post
   Reading: "Metric System"
     —The World Book Encyclopedia
    Exercises

SECTION FIVE
THE POWER OF SUGGESTION / 129

Figurative Language / 131
ADJECTIVES THAT BORROW / 131
    Exercise
WORD CLASS SHIFTS: THE X = Y FORMULA / 132
    Exercises
   Reading: "Indy Ripe for Change"
     —Jim Murray, L.A. Times
    Exercise
TELEVISION REVIEW / 138
    Exercise

  Reading: "Van Dyke's Show Bows Tonight at 9"
   —*Aleene MacMinn, L.A. Times*
  Questions
Movie Review / 140
  Exercise
  Reading: "The Lively Arts" (Cabaret)
   —*Margaret Ronan, Senior Scholastic*
  Questions
Book Review / 143
  Exercise
  Reading: "A Hairy Mirror" (In the Shadow of Man)
   —*Time, the Weekly Newsmagazine*
  Questions

SECTION SIX
POWER THROUGH INTEGRATION / 149

Critical Reading / 151
  Exercise
  Reading: "Rodeo Cowboys Don't Take Their Hats Off to Anybody"
   —*Robert Meyers, Westways*
  Questions
  Exercise
  Reading: "Rodeos: Sport or 'Spectacles of Brutality'?"
   —*Charles Hillinger, L.A. Times*
  Reading: "Today's Rodeo: Top Cowboys are Airborne"
   —*David Lamb, L.A. Times*
  Questions
  Exercise

Study Skills / 163
  Exercise
  Reading: "Heredity and Environment"
   —*Psychology, Engle and Snellgrove*
  Questions and Exercises
The Essay Question / 184
  Exercises

Talking About Short Stories / 187
  Reading: "A Diamond Guitar"
   —*Truman Capote*
Characters / 195
  Exercise
Setting / 195
  Exercise
Plot / 196
  Exercise
Imagery / 196
  Exercises

THE TITLE / 199
　　Exercise
　　Questions for Discussion

APPENDIX A:
ANSWERS TO SELECTED EXERCISES / 201

APPENDIX B:
INSERT FOR INSTRUCTOR / 217

Appendix to Section One / 218

WORD RECOGNITION GENERALIZATIONS / 218
　　Spelling Patterns
　　Guidelines for Breaking Words into Syllables
CONSONANTS / 220

To The Student

The beginning reader learns to interpret in print what he already understands in speech. Becoming a fluent, mature reader involves developing an increasing awareness of the richness and fine shadings of meaning present in everyday speech. At the same time, it involves learning to interpret, from print, language that appears in varied forms that are often more complex than spoken English. Learning to read with ease, pleasure, and accuracy is a continuing, life-long process. It requires active, aware involvement with language. The purpose of this text is to provide that involvement, accompanied by meaningful guidance. The wide variety of reading selections taken from magazines, newspapers, and current books should offer suggestions for continuing the involvement after you have gone through the text. *The Power of the Word* was put together with great confidence in you and what you can already do. I hope that you will work through it with equal confidence in yourself and your potential.

To the Instructor

Increasing numbers of high-school students are expressing a desire to continue formal schooling, and there is undeniable evidence that language instruction needs new directions to fill the needs of many of these students. This is a mandate for all those involved in language instruction to take a hard look at traditional practices. *The Power of the Word* combines durable practices in reading and language teaching with concepts from linguistic scholarship that seem particularly relevant to students' immediate needs.

Students placed in required reading classes in secondary schools and junior colleges are often somewhat inaccurately labelled as "remedial." The progress of most of these students has been arrested because problems connected with late maturation or slow development have deprived them of instruction at an appropriate time or at a rate at which it could be assimilated. Most of these students need a *truly* developmental program that is based on various stages of growth within the individual student and that revolves around an integration of progressively refined skills. *The Power of the Word* provides continuing instruction for the older student and intervenes at points in the reading process where intuition does not give sufficient direction. The goal of this text is to help the student along the road that leads to mature, fluent reading. Becoming a fluent reader is a long process. The exercises in this text provide drills for the student who requires time to absorb new concepts, but the exercises are not repetitive of work given in the earlier school years.

The Power of the Word is comprehensive. It is designed to cover a full semester's work, and it encompasses a wide variety of skills, which range from the mechanics of word recognition and the interpretation of punctuation marks to the integrated application needed for studying a textbook and reading a short story. It builds in difficulty from front to back and within each section. After the student has worked though the text—with guidance from you and with the stimulation that arises from interaction with his fellow students—he should have acquired specific skills, increased confidence, and some basic concepts that should induce further growth with or without formal instruction.

The text is highly inductive, and students should be allowed the time necessary to make deductive conclusions. I strongly believe that reading is something we should *do*, not something we should just talk about, so there is a minimum of instructional text and a maximum of supportive and directive practice. The student must, in my opinion, be regularly involved in the reading process, but only occasionally, and often just temporarily, does the process itself need to be at the threshold of attention. Because I feel that all language skills interact, the various sections of this text are geared toward a spiraling type of growth rather than toward a mastery of any one skill.

The word recognition section is based on the spelling pattern approach advanced in Charles Fries' *Linguistics and Reading*. The terms used in this section constitute the tools for a method of learning and should not be considered absolutes. An effort has been made, however, to avoid unnecessary confusion about terminology. Labels from traditional and modern language methods have been used where they are appropriate. Energy spent in teaching or learning word recognition techniques should be directed toward improved performance rather than toward rote learning of rules or terminology. The exercises in word recognition can provide a helpful overview of the language for the student who may need only a little more confidence in his approach to pronouncing new words, or they can provide extensive drill for those who are severely handicapped.

The spelling pattern method as presented in this text is based on two strong premises. The first is that the older student, no matter how handicapped he may appear to be, is probably not a nonreader. The second is that this student has been exposed to considerable instruction in school and to extensive language experiences. He knows what looks like English and what sounds like English. The design of the entire section seeks to take advantage of latent learning by organizing previous experiences into manageable concepts.

The fact that the student *does read* accounts for a salient feature of the method. All patterns are taught from the known to the unknown. The student *listens to himself* pronounce a reference word in order to derive the needed response. This precludes any problems with differing accents or inexact descriptions of sounds. In order for a student to learn word recognition skills and not merely pronounce words from sight, he must work with unfamiliar words. The older student usually has a rather large sight vocabulary learned as his needs have dictated. Gathering unfamiliar words of the appropriate length and form to provide sufficient practice for such a student requires the use of many low-frequency words. Therefore, this material should not be viewed as vocabulary study. You must make every effort to have students say words aloud. It is doubtful if the work will serve any useful purpose if you do not. Volunteers and paraprofessionals can assist in providing encouragement and checking responses if they are properly trained. I have had considerable success with having individual students recite into a cassette recorder for the approval of the class or a small group. I have also had surprising success with entire classes reciting in unison.

The exercises on affixes (Section II) represent an attempt to use conventional subject matter to achieve different goals than those to which the teaching of affixes is most often directed. Teachers have long thought of the teaching of roots and affixes as one of the most practical aspects of reading instruction. It has been my experience, however, that students in the most formative stages learn word meanings as wholes, and that any attention to or interest in the meanings of word parts is somewhat an accessory after the fact. Furthermore, even a cursory study of etymology reveals how much historical changes in spelling and semantic driftings have obscured the contributions of word parts to word meanings except for someone who is truly interested in etymology or gifted in the analytic approach. In this text, affixes are taught as operants. Recognition of word function as discernible through affixes is one way to help the student develop a sense of syntax. Working with word variants can also be looked upon as a reinforcement to word recognition and an opportunity to provide students with a background of word forms that stem from the same roots. Facility with this form of redundancy—so common in English—will improve a student's reading ability and will contribute to his ability to speak and write as well. The exercises on sentence relationships (Section III) shift the focus from conjunctions as connectives in a somewhat weak role to the strong role they play in comprehension when they are looked upon as "structure words." Linguists have long urged greater attention to these words in reading instruction.

If the student is to become a really skillful reader, he must look upon reading as a part of his daily life—not just something he does in school. The many reading selections in the text were chosen for their relevance to the interests of the students. The sources of the selections (newspapers, magazines, and current paperback books) suggest an easy transition to additional personal reading. I hope that working with your students on the exercises I have devised for these selections will produce for you—as they did for me while they were being developed—that most exciting of situations in which both instructor and students learn.

Section One

Power Through Growth and Accuracy

Word Recognition Techniques

The purpose of studying word recognition techniques, sometimes called *phonics,* is to improve your ability to pronounce unfamiliar words. If you can already pronounce a word, it is part of your sight vocabulary and you do not need to know how it got there. A good reader is always increasing his sight vocabulary. It is possible that a word may have meaning to you even though you do not know how to pronounce it. However, inability to pronounce a word may encourage you to skip over it or to not take from the word the maximum depth of meaning. A large part of your total vocabulary—all the words you understand—comes to you through the ear, through listening. Failure to recognize, when you read, any word that has meaning for you when you hear it is to lose an opportunity to add strength to your language skills. *The Power of the Word* will give you instruction and practice that will help you to organize and add to the language skills you already have.

No matter how long or complex an English word may look, it usually can be analyzed as a series of spelling patterns. These spelling patterns are made up of one or more of the five vowel letters, "framed" by consonants.* The most common spelling patterns are described in this section of the text and the descriptions are followed by practice exercises. In describing the patterns, the symbol *C* is used for a consonant or a group of consonants, and the symbol *V* is used for *each* vowel within the frame. Thus, the formula *CVC* means consonant-vowel-consonant. A common example of this pattern is *hat*.

CVC
h a t

Making correct oral responses to consonants offers very little difficulty to most readers because the response to a consonant is usually the same in each instance. For example, once you have learned to respond to the letter *f* in one word, such as *fan,* your response to *f* will be the same in all words. Furthermore, your response becomes automatic. Some consonants, when they appear in groups of two or three, *may* call for a slight "trick of the tongue" before you can make a quick response to them. However, if you are very confident in your responses to the vowel or vowel combinations, you will soon master any consonants or combinations of consonants that bother you.

The key to the pronunciation of all the spelling patterns is the vowel. Although there are only five vowels, any change of the vowel or of the combination of vowels within the frame can produce a very different response. For example, pronounce these two groups of words:

bit, bat, bet
bat, boat, bout

If you pronounced these words correctly, you are responding to the spelling pattern principle rapidly and automatically. It is easy to see that the only difference in the six words is the vowel: the consonant frame is the same for all. Now pronounce these words:

gat, groat, grout

---

* The vowels are *a, e, i, o,* and *u*. When *y* is used like *i,* it is considered a vowel (*sin; syntax*). *W* is sometimes used like *u* and is then considered a vowel (*out; cow*).

Did you respond to each of these words as rapidly as you did to those in the first group? You should have. Response to the spelling pattern principle should be automatic. If you hesitated in giving a response to these words, you may be relying on sight techniques or you may not have had enough practice in recognizing slight differences within the same pattern to produce high-speed responses.

Your mind has many other things to do while reading besides responding to words. These other things have a great deal more to do with the actual task of reading. Therefore, quick and automatic responses to spelling patterns—which means quick and accurate responses to an ever-increasing number of words—is an important skill in reading, even though it is *not* reading.

The spelling pattern principle applies to a large percentage of one-syllable words and to parts of thousands of multisyllable words. Of course, there are words and parts of words for which it does not apply, but your mind has other ways of supplying you with needed responses and will "key punch" another method when you need it.

The method used in this text is to present a generalization and a list of reference words (known words) for each response you are learning. Since the approach focuses on response to vowels, you should first determine the pattern of the word you are to pronounce, then concentrate on pronouncing the vowel in the new word in the same way that *you* pronounce the vowel in the reference word. By learning a reference word for each vowel or vowel team in each pattern and listening to your own pronunciation of reference words you can always keep your method with you and not hidden in a textbook. This method also avoids any confusion that might arise from the different pronunciations given to words or to English spelling patterns in different parts of the country. If you learned the response by listening to someone else pronounce a reference word, you might not be able to imitate his response because it would be unnatural for you to do so. Or you would be giving a response that would be unlike the response you give to other words of the same pattern.

Assume that the word *tamp* is an unfamiliar word. It represents the *CVC* pattern. Note that its single vowel *a* is framed by consonants and that *mp* is considered to be one consonant because *mp* is a frequently seen team of final consonants in English words. The reference word is *hat*. Say it to yourself. Transfer the response you hear yourself giving the vowel *a* in hat to the new word *tamp,* framing the vowel sound with the natural responses to *t* and *mp*. If English is not your native language, or if you have difficulty responding to some consonant teams, you may want to refer to the list of common consonant teams that call for unexpected responses (page 206) before you do Exercise 1.

If you can become very confident in giving the correct response to all vowels and vowel teams, you should soon be able to conquer any difficulty you may have with consonants. In order to develop this confidence, you must

DETERMINE THE SPELLING PATTERN
MEMORIZE REFERENCE WORDS
PRONOUNCE ALL WORDS IN EXERCISES
LISTEN TO YOURSELF.

All the patterns and generalizations you will work with are grouped, for reference and review, in the Appendix to Section I on page 218. In addition, each generalization is presented individually in the text with plenty of opportunity for practice. Generalizations are given in a sequence designed to give you insight into the construction of English words.

English Spelling Patterns

GENERALIZATION 1

CVC Pattern

The most common spelling pattern in the English language consists of consonant-vowel-consonant. This pattern is found in hundreds of one-syllable words and is a part of hundreds more multisyllable words. In all patterns the symbol *C* is considered to be a consonant whether it is a single consonant or two or more consonants pronounced together. In this pattern the vowel is pronounced as you say it in the following words:*

REFERENCE WORDS

a as in *hat* and in *flat*
e as in *bed* and in *trench*
i as in *sit* and in *skin*
o as in *hot* and in *shot*
u as in *jump* and in *brush*

EXERCISE 1A

The words listed are examples of the *CVC* pattern. In the table that follows, classify the words according to the vowels between the consonant frames, writing each word in the columns provided. After your lists are complete, pronounce each word to yourself, using your own pronunciation of the reference words as guides. If your classroom has a tape recorder, record the words on tape for a classmate to check. Do not concern yourself with word meanings. Your objective in this section is to learn to make quick oral responses to common spelling patterns.

ban	snob	glint
rev	trek	hunch
lax	clad	clan
hex	bronc	filch
sod	glum	smug
zest	crunch	glib
hasp	gild	prod
smut	spat	glen
flex	belch	winch
rasp	stomp	wend
brisk	grim	gland
sprint	flick	hemp
stint	slab	geld
clod	broth	bilk
slit	cob	cult
snub	slat	strut

* *r* following a vowel puts a word into another pattern.

Supply Reference Words

a	e	i	o	u
ban	rev			

EXAMPLES:

Test your skill:
Pronounce these "funny" words as rapidly as you can.

flimflam   chitchat   mishmash
humdrum   bric-a-brac clip clop

EXERCISE 1B   For extra drill, write these words in columns according to the vowel. Pronounce them to yourself.

rift	whiff	whet	chimp	blimp	shunt	primp
spat	posh	flog	floss	quip*	simp	grog
fret	waft	nib	scum	writ	scamp	scalp
cult	drench	stench	glut	kelp	thrush	weft

Supply Reference Words

a	e	i	o	u
spat	fret			

EXAMPLES:

* Consider *u* a consonant when it follows *q*.

EXERCISE 2

In order to make accurate oral responses to spelling patterns, you must be a good listener. By listening you can train yourself to hear fine differences in sounds. By listening to yourself you can check whether you are producing the response to a spelling pattern that the letters are signaling you to produce. In this exercise you are asked to spell words containing the *CVC* pattern. Listen very carefully to your instructor as the words are pronounced. When your instructor spells the words for you, place a ✔ after those in which you have made an error. This will help you to diagnose any sound that you cannot match with a vowel. Use the *CVC* pattern only—not some other unusual spelling pattern you may be familiar with. In some instances you may not be able to tell whether to use *c* or *k*.*

A. 1. _____   6. _____
   2. _____   7. _____
   3. _____   8. _____
   4. _____   9. _____
   5. _____ 10. _____

B. 1. _____   6. _____
   2. _____   7. _____
   3. _____   8. _____
   4. _____   9. _____
   5. _____ 10. _____

C. 1. _____   6. _____
   2. _____   7. _____
   3. _____   8. _____
   4. _____   9. _____
   5. _____ 10. _____

Group D illustrates one of the ways in which English words are built—with the use of prefixes. Numbers 5 and 10 are built by combining common prefixes *and* suffixes with the *CVC* pattern.

D. 1. _____   6. _____
   2. _____   7. _____
   3. _____   8. _____
   4. _____   9. _____
   5. _____ 10. _____

* *Note to Instructor:* Spelling words are in Appendix B.

CVC Pattern with Affixes

English is a rich language because it contains so many words. However, a few spelling patterns appear again and again at the beginning and at the end of words. You see these spelling patterns so frequently that your response to them is automatic. Therefore, response to words of more than one syllable is often just as easy as response to words of one syllable. You merely detach the common beginning or ending spelling pattern and focus on the rest of the word. These introductory and final spelling patterns often carry meaning and are known as *prefixes* (beginnings) and *suffixes* (endings), or *affixes* (both beginnings and endings). Studying their meanings can be very interesting, but the goal here is to learn how to use them as an aid to quick recognition of words of more than one syllable. Listed below are some common beginning and ending spelling patterns. (There are actually many more than those listed.)

Common Affixes

Beginning Spelling Patterns (Prefixes)		*Final Spelling Patterns (Suffixes)*	
in	inspect	tion	fraction
re	regret	er	faster
dis	dismiss	et	rocket
con	consent	y	funny
de	defend	ly	badly

GENERALIZATION 2

A *syllable* is a part of a word that can be pronounced; it must contain a vowel. Prefixes and suffixes are usually considered separate syllables and do not affect the manner in which a word is divided for pronunciation.

EXAMPLE:

	prefix	*CVC*
inspect	in	spect

EXERCISE 3A

Dictionaries separate double consonants because their concern in dividing a word into syllables is to provide a standard code for use in writing and printing. For accurate pronunciation, keep double consonants together. Dividing a word in this way shows that only one consonant is pronounced and serves to clearly define the affix. In the following words the part of the word that remains after the affix has been taken away represents the *CVC* pattern. Break each word into syllables for the purpose of pronunciation by separating the affix from the rest of the word. Pronounce each word.

EXAMPLE:
struggle   strugg le

faction	_____	rebuff	_____
revamp	_____	distaff	_____
convex	_____	dabble	_____
skinny	_____	dispatch	_____
dispel	_____	fraction	_____
pesky	_____	concoct	_____
gusset	_____	pallet	_____
crafty	_____	rebut	_____
unrest	_____	traction	_____
lofty	_____	shudder	_____
recant	_____	infest	_____
deftly	_____	deflect	_____
decamp	_____	buffet	_____
billet	_____	grapple	_____
pellet	_____	swelter	_____

EXERCISE 3B Additional Practice

induct	_____	canter	_____
nugget	_____	sprocket	_____
prattle	_____	regress	_____
moppet	_____	disrupt	_____
fettle	_____	raptly	_____
roster	_____	sprinter	_____
influx	_____	skinny	_____
splinter	_____	soggy	_____
goggle	_____	rudder	_____
nifty	_____	mallet	_____

Three-syllable words

induction	_____	refraction	_____
inception	_____	deflection	_____
defender	_____	contender	_____

CVC plus CVC

The parts, or syllables, of words are easily seen when prefixes and suffixes are separated from the base, or root, of the word. Other words of more than one syllable can be broken into parts for the purposes of pronunciation by dividing them between two consonants that are not pronounced together. Each part, of course, must contain a vowel, because it is the vowel that makes the group of letters a unit that can be pronounced. Dividing words into syllables makes the spelling patterns of each syllable clear and is a strong guide to pronunciation.

GENERALIZATION 3

When two separately sounded consonants appear between two sounded vowels, words are usually divided between the consonants for the purposes of pronunciation.

EXAMPLE:

	CVC	*CVC*
mascot	mas	cot

EXERCISE 4   Each of the syllables in the words listed below represents the *CVC* pattern. Underline the first syllable of each word by applying the principle in Generalization 3. Pronounce each word and read the sentences aloud. "Attacking" a word is the most difficult step in word recognition. If you are able to pronounce the first syllable, you will probably have little trouble with the second.

In this exercise you may notice that you tend to pronounce some of the second syllables a little less loudly than the first syllables. This is a rhythm in English words that seems natural to native speakers. When you are working at building accuracy in your word recognition skills, you should not be particularly concerned about this rhythm, or stress—it will tend to emerge when words are put into sentences and the meaning is clear. Further attention is given to rhythm (accent or stress) later in this section and in the dictionary unit in Section IV.

1. gambit
2. tandem — A tandem is a bicycle built for two.
3. frantic
4. rancid — Butter gets rancid when it is not kept cold.
5. vandal

6. drastic
7. random — The speaker selected five people at random and asked them the same question.
8. transit
9. candid — A candid remark is a truthful remark.
10. bedlam

11. pundit
12. transom — He got out of the room by crawling through a transom.
13. pontiff
14. weskit — A weskit is a vest.
15. damsel

16. caftan
17. scalpel — No one wants to submit to the doctor's scalpel.
18. bodkin
19. dictum — Most people respect the dictum of the law.
20. strumpet

21. gremlin — Every family needs a gremlin on whom to place the blame for misplaced articles.
22. pectin — Some fruits contain more natural pectin than others.
23. tendril — She nervously wound a tendril of hair around her finger.
24. tranquil — The sky was tranquil after the storm.
25. gambrel — The building has a gambrel roof.

26. bombast — The speechmaking proceeded with bombast and ceremony.
27. cryptic — His answer was short and cryptic.
28. skeptic — She questions everything. She is a real skeptic.
29. nostalgic — Some people are nostalgic about their childhood.
30. incumbent — It is difficult to defeat an incumbent in an election.

Can you respond to the *CVC* pattern when it is incomplete? Look at this list of common words and say them to yourself.

> ant
> end
> ill
> off
> up

These words represent the *CVC* pattern in incomplete form (¢*VC*). The response to the vowel is the same as when the pattern is complete. Now pronounce these two-syllable words that begin with the incomplete *CVC* pattern.

> <u>a</u>dder
> <u>e</u>nvy
> <u>i</u>nner
> <u>O</u>scar
> <u>u</u>ltra

EXERCISE 5 This exercise gives you practice in "attacking" a syllable beginning with a vowel (*CVC* pattern). Pronounce all of the following words. Record the number of syllables in each word. If any word has more than one syllable, separate it into syllables in the space provided.

	Word	Number of Syllables	Syllables
EXAMPLES:	ebb	1	ebb
	antics	2	an tics
	apt		
	ethnic		
	amble		
	Ibsen		
	emblem		
	ilk		
	anvil		
	ingot		
	ascot		
	aspic		
	ostrich		
	inept		
	opt		
	addle		
	imp		
	ample		
	Islam		
	Aztec		
	aspect		
	isthmus		
	epsom		
	Aspen		
	optic		
	umbel		
	Ops		
	preempt		

Contrasting Patterns—CVCe Pattern

By now you should be making automatic responses to the *CVC* spelling pattern. However, you probably are aware that the vowels often seem to call for responses that are quite different from those you have learned for the *CVC* pattern. This is because contrasting spelling patterns call for contrasting responses. Pronounce the following words, which you probably know, and take note of your responses to each vowel between the consonants.

a	*e*	*i*	*o*	*u*
bat	pet	tin	cop	cup
back	deck	tick	clock	cluck
bake	Pete	fine	Coke	cube

EXERCISE 6A

Use the groups of words above as reference words for spelling patterns. Be sure that your responses to the vowels match the responses you gave to the reference words that have similar spelling patterns. Pronounce the following groups of words.

tin	hop	slim	slat
tick	hock	slick	slack
tine	hope	slime	slate
dub	clop	spat	strip
duck	cloth	spatter	strict
dude	cope	spate	stripe
stop	met	shod	strap
stock	mecca	shock	straddle
stoke	mete	shone	strafe
rub	trod	snip	ban
ruff	throttle	snicker	banner
rube	strode	snide	bane
thrip	scuff	chip	slit
thriller	scuffle	chick	slither
thrive	in*trude*	chide	site
throb	mutt	shred	grit
throttle	mutter	heckle	grist
strobe	mute	re*plete*	gripe

If you pronounced these words correctly, you have started to generalize independently about spelling patterns and the responses they call for. Can you put into words what you have done in pronouncing the above sets of words? Try to explain to yourself why you gave a different response to the vowel in the first two words in each list than you gave to the vowel in the third word.

EXERCISE 6B

Additional Drill

bad	mit	staff	spat
badger	mitten	staffed	spatter
bade	mite	stave	spate

bod	fill	razz	rot
boggle	filter	rash	rotten
bode	file	raze	rote
spill	dub	din	stock
sprint	duffle	dimple	sprocket
sprite	dupe	dine	stoke
muss	rub	bid	brim
muster	rudder	bicker	brink
muse	rude	bide	brine
Bal	trick	enmesh	disbud
ballot	trickle	deflect	rebuttal
bale	trite	delete	rebuke
glib	thrift	smit	ken
glitter	thicket	smitten	cent
glide	thrive	smite	cede

GENERALIZATION 4

When the *CVC* pattern is followed by an *e* (*CVCe*), the vowel between the consonants is given the sound that the letter is given when spoken alone—as in reciting the alphabet.

EXAMPLES:

a as in *blame*
e as in *Pete*
i as in *ride*
o as in *stone*
u as in *cube* or *rude*

In order to respond properly to verbs of the *CVC* pattern and the *CVCe* pattern, you should become familiar with changes in spelling that take place when endings are added. Note what happens when endings are added to these verbs.

knot She *knotted* the rigging with great care.
I am *knotting* this rope every three inches to provide extra strength.

file The student *filed* the instructions for writing his term paper but couldn't remember where he *filed* them.
I am *filing* all my history notes under the heading "Civilization."

outline I am *outlining* the chapters in my history book.

EXERCISE 7A

After observing what has happened in the italicized words above, supply the missing words in the following sentences.

1. Verbs spelled according to the *CVC* pattern with a single concluding consonant _____ the final consonant when adding a verb ending.
2. Verbs spelled according to the *CVCe* pattern _____ the final *e* when adding an ending.

EXERCISE 7B Add to the following words the endings that are indicated above the columns. Pronounce the words first alone and then with the endings you have added.

	ed	*ing*
1. mop	_____	_____
2. mope	_____	_____
3. gap	_____	_____
4. gape	_____	_____
5. lop	_____	_____
6. lope	_____	_____
7. strip	_____	_____
8. stripe	_____	_____
9. plan	_____	_____
10. plane	_____	_____

EXERCISE 7C In the blanks write the word in parenthesis as it would be spelled with the addition of the ending provided. Read each sentence aloud. The correct pronunciation of the word you have written in the blank should be clear if you first say to yourself the word to which you added the ending.

Ending	New Word	
ing	_____	1. The pet fox is (*thrive*) on a diet of baby food and raw meat.
ing	_____	2. Students enrolled in sociology classes are (*plan*) field trips to all public agencies whose activities have anything to do with juveniles.
ed	_____	3. Scores of motorcycles (*glut*) all traffic lanes, making any normal flow of traffic impossible.
ing	_____	4. Interest in handmade accessories tends to be (*wane*) in favor of the more conventional machine-made articles.
ed	_____	5. In reading textbooks there is a danger of getting (*bog*) down in details without ever realizing the overall principles to which those details are related.
ing	_____	6. The candidate was still (*chafe*) at the personal remarks made by his opponents.
ed	_____	7. The Model T (*chug*) along as if it had just come off the assembly line.

ing	_____	8. The military is (*phase*) out many of the regulations that create sharp social divisions between officers and enlisted men.
ed	_____	9. The officers (*chastise*) the motorist unmercifully for not stopping at the stop sign, but he did not issue a citation.
ing	_____	10. The cover can be removed by (*grip*) the handles tightly while holding the box firmly with your knee.
ed	_____	11. The strip of land (*jut*) into the sea like a crooked finger.
ing	_____	12. (*Gripe*) is unconstructive; that is, it accomplishes nothing.
ed	_____	13. The child (*chafe*) at the reprimand, but it was apparent that he realized he was guilty of wrongdoing.
ing	_____	14. Some people are always (*connive*) to get out of work rather than applying themselves to doing the work.
ed	_____	15. Many cities on the coast are (*fog*) in for many months during the summer.
ed	_____	16. The directions for using the machine were (*tape*) to the inside of the carrying case.
ing	_____	17. Constant (*snipe*) from windows and parked cars made any exploration of the area dangerous.
ing	_____	18. The (*mat*) used for the picture brought out its deeper tones.
ing	_____	19. A regular (*tap*) of the suspect's foot was his only indication of nervousness.
ed	_____	20. The comedian's career (*span*) three generations.

Other Spelling Patterns

By now you are probably looking at unfamiliar words very carefully and you know that the key to unlocking pronunciation is the vowel. You should now be ready to handle more complex patterns. In the *CVVC* pattern, teams of *two* vowels give us *one* sound. You can remember this sound by thinking of a word you already know that has the same vowel team.

EXERCISE 8

Pronounce the words in the right-hand column after pronouncing the reference word of the same number in the left-hand column. Try to fix in your mind the sound each vowel team represents. Memorize the reference word for *each* vowel team.

Reference Words	New Words
1. coat	1. shoat
2. rain	2. staid
3. play*	3. bray
4. meat	4. bleat
5. boy*	5. ploy
6. boil	6. roil
7. house	7. flout
8. caught	8. taut
9. saw*	9. spawn
10. cow*	10. renown

Pronounce the pairs of words again. Think to yourself the sound each vowel team represents. Use this page as a reference page when you come to Exercise 9, where you will be asked to handle several patterns at one time.

GENERALIZATION 5

CVVC Pattern
When two vowels appear together framed by two consonants (*CVVC*), they usually have the sounds that you give to the teams when you say the words listed below.
EXAMPLES:

ea	as in	*team*	*ow*	as in	*cow*†
oa	as in	*boat*	*oi*	as in	*boil*
ai	as in	*wait*	*oy*	as in	*boy*†
ay	as in	*stay*†	*au*	as in	*fraud*
ou	as in	*house*	*aw*	as in	*crawl*

* Sometimes a pattern will be incomplete—*CVV* instead of *CVVC*—but the sound of the vowel team remains the same.

† Sometimes a pattern will be incomplete—*CVV* instead of *CVVC*—but the sound of the vowel team is the same.

EXERCISE 9

Can you respond to many spelling patterns in words of more than one syllable? Words of more than one syllable can be very easy to pronounce because often you can focus only on one syllable where you see a common spelling pattern. Other syllables may be common affixes to which you already respond automatically.

EXAMPLES:

Reference Words	New Words
boy	employ
house	devout
rain	refrain

Try these pairs of words. Hold in your mind the sound each vowel or vowel team represents.

1. meat	1. squeam(ish)	squeamish
2. coat	2. oaf(ish)	oafish
3. rain	3. (con)straint	constraint
4. tray	4. (de)fray	defray
5. house	5. oust(er)	ouster
6. boy	6. (de)ploy	deploy
7. boil	7. (de)void	devoid
8. taught	8. auc(tion)	auction
9. Pete	9. (re)plete	replete
10. wise	10. (sur)mise	surmise
11. use	11. (be)muse	bemuse
12. mine	12. (de)cline	decline
13. neck	13. (in)vect(ive)	invective
14. sick	14. (con)vic(tion)	conviction
15. out	15. vouch(er)	voucher

One letter, the letter *r*, can spoil an almost perfect "case." Listen to these common words: farm, term, girl, form, fur. These words are good examples of the way the vowels are usually pronounced when followed by *r*.

EXERCISE 10A

Pronounce the reference word before pronouncing the new word. Listen to your responses carefully.

	Reference Words	New Words	
	farm	churl	smirk
	term	serf	pert
	girl	snarl	shard
ar	form	gird	burl
er	fur	murky	irk
ir		berm	smirch
or		snort	shorn
ur		blurt	firth

18

EXERCISE 10B FILL IN THE BLANKS:

1. __r__, __r__, and __r__, are pronounced the same.
2. The response to __r__, __r__, and __r__ is the same sound heard in the word _____. (*Supply word not already on this page.*)

GENERALIZATION 6

CVrC Pattern

A vowel followed by *r* usually has a different sound than when it is followed by any other letter. The following words illustrate the most common sounds for each vowel in the *CVrC* pattern.

EXAMPLES:

ar as in *car**
er as in *term*
ir as in *bird*
or as in *Ford*
ur as in *curl*

* Although this pattern often may not have another consonant following *r*, as in *car* and *for*, it remains a *CVrC* pattern. The important thing to remember is that the *r* affects the response given to the vowel. The initial or final consonant may also be omitted in syllables of words of more than one syllable.

EXAMPLE:

	₡Vr₡	CVr₡
armor	ar	mor

EXERCISE 11A Can your "computer" mind "sort" the spelling patterns rapidly? Classify each word in the following list by spelling patterns and vowel teams as shown by the examples in the chart below. Consider *u* a consonant when it follows *q*. If the word has more than one syllable, classify it according to the underlined syllable. After you have written the words in columns, pronounce them to yourself.

maim	cau<u>l</u>dron	probe	quirk	chess	con<u>cise</u>
mime	bland	plau<u>d</u>it	taint	ream	blurb
frond	gloat	drone	flaunt	<u>mar</u>vel	grist
brunt	<u>scur</u>vy	flout	<u>rai</u>ment	girth	ingrate
prawn	re<u>coil</u>	de<u>lete</u>	quoit	blithe	mirth
frenzy	shoat	crux	<u>tren</u>chant	gird	<u>floun</u>der
churl	de<u>void</u>	dint	<u>sor</u>did	wreak	trite
rife	yawl	<u>der</u>vish	bleak	croze	glut
prod	spate	smirk	<u>dor</u>sal	grail	scribe
strafe	foil	sloyd	<u>fur</u>bish	shoal	shorn
re<u>cede</u>	taunt	smite	bloat	shroud	fraud
wrath	gist	trump	grid	thane	scowl
<u>throm</u>bus	tithe	goad	wren	carp	un<u>daun</u>ted

EXAMPLES

CVC	CVCe	CVVC oa ea ai oi oy	CVVC ou ow au aw	CVrC
frond	mime	maim	prawn	churl

20

EXERCISE 11B   Additional Drill

wren	groil	clout	girth	wen	morph
lout	tarp	morsel	raucus	brackish	awl
vibe	chide	laud	grog	whelp	thrip
bard	plait	refute	grope	snipe	refurbish
tram	slurp	dram	bleat	knack	
groin	blimp	stench	grim	gnome	
shay	jibe	Crete	kelp	hurly-burly	

CVC	CVCe	CVVC	CVVC	CVrC
		oa ea ai	ou ow	
		oi oy	au aw	

In the *CVVC* pattern there are some vowel teams other than those presented in the preceding exercises. You might like to generalize about these vowel teams: recognizing them will mean you may apply the spelling pattern technique to a higher percentage of word parts. As you become more skillful, more and more words will become part of your sight vocabulary; that is, recognition will be so fast that you will no longer be aware of seeing individual letters. The fluent reader, however, continues to have the need to bring to the surface the ability to see words in meaningful parts and to apply the spelling pattern technique whenever he sees an unfamiliar word.

EXERCISE 12   List five examples of words containing the vowel teams given below. Make your own generalizations about the responses these vowel teams call for and watch for words or word parts containing these teams in your reading.

ee	*oo*	*ue*	*eu* or *ew*	*ui*
EXAMPLES:				
feel	fool	blue	grew	fruit
1. ___	___	___	___	___
2. ___	___	___	___	___
3. ___	___	___	___	___
4. ___	___	___	___	___
5. ___	___	___	___	___

Syllabication

By now you should be making high-speed responses to several spelling patterns. You can respond to these patterns when they appear in words of one syllable and in words of more than one syllable. Up to this point the words of more than one syllable in the exercises have been made up of two syllables representing the same spelling pattern (hec tic—*CVC CVC*) or one spelling pattern plus an affix (dis pute—*CVCe*). More practice is all that you need to respond with confidence to many spelling patterns in a variety of combinations.

EXERCISE 13

Using the guidelines for breaking words into syllables (Generalizations 2 and 3), break the following words into syllables. Determine the patterns you see in each syllable of every word before you pronounce it. Listen to yourself carefully and record the number of syllables in each word.

	Word	Syllables		Number of Syllables
EXAMPLES:	rampage	*CVC* ram	*CVCe* page	2
	rebuke	*affix* re	*CVCe* buke	2
1.	confiscate			
2.	turgid			
3.	stampede			
4.	imbibe			
5.	spectrum			
6.	urban			
8.	conclave			
9.	thrush			
10.	blaspheme			
11.	sordid			
12.	churlish			

13. arcane   _____   _____

14. contraction   _____   _____

15. mundane   _____   _____

16. confection   _____   _____

17. nocturnal   _____   _____

18. incandescent   _____   _____

19. scoundrel   _____   _____

20. surrogate   _____   _____

GENERALIZATION 7

CV Pattern

When *one* consonant appears between two sounded vowels, the word is usually divided before the consonant for the purposes of pronunciation.

EXAMPLE:

        hu   man

a. When a word has been separated into syllables for the purposes of pronunciation according to the above generalization, the vowel at the end of a syllable will usually be pronounced as it is pronounced when referred to as a letter.

EXAMPLE:

    va   por
    fe   tus
    vi   brate
    mo   sa   ic
    Cu   ban

b. There are many exceptions to this generalization, but always try it first. If your response to it does not produce a word that sounds right to you, break the word so that the first syllable forms the *CVC* pattern (habit; hab it). Your response to the vowel will then be the usual response to the vowel in that pattern.

EXAMPLE:

    panic   pan   ic

EXERCISE 14

Rewrite the words below in the spaces provided. In the left-hand column, write the words as they appear in the list; in the left-hand column, divide the words into syllables for pronunciation. Pronounce each word.

EXAMPLE:

                vapor   va   por

1. nomad	7. cobra	13. lethal	19. natal	25. mogul
2. matron	8. siphon	14. croton	20. egret	26. fracas
3. wily	9. scuba	15. putrid	21. matrix	27. blatant
4. vagrant	10. docent	16. Midas	22. lunar	28. quasi
5. tyrant	11. sacred	17. modal	23. solar	29. flagrant
6. bison	12. potent	18. cretin	24. Tiber	30. pogrom

1. _____ _____
2. _____ _____
3. _____ _____
4. _____ _____
5. _____ _____

CIRCLE ONE: In the *CV* pattern I pronounce *i* as in (win, wine).

6. _____ _____
7. _____ _____
8. _____ _____
9. _____ _____
10. _____ _____

CIRCLE ONE: In the *CV* pattern I pronounce *o* as in (tot, tote).

11. _____ _____
12. _____ _____
13. _____ _____
14. _____ _____
15. _____ _____

CIRCLE ONE: In the *CV* pattern I pronounce *u* as in (muss, muse).

16. _____ _____
17. _____ _____
18. _____ _____
19. _____ _____
20. _____ _____

CIRCLE ONE: In the *CV* pattern I pronounce *e* as in (pet, Pete).

21. _____ _____
22. _____ _____
23. _____ _____
24. _____ _____
25. _____ _____

CIRCLE ONE: In the *CV* pattern I pronounce *a* as in (flak, flake).

26. _____ _____
27. _____ _____
28. _____ _____
29. _____ _____
30. _____ _____

Accent

When a word has more than one syllable, it is natural to pronounce one syllable with more force, or stress, than other syllables in the word. This force is called *accent*. When there is a need to communicate in writing about accent, as the writers of a dictionary need to do, the syllable to be stressed is marked with an *accent mark* (´). Most of the two-syllable words you have worked with up to this time have had the accent on the first syllable.

Listen to yourself as you pronounce the following words and note where the accent mark is placed.

som´ber   shod´dy
pes´ky   rasp´y
shud´der   nug´get
dab´ble   fid´dle

EXERCISE 15

Turn back to page 8 and write the first twenty words in Exercise 3A in the blanks below. As you write each word, say it to yourself and place an accent mark over the part of the word that you pronounce with the most stress.

1. _____   11. _____
2. _____   12. _____
3. _____   13. _____
4. _____   14. _____
5. _____   15. _____
6. _____   16. _____
7. _____   17. _____
8. _____   18. _____
9. _____   19. _____
10. _____ 20. _____

The Reduced Vowel

EXERCISE 16

Read the words below and listen carefully to yourself as you pronounce them. You should be able to pronounce them all because they have been broken into syllables for you. Also, they all have the same first syllable, and the second syllables represent familiar spelling patterns.

1. afire — a fire´
2. agree — a gree´
3. avoid — a void´
4. abet — a bet´
5. abash — a bash´
6. abode — a bode´
7. avail — a vail´
8. abound — a bound´
9. ahoy — a hoy´
10. amuck — a muck´
11. avow — a vow´
12. abate — a bate´
13. adrift — a drift´
14. ajar — a jar´
15. alert — a lert´
16. atone — a tone´
17. aloft — a loft´
18. avenge — a venge´
19. askance — a skance´
20. adroit — a droit´

Pronounce the words again. Take note of how you pronounced the vowel *a*. If you are a native speaker, you probably touched the vowel lightly with a sound like "uh" and gave your attention and energy to the accented syllable.

Generalization 8

The Reduced Vowel

When any of the five vowels appears in an unaccented syllable, it may have a sound that is similar to the sound "uh" as heard in the first *a* in *away*. This is known as the *reduced vowel*. Most dictionaries indicate this sound by the symbol ə called the *schwa*.

EXAMPLES:

a as in *ago*
e as in *open*
i as in *sanity*
o as in *contain*
u as in *focus*

The fact that some syllables are accented and some are unaccented is only one of the factors that make it necessary for you to be flexible in your approach to pronouncing unfamiliar words. In Exercise 16 you gave a different response to the vowel *a* than you had given in any previous exercise. This is because in the words for Exercise 16 the letter *a* constituted an unaccented syllable. In later exercises you will be given examples of other factors that will call for flexibility on your part, but before you go on to those exercises you will be given the opportunity to become more aware of accent. From this point on, your consideration of what syllable is to be accented should be part of your word recognition techniques.

EXERCISE 17A The following words have been broken into syllables. Listen intently as your instructor pronounces each word for you, and place an accent mark over the syllable that your instructor pronounces with the most stress.

EXAMPLES:

sister   sís ter
discuss   dis cusś

1. culprit	cul prit	11. compact	com pact
2. egress	e gress	12. rapport	rapp ort
3. morass	mo rass	13. pedant	ped ant
4. largess	lar gess	14. augment	aug ment
5. cretin	cre tin	15. nadir	na dir
6. distaff	dis taff	16. tepid	tep id
7. compact	com pact	17. egret	e gret
8. conduct	con duct	18. tensile	ten sile
9. gamut	gam ut	19. malign	ma lign
10. prowess	prow ess	20. conduct	con duct

EXERCISE 17B Read the following sentences and place an accent mark over the syllable of the underlined word that you hear yourself stressing.

1. Mr. Jones does not know how to conduct a class.
2. The child's conduct in class was disturbing to other children.
3. The girl carried a compact and used every opportunity to take it out, powder her nose, and admire herself in the mirror.
4. The campus is very compact; therefore it does not take much time to get from one class to another.

EXERCISE 18A Listen intently to these words as they are pronounced for you. Supply the accent marks. Note that all these words have at least three syllables.

1. diadem   di a dem
2. forensic   fo ren sic
3. ignoramus   ig no ra mus
4. infamous   in fa mous
5. combatant   com ba tant
6. municipal   mu ni ci pal
7. preferable   pref er a ble
8. remonstrate re mon strate
9. diffidence   diff i dence
10. lethargic   le thar gic
11. succulent   succ u lent
12. posthumous post hu mous
13. prodigious pro di gious
14. semantics   se man tics
15. carnivorous car ni vor ous
16. apostate   a pos tate
17. bibulous   bib u lous
18. impious   im pi ous
19. antipathy   an ti pa thy
20. cognizance cog ni zance

EXERCISE 18B   Read the following sentences and place an accent mark over the syllable of the underlined word that you hear yourself stressing.

1. He said he thought the nickname I had given him was an insult.
2. I did not intend to insult him.
3. I do not object to people coining nicknames for me.
4. The child picked up a small object in the street, never realizing it was the valuable gem everyone was looking for.

EXERCISE 19A   Two syllables are stressed in the following words. Can you hear both accented syllables when they are pronounced for you? One may be stronger than the other. Dictionaries show the difference between the amount of stress given in accented syllables by making one mark heavier than the other. In this exercise mark each accented syllable in the same way.

1. culinary	cu li nar y
2. enigmatic	en ig mat ic
3. moratorium	mo ra tor i um
4. probability	pro ba bil i ty
5. aberration	a berr a tion
6. emaciation	e ma ci a tion
7. oligarchy	ol i garch y
8. constellation	con stell a tion
9. supercilious	su per ci li ous
10. predecessor	pre de cess or
11. coalition	co a li tion
12. countermand	coun ter mand
13. incidental	in ci den tal
14. paraphernalia	par a pher na li a
15. incoherent	in co her ent
16. hypochondria	hy po chon dri a
17. degradation	deg ra da tion
18. malformation	mal for ma tion
19. polytechnic	pol y tech nic
20. pusillanimous	pu sill an i mous

EXERCISE 19B   Read the following sentences and place an accent mark over the syllable of the underlined word that you hear yourself stressing.

1. The old man has been an invalid for many years.
2. The permit is invalid without the signature of either an instructor or a counselor.
3. It is difficult to refuse to lend a book when you know the person making the request really will read it.
4. We were ashamed of the park because of the refuse left on the ground by former users.

EXERCISE 20   Pronounce the following words to yourself. Remember all the spelling patterns and what you know about accent.

1. continent	con ti nent
2. connive	con nive
3. redundant	re dun dant
4. dormant	dor mant
5. foment	fo ment
6. rotunda	ro tun da
7. resident	res i dent
8. parental	pa ren tal
9. arsenal	ar se nal
10. sordid	sor did
11. spontaneous	spon ta ne ous
12. empathy	em pa thy
13. solvent	sol vent
14. entertainment	en ter tain ment
15. tantamount	tant a mount

In the left-hand column write the words in which you hear a reduced vowel. You may hear a reduced vowel in more than one syllable. Write the syllable numbers in the right-hand column. If you do not hear a reduced vowel in any syllable write "none."

	Word	Syllable Number
EXAMPLE:	fiscal	2d
1.	_____	_____
2.	_____	_____
3.	_____	_____
4.	_____	_____
5.	_____	_____
6.	_____	_____
7.	_____	_____
8.	_____	_____
9.	_____	_____
10.	_____	_____
11.	_____	_____
12.	_____	_____
13.	_____	_____
14.	_____	_____
15.	_____	_____

Flexibility

Now that you are skillful at recognizing patterns and the common vowel teams, you are ready to look at some words in which vowels are seen side by side but are not teams. Two vowels together do not always represent one sound. Sometimes each vowel is sounded. In some instances two *sounded* vowels side by side can represent a *vowel team* reversal.

Pronounce these words:

dial   vial

Note: You have sounded each vowel and these are two-syllable words:

di al   vi al

In these words the two vowels *i* and *a* are a reversal of the more frequent *a i* team. A reversal of the vowels from a common vowel team *may* be a signal that each of the vowels may be sounded and thus they will belong to two separate syllables, for there is only one sounded vowel in a syllable.

EXERCISE 21

The following words contain two vowels in succession that reverse a customary pattern. Break each word into syllables and pronounce it. Place an accent mark over the syllable where stress seems natural.

	Word	Syllables	Vowel Team Reversal
EXAMPLE:	trial	tri al	ai to ia
1.	pliant		
2.	dual		
3.	friar		
4.	denial		
5.	iambic		
6.	nuance		
7.	chaos		
8.	iodine		

EXERCISE 22

Because familiar patterns can sometimes be split and the spelling pattern may not apply in all situations, you must remain flexible in your approach to unfamiliar words. In such cases you must test the sound of your response. If you make several attempts and still are not confident of your response, consult a dictionary. In the following words *common vowel teams* are split; that is, each vowel in the team is pronounced. The words are divided into syllables. Note the divisions carefully and pronounce the words. In the middle column supply accent marks; in the right-hand column indicate the vowel team split.

	Word	Syllables	Vowel Team Split
EXAMPLE:	meander	me an der	ea to e a
1.	fluent	flu ent	

2. oasis	o a sis		
3. permeate	per me ate		
4. cruet	cru et		
5. caveat	cav e at		
6. panacea	pan a ce a		
7. Moab	Mo ab		
8. gruel	gru el		
9. oleander	o le an der		

Sometimes if the letter *i* is unaccented and followed by another vowel it will be pronounced like *e* in the *CVCe* pattern (helium he′li um). Vowels may be separated from other vowels for the purposes of pronunciation when the second vowel is the first letter of a suffix. If you maintain a careful, flexible approach, you are almost certain to come quite close to the accepted pronunciation. Then you will carry a strong image of the word in your mind and will recognize it when you hear it spoken. Later exposures to the word and, of course, consulting a dictionary will clear up any troublesome spots.

The spelling of some words produces combinations that call for the separation of vowels. Your familiarity with the language should provide a reasonable check on your pronunciation of a word or letter if you pronounce carefully, are flexible enough to try alternate pronunciations, and listen to yourself attentively.

EXERCISE 23

Break the following words into syllables. Blanks are provided for each syllable, and the syllable to be accented is marked. Supply the other information asked for. Star any syllable introduced by a vowel split that is a common suffix.

Word

EXAMPLE: continuous
1. ambiguous
2. fluctuate
3. podium
4. pandemonium
5. defiant
6. intermediary
7. pediatrics
8. extraneous
9. strontium
10. strenuous
11. voluptuous
12. viable
13. grandiose
14. fatuous
15. peon
16. fiasco
17. continuum
18. promiscuous
19. maniacal
20. repudiate

Syllables				*Vowel Split*	*Syllable Introduced by Second Vowel*
con tin' u ous				u o	ous

1. ___ ___' ___ ___   ___ ___
2. ___' ___ ___   ___ ___
3. ___' ___ ___   ___ ___
4. ___' ___ ___' ___   ___ ___
5. ___ ___' ___   ___ ___
6. ___ ___ ___' ___' ___   ___ ___
7. ___' ___ ___' ___   ___ ___
8. ___ ___' ___   ___ ___
9. ___' ___ ___   ___ ___
10. ___' ___ ___   ___ ___
11. ___ ___' ___ ___   ___ ___
12. ___' ___ ___   ___ ___
13. ___' ___ ___'   ___ ___
14. ___' ___ ___   ___ ___
15. ___' ___   ___ ___
16. ___ ___' ___   ___ ___
17. ___ ___' ___ ___   ___ ___
18. ___ ___' ___ ___   ___ ___
19. ___ ___' ___ ___   ___ ___
20. ___ ___' ___ ___   ___ ___

EXERCISE 24

In this exercise you must decide independently on the number of syllables. Break each word into syllables. Each word contains a vowel split. Listen to yourself carefully to check your response and to determine the most natural rhythm (accent). Supply an accent mark.

Word	Syllables
1. suet	_____
2. scion	_____
3. insidious	_____
4. sumptuous	_____
5. mausoleum	_____
6. nauseate	_____
7. substantiate	_____
8. gratuity	_____
9. pediatrics	_____
10. parsimonious	_____
11. contemptuous	_____
12. viable	_____
13. iota	_____
14. obsequious	_____
15. biopsy	_____
16. promiscuity	_____
17. striated	_____
18. choreography	_____
19. diaphanous	_____
20. coerce	_____

Pronounce the following words rapidly. If you can say them at first glance without error, you have proved to yourself that you have a "computer" mind. This means that you have "programmed" in your mind some of the most important spelling patterns of English and can produce quick and accurate oral responses as well as incorporate some flexibility into your approach to making responses.

| mode | modal | census | rostrum | gene | genus |
| model | medial | sensuous | scrontium | gentle | genius |

EXERCISE 25

Now try the words below. Some of them you may know; others you may not know, so they have been separated into syllables for you. Listen to yourself and see if you can determine any reason why the suffix *ous* sometimes stands alone and sometimes is combined with other letters to produce a syllable.

conscious	con scious
meritorious	mer i tor i ous
obnoxious	ob nox ious
spurious	spur i ous
conscientious	con sci en tious
imperious	im per i ous
fallacious	fal la cious
scrumptious	scrump tious
rambunctious	ram bunc tious

When the suffix *ous* is preceded by *i*, the presence of the letters *t, c, sc,* or *x*, before the *i* produce an *s* sound and the entire syllable (*tious, cious, scious,* or *sious*) is pronounced *shus*. Can you think of any other word in which you respond to similar spellings with *shus?*

English is a rich language with a long history that has involved many changes in form and in spellings and has reflected the influences of many other languages. It is said by some that the spelling of English is totally inconsistent. Your work in this section has shown you that English words are made up of spelling patterns that make it possible to predict the pronunciation of most words. Practice and the confidence that comes with practice will produce the flexibility you need to handle inconsistencies. The spelling patterns you have worked with are those most frequently seen. There are others that you may want to generalize about as you read. Breaking words into syllables has helped train you to see words in meaningful parts. As you become more skilled in word recognition, you will become more aware of how smoothly all the parts of a word flow together and how much the natural rhythm of English sentences contributes to the pronunciation of individual words. You will also find it less necessary to pause so frequently to think about spelling patterns or syllabication or to be too concerned about whether a letter is part of one syllable or another. However, everyone must resort occasionally to careful analysis of unfamiliar words when he is uncertain of their pronunciation.

Final Test

EXERCISE 26   Break the following words into syllables according to the generalizations presented in this text and pronounce them. You should be able to pronounce all of these words without consulting a dictionary. Place an accent mark where it seems natural to stress a syllable. Indicate the number of syllables.

Word	Syllables	Number of Syllables
EXAMPLE: ostracize	os tra cize'	3
1. caustic		
2. prognosis		
3. obfuscate		
4. prognosticate		
5. syndrome		
6. shibboleth		
7. espouse		
8. gazebo		
9. flaccid		
10. bordello		
11. placebo		
12. consensus		
13. confiscate		
14. skirmish		
15. shrift		
16. stringent		
17. preposterous		
18. morpheme		
19. ingrate		
20. gargoyle		

EXERCISE 27 Break the following words into syllables according to the generalizations presented in this text. Pronounce each word. Indicate the number of syllables. Remember the need for flexibility and the effect that accent can have on vowel sounds.

Word	Syllables	Number of Syllables
1. ombudsman		
2. malleability		
3. extemporaneous		
4. imminent		
5. emanate		
6. misanthrope		
7. renegade		
8. foible		
9. dyspeptic		
10. immolate		
11. eclectic		
12. blasphemous		
13. promiscuous		
14. fallacious		
15. obsolescence		
16. obsolete		
17. pontificate		
18. accolade		
19. loquacious		
20. coincide		
21. tenacious		
22. emphysema		
23. termagant		
24. phantasmagoria		
25. succinct		

Improving Comprehension

Paragraph Analysis

Good writers are well organized! They group related ideas and facts together and tend to stress one idea or fact at a time. Throughout this text you will be given paragraphs or groups of paragraphs to read and analyze. These paragraphs—taken from books, magazines and newspapers—are similar in organization and style to many others you will encounter in your reading. Analyzing them should give you valuable reading practice and an opportunity to develop a personal technique for comprehending what you read.

The exercises serve as performance tests so that you, your instructor and your classmates will have some basis on which to evaluate reading comprehension.

All exercises take you through basically the same steps, but the tasks in the exercises may be quite different, so it is important that you *always read directions* carefully.

Following are the steps you will be asked to take in all comprehension exercises.

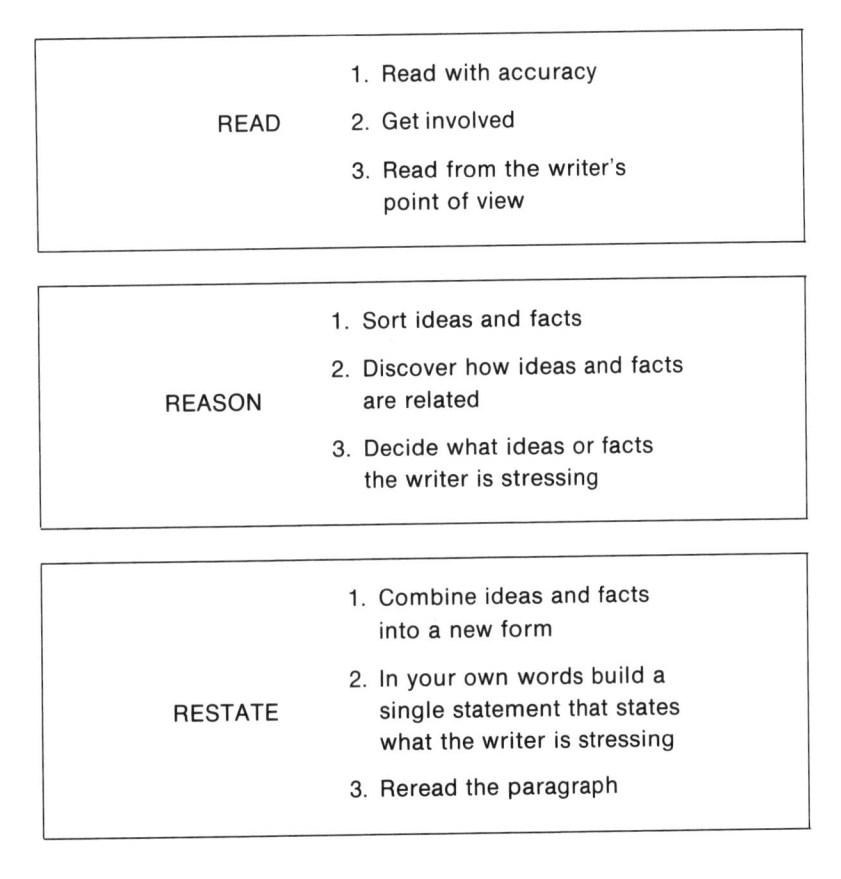

READ	1. Read with accuracy
	2. Get involved
	3. Read from the writer's point of view

REASON	1. Sort ideas and facts
	2. Discover how ideas and facts are related
	3. Decide what ideas or facts the writer is stressing

RESTATE	1. Combine ideas and facts into a new form
	2. In your own words build a single statement that states what the writer is stressing
	3. Reread the paragraph

Read the following article. Doing the exercises that follow each paragraph of this article will give you insight into the thought processes necessary to be a good reader. Be sure to apply the three steps discussed above.

Read Paragraph I. In the spaces provided build two statements that tell in a different way what idea the writer is stressing in the paragraph. A good statement consists of two parts: the first part tells what the statement is about, and the second part makes the statement—that is, it tells something about the first part. For this paragraph build your statements by combining a choice from the list provided for Part I with a choice from the list provided for Part II. Write out each statement.

What Camper Fits Your Family?

READ

[PARAGRAPH I]

Camping families should take stock of their camping needs before purchasing a recreation vehicle. Many types of recreation vehicles are available—vacation trailers, motor homes, pickup campers, converted vans, and camping trailers. Which camping vehicle is best for you depends on several factors: how often your family plans to go camping, how long you intend to spend in each place, and how much comfort you demand. If you take a two-week vacation once every three years, you won't need a $14,000 motor home. On the other hand, if you try to get away every weekend and like to take the whole family on a major vacation trip every year, a stripped down tent trailer isn't going to answer your needs. The solution is to custom-fit a camping system to your family's camping needs.

Adapted from *Better Homes and Gardens,* November, 1970. © Meredith Corporation, 1970. All rights reserved.

Part I
A. A $14,000 motor home
B. Recreation vehicles
C. Camping families
D. Converted vans
E. The choice of a camping system

Part II
A. should be determined by a family's camping needs.
B. are available in many styles and prices.

REASON
C. should take stock of their camping needs before purchasing a recreation vehicle.
D. is not the camping vehicle for the family who camps only occasionally.
E. do an amazing job as camping vehicles with the space available.

                Part I   Part II

1. _____ / _____

RESTATE

2. _____ / _____

To check the accuracy of your choices reread the two statements you have written. Even though they are worded differently they should say essentially the same thing. Occasionally in this text you will be asked to *restate* the central idea of a paragraph in two different ways. Readers may choose quite different words to talk *about* what they have read, but in all except the most complex material readers should be able to agree on what a writer has said.

Read the remaining paragraphs of the article. After reading each paragraph, *restate* what the paragraph says in the spaces provided. Build your restatement by deciding who or what is being talked about in each paragraph and writing that in your own words in the blank for Part I. From the choices offered you for Part II of your statement, select the one that most accurately states what the writer is saying about Part I and write it in the blank for Part II. A restatement of what a writer says in a paragraph actually represents a combination of the ideas and facts written within the paragraph. By the time you have finished you will have already gained skill in analyzing the paragraph and will be familiar with the techniques used in this text to help you improve comprehension.

[PARAGRAPH II]

Vacation trailer families are a special breed. They enjoy traveling for its own sake. They don't like the restrictions that go along with staying in a hotel or motel from the viewpoint of cost, location and freedom. For them, a place to stay should be as close as a place to stop. They have been largely responsible for the development of public campgrounds, and have helped change the concept of camping, which used to be thought of as "tenting." Because vacation trailer families enjoy traveling so much and are true nature-lovers, they don't mind the lower speed limits imposed on cars towing a trailer.

                Part I   *Part II*

3. _____ / _____

Part II
A. are a special breed.
B. enjoy traveling so much they don't mind a few inconveniences.
C. were responsible for changing the concept of camping.

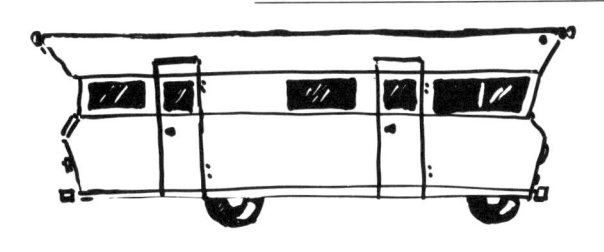

[PARAGRAPH III]

Motor home families like to get away from home as often as possible, but they don't like to leave comfort behind. They've chosen their specialized vehicle because it's ready to go whenever they are. As large as it appears, a motor home is really almost as easy to drive as the family car. Maximum speed restrictions are generally the same as for automobiles. Traveling in a motor home is so comfortable the kids will never ask, "How much longer till we're there?" And breaking camp is as easy as starting the engine.

	Part I	Part II
4.	_____	/ _____
	_____	

Part II

A. like a recreation vehicle that is ready to go when they are.
B. do not have to conform to any special speed restrictions.
C. like a recreation vehicle that is both comfortable and ready to go when they are.

[PARAGRAPH IV]

Pickup camper users have changed over the years. At first this group was made up of wool-shirted, hairy-chested outdoorsmen. They got together with other men of similar interests, threw a shell over a pickup frame, and took off on a fishing or hunting trip. Apparently, the families left at home didn't want to be left behind, and whole families started going along. Manufacturers responded with units that matched the travel trailers in convenience and still fit into the pickup truck frame. Families took to the idea so enthusiastically that truck manufacturers followed with pickups having suspension systems suited to the heaviest camper units. And they added options such as automatic transmissions, power steering and brakes, and interiors with many luxuries.

	Part I	Part II
5.	_____	/ _____
	_____	

Part II

A. usually put together their own recreation vehicle.
B. have changed over the years.
C. were mostly hunters or fishermen.

[PARAGRAPH V]

The converted van family has the same needs as the motor home family—only on a modest scale. The van can do an amazing job with the space it has, but it's a little too cozy for a large family on a rainy day. On the other hand, the converted van is no more expensive and no harder to drive than an automobile, so it's a sound investment as a second car. Like its big brother, the motor home, it's ready to go whenever its owners are.

	Part I	Part II
6.	_____	/ _____
	_____	

Part II
A. is interested mainly in economy.
B. is looking mainly for a second car.
C. likes convenience, flexibility and economy in a recreation vehicle.

[PARAGRAPH VI]

Camper trailer families are a hardy lot, but they still enjoy comforts and conveniences the tent camper can only dream about. Camping trailers are basically light trailers that open up into a suitable shelter and also carry all necessary camping equipment. Unlike tent-campers, camper trailer families always have a dry bed off the ground and extra room in the car while traveling. The luggage can be stashed in the trailer. Getting a camper-trailer is a great way to start making camping a family thing. You can tow the unit wherever your car will go, but the car is always ready to take off on a sight-seeing adventure. Most important, many models are priced well within the average family budget.

Part I   *Part II*

7. _____ / _____

Part II
A. can try camping without making too big an investment.
B. must be prepared for all the problems of the tent-camper.
C. must be as hardy as the family who still prefers tent-camping.

Look back at the restatements you have built. Which of the six statements is the most general? That is, which emphasizes a general idea or principle rather than giving specific examples of a general principle or idea? Write the most general statement in the frame below. Each of the other statements should deal with one aspect of the idea expressed in the frame. Write Part I of each of the remaining statements opposite the letters below the frame.

I

A.
B.
C.
D.
E.

41

You now have an outline of the entire article, which is similar in form to notes you might take on a lecture, a portion of a textbook or selections you might read in preparation for making a report. Note that the article has a definite pattern. In this instance the first paragraph introduces the subject of the article and each paragraph that follows deals with one phase of the subject. This is a common pattern. However, the reader must not try to make either paragraphs or groups of paragraphs conform to any preconceived pattern. Instead, the reader must develop skill in determining the writer's pattern.

"Remember when camping meant pitching a tent and cooking on a campfire—and trails were for walking?"

Editorial cartoon by Frank Interlandi. Copyright 1971, *Los Angeles Times*. Reprinted with permission.

EXERCISE 28

Read the following paragraph.

Children should have many more opportunities for free play. Not only would they enjoy their childhood more, but they would be better able to cope with the complex problems of adult life. When a child is allowed to play without adult supervision, he is allowed to express his personality and release the feelings that have been pushing to get out into the open. Each child needs to prove himself and to experience success at some game and activity. When he does so, he gains respect for himself as well as for others. In free play, the child learns to share and to blend his personality into that of the group. Free play offers many opportunities for social interaction and is a training ground for coping with competition. The way children play can save their mental health.*

* Adapted from "The Way Our Children Play Can Save Their Mental Health" by Arthur Weider, Ph.D. In *Family Weekly*, July 4, 1971.

1. Restate what the author is saying by supplying Part II from the three phrases listed.

Part I   *Part II*

Children / _____

Part II
A. need to compete more.
B. need to play more.
C. need to play more without supervision.

2. Restate the paragraph again by supplying Part II from one of the three phrases listed.

Part I   *Part II*

Free play / _____

Part II
A. teaches a child to share.
B. can improve a child's mental health.
C. teaches a child to cope with competition.

Sometimes a writer states his main point in one sentence and devotes the rest of the paragraph to convincing the reader of his point or giving examples or illustrations of what he has said.

EXERCISE 29

Read the following paragraph and write in the space provided below it the sentence that best states what the author is saying. Separate Part I and Part II of the sentence in the same way as in previous exercises. A guideline for selecting a sentence that states the central idea is to check whether all points made or examples given in other sentences are related to the sentence you have chosen.

> Results of an intelligence test should never be taken automatically at face value—and they certainly are not by those who understand the limitations of the test and its purpose. An intelligence test score should be viewed as only one of many bits of information collected by a school and kept on file. Along with it would be a great deal of other data needed to round out the picture of a student's educational potential and needs. The grades he has earned in class, his physical health, out-of-school work experience, participation in extra-curricular activities, evidence of his emotional health, attitudes and interests—all must be weighed if a student is to get the instruction and guidance that will best develop his potential.*

_____

_____

Sometimes a writer will state twice within a paragraph—in two separate sentences—what the paragraph is about. He does this to convince his reader. In these two sentences he will usually say *almost* the same thing but *not exactly* the same thing.

* Adapted from *Better Homes & Gardens*, November, 1970. © Meredith Corporation, 1971. All rights reserved.

EXERCISE 30   Read the following paragraph and write in the spaces below it two sentences from the paragraph that state what the author is saying. Place first the sentence that you think makes the most direct and comprehensive statement.

    The popularity of the guitar is going a long way toward changing the old-fashioned notion that the guitar is for show and not for acquiring the basics of music. Actually, the guitar is as versatile musically as the piano, and it also offers something many instruments don't—portability. The guitar can provide all the basics needed for an excellent start in instrumental music. One of the easiest instruments to grasp (mentally and physically), the guitar can encourage a beginner or a "switcher" by letting him master some simple chords in a few lessons. Once he's actually creating music on the guitar, he'll feel a sense of accomplishment that often carries over to another instrument.*

Sentence 1. _____

Sentence 2. _____

A writer may appear to include many things that are not directly related to a single idea but he will have a purpose for including them. He may include facts, ideas, or descriptive words and phrases to arouse your interest, or he may relate his point to a recent event or news item. Including such items can provide a buildup that helps to emphasize the central idea.

EXERCISE 31   Read the following paragraph. In the space provided, using one of the three choices offered for Part II, build a sentence that best expresses the idea the writer is stressing.

    Louis Armstrong, famed jazz trumpeter, was mourned throughout the world when he died July 6, 1971. He was one of the major architects of contemporary popular music. Millions knew him in his later years as one of the most loved of all entertainers—with his rough gravel voice, huge rolling eyes, and the inevitable large white handkerchief he used to mop his brow. But to people who charted the history of popular music—and to the musicians who played it—Armstrong was far more than an entertainer. He changed the whole face of jazz, and with it popular music, by stressing the role of the soloist in what had been until his time primarily a type of music where the group was the center of attention.**

Part I   *Part II*

Louis Armstrong / _____

* Adapted from "Try the Guitar for an Ice Breaker," *Better Homes and Gardens,* March, 1971. © Meredith Corporation, 1971. All rights reserved.
** Adapted from *L.A. Times,* July 7, 1971. © Reuters Limited. Printed with permission.

Part II
A. was known to all as an architect of contemporary popular music.
B. was one of the most loved of all entertainers in contemporary music.
C. changed jazz and other popular music by bringing attention to the solo performer.

The single idea stressed by a writer is usually quite general. Good readers are constantly generalizing. A reader who is skilled at generalizing will recognize when a generalization is so broad that it touches on little of what is in the paragraph. He will also know when a generalization is not broad enough to touch on all the parts of the paragraph.

EXERCISE 32A Read the following paragraph. Below the paragraph, circle the statement (1, 2, or 3) that, in your opinion, generalizes the most effectively about the contents of the paragraph.

After July 1, 1975, the enlisted man of the U.S. Navy will no longer wear the round hat, square-collared blouse, and bell-bottomed trousers of the familiar "sailor suit." This costume will be replaced by a dark blue double-breasted suit and a white, standard peaked military hat now worn by officers. The style features of the old uniform have a long history. It is reported that in 1745 a British naval officer, charged with the duty of designing a uniform for the British sailor decided on the colors blue and white when he was attracted by a pretty girl walking by in a snappy blue and white riding habit. The general style of the British uniform was later adopted by the U.S. Navy and has been given only minor changes by the U.S. Navy up to the present. Along with the color, the U.S. Navy man got several practical style features. The large square collar had been designed to protect sailors' necks from the oil with which they tarred their wigs. The black neckerchief was useful as a sweat rag, as of course black did not show the dirt. The bell-bottomed trousers could be easily rolled up while swabbing the deck or quickly shed if the sailor had to jump ship. Nobody is quite sure why the trousers had two front closings with thirteen buttons—some say the thirteen buttons represented the thirteen original colonies. The new uniform, according to naval officers, will improve morale and present the concept of "one Navy."

Circle one:

1. After 1975 the traditional "sailor suit" will no longer be the uniform of the U.S. Navy enlisted man.
2. The style features of the uniform of the U.S. Navy enlisted man have a long and interesting history.
3. Most of the style features of the uniform of the U.S. Navy enlisted man were borrowed from the British navy and remained much the same up to the 1970s when a new uniform was adopted.

Seaman   Lieutenant   Petty Officer

U. S. Navy, Service Dress, 1862–1863

Permission to reprint and including printing for public sale by the Superintendent of Documents, Government Printing Office, courtesy of The Company of Military Historians and H. Charles McBarron.

EXERCISE 32B

Details to be remembered may differ from one reader to another according to the reader's purpose for reading. Beside the letters A and B in the left-hand column write two details that you might put in notes from your reading if you were preparing a paper for a social science class on the subject "Attitudes Within the Military." Beside the letters A and B in the right-hand column write two details you might select if you were an art student writing a paper on "Historical Sources for Fashion Details."

46

Attitudes Within the Military	Historical Sources for Fashion Details
A. _____	A. _____
B. _____	B. _____

EXERCISE 33

Read the following paragraph. Build two generalizations about the subject of the paragraph by writing in your own words a Part II to complete each Part I provided for you.

Loch Ness is a lake in northern Scotland. It is best known as the home of the Loch Ness Monster. Reports of this sea monster date back to the 1200's and have increased since the 1930's. After centuries of myth and speculation, there appears to be evidence that some kind of large creature—or creatures—may roam the depths of Loch Ness. A number of people claim to have seen the monster, which they describe as a scaly creature about 30 feet long. In 1934 a doctor, vacationing in Scotland, brought back a photograph of a long-necked creature making waves in the lake. In 1968, a team of British scientists, using sonar equipment, detected the sound patterns of large moving objects in the deep waters of Loch Ness. In 1970 three Americans went to Scotland with a "love potion" with which they hoped to lure Nessie to the surface of the lake. Although no monster came near the surface to sniff the potion, the Americans brought back a recording, taken at the depth of 250 feet, of a strange sound apparently made by a large animal. The Americans, as well as others, plan future expeditions in quest of "Nessie."

Generalization 1.

A mysterious monster / _____

_____

Generalization 2.

Scientists and amateur explorers / _____

_____

Wide World photo

Photograph of Loch Ness monster

Section Two

Power from Signals

Affixes

In Section One you learned to see words in meaningful parts for the purposes of pronunciation. In this section you will work with word parts as signals to word meaning and word function. You must use every available means to gain understanding of words as units and as functioning parts of sentences if you want to read with ever-increasing power.

Prefixes

Many words are merely variations of words that are already familiar to you. The meaning of a basic word is changed by the use of a *prefix*—a word part added (*fixed*) to the beginning of a word. For instance, when you read that the summer television programs will be mainly *reruns,* you know immediately that programs that have already been run once will be run again. The *re* is a clue that signals another meaning of the basic word. Quick recognition of such signals will help you to read with improved comprehension and speed.

EXERCISE 1A Prefixes that give the most definite clues to word meaning are those meaning *no* or *not*. Although there really are not many different forms of these negative prefixes, you may think there are because the influences of different languages on English have varied the spelling of many prefixes. In the list below, each prefix brings the meaning *not* to the word to which it is affixed. Say each word as you circle the prefix.

1. unwilling
2. nonskid
3. disagree
4. unsolved
5. indefinite
6. irregular
7. immature
8. unemployment
9. discontented
10. illegal
11. unmade
12. imperfect
13. unconscious
14. impractical
15. inexact
16. nonprofit
17. disapprove
18. incapable
19. ungrateful
20. illegitimate
21. irreplaceable
22. dissatisfied
23. irresistable
24. immoveable
25. illiterate
26. noncombatant
27. nonunion
28. unsuccessful
29. immobile
30. irrational

EXERCISE 1B List the different negative prefixes you found in the thirty words in Exercise 1A.

Common Negative Prefixes

1. _____
2. _____
3. _____
4. _____
5. _____
6. _____
7. _____

Sometimes, although the word *not* cannot be substituted for a prefix, the prefix will still give the suggestion of *not* or *no*.

EXAMPLE:

Disrupt means to throw into confusion; therefore it gives a strong negative impression.

EXERCISE 1C

From the following list of words select the most appropriate word to fill the blanks in the following sentences. Add an *s* where a word is used in the plural. Consult a dictionary for meanings when necessary.

1. disappear   8. disbud
2. disband   9. disability
3. disbar   10. disadvantage
4. disavow   11. disgust
5. disbelief   12. dismay
6. discard   13. disarray
7. discord   14. disperse

1. The crowd was disorderly and was ordered by the police to _____.
2. Although plastic, a synthetic product, has several advantages over some natural materials, it also has many _____.
3. The wounded veteran receives a _____ pension.
4. It was clear that someone had been in the apartment during her absence because her possessions were in _____.
5. You will get more and better blooms from a camellia if you _____ the plant soon after buds appear.
6. The fear of severe punishment caused him to _____ any knowledge of the missing books.
7. The club was declared illegal according to school regulations, so the group was forced to _____.
8. The aircraft company was forced to _____ their plans for the new plane when they learned a competing company had a similar plane in production.

9. Everyone looked up in _____ when the instructor announced that the class clown had received the highest score on the examination.
10. The students had not been able to agree on the reasons for their discontent with the school or on what changes they wanted made. This _____ among members of their own group prevented the student dissidents from taking their rightful part in the decision-making.

There are scores of prefixes in the English language. Most of them you recognize by sight, and you may associate meanings with many of them without being able to define them. The meanings of others have become vague, as spellings or word forms have changed throughout the many years that the language has been developing. The meanings of some prefixes are worth learning because of the sharp changes they can create when added to "base words." Furthermore, the similar spellings of some prefixes with very different meanings sometimes cause confusion and therefore deserve special attention.

Look at the meanings of the prefixes in the chart below.

Look Alikes	Opposites
anti—against	homo—same
ante—in front of	hetero—different
inter—between	hyper—over (in amount)
intra—within	hypo—below (in amount)
pre—before (in time)	pre—before (in time)
pro—in favor of	post—after (in time)

Now notice the very precise and sharply different meanings words can have when different prefixes are combined with the same base word.

1. The judge met with the anti-war demonstrators in the ante-chambers of the courtroom. Although there were many people in the community with pro-war sentiments, they did not band together in any kind of formal organization.
2. The new recruit attracted little attention during the pre-season training period. Few people would have predicted that he would be a star in the post-season All-Star game.

Although it is usually not wise to try to create your own words on the basis of your knowledge of word parts, a few prefixes are often used rather freely in combination with other words to convey precise word meaning and to express ideas in a brief and a direct manner.

Prefixes Useful for Do-It-Yourself Words	
anti—against	intra—within
pre—before	pseudo—false, fake
post—after	mal—bad, wrong
pro—in favor of	sub—beneath, below
inter—between	

EXERCISE 1D Read the sentences in the left-hand column and create a new word by combining one of the above prefixes with a word inside the parentheses. Write the new word in the blank provided for it in the right-hand column.

New Word
EXAMPLE: *Inter-office mail*

Sentence
A boy works three hours a day just delivering mail (between offices).

New Words

1. _____ hearings

2. _____ meetings
   _____ meetings

3. _____ permit
   _____ permit

4. _____ study

5. _____ suits

6. _____ weather

7. _____ of the brain

8. _____ buildup
   _____ adjustments

9. _____ workers
   _____ workers

Sentences

1. Children are often not allowed to testify at regular court trials. Their statements are taken at hearings (*held before the trial*).

2. Meetings held (*before a convention*) are usually better attended than those held (*after a convention*).

3. The newly formed trucking company was able to get a permit (*to drive within the state*) but was not able to get a permit (*to drive from one state to another*).

4. Body science, in the opinion of many, is a study (*pretending to be scientific*).

5. Professional people, such as doctors or lawyers, fear being involved in suits (*accusing them of bad or wrong practice*).

6. Everyone is stimulated by changes of the seasons, but few are excited by the stimulation of weather (*that goes below zero*).

7. The doctor could not determine whether the child's abnormal behavior was caused by emotional disturbance or a brain (*that did not function properly*).

8. A buildup in the economy (*before the war*) left the people unprepared for the necessary adjustments (*after the war*).

9. The audience was equally divided between workers (*in favor of the union*) and workers (*who opposed the union*).

Suffixes as Clues to Word Class and to Sentence Meaning

Often a base word, with the addition of a *suffix* (word part added to the end of a word), becomes a different word and performs a different function in the sentence than the original base word. Suffixes can be an important clue to word function, and recognition of word function has a great deal to do with understanding sentence meaning. Word function (the job that a word does) in sentences separates words into classes called nouns, verbs, adjectives, and adverbs. These classes are often called *word classes,* or *form classes*. In the statements you built to restate the paragraphs in the comprehension exercises, the key words in Part I were *nouns*. The key words in Part II of all these statements were *verbs*. The verbs in Part II may have needed a noun or an adjective to complete the meaning or carry the job through to completion. For instance, look at the different jobs the base word *help* (verb) does as it changes to *helper* (noun) in the following sentences.

    (noun)   (verb)   (noun—completes job of verb)
1. Children / help their parents.

    (noun)   (verb)   (noun—completes job of verb)
2. Many helpers / make light work.

    (noun) (verb)   (noun—completes job of verb)
3. Parents / need many helpers.

There are many ways to communicate about word classes because of the many approaches to analyzing sentences. These approaches are called *grammar*. Your particular concern in this section will be to take note of how words change their form classes with an addition of a suffix or a change of suffix. By noting this change of form class you can both increase your vocabulary building power and also your sentence comprehension power.

In the following exercises you will be asked to label nouns according to their job function. The labels are used only to check accuracy, not to teach any particular system of grammar. Key words are underlined in the following sentences, and their form class is given, that is, noun, verb, adjective. Note the labeling of nouns.

    I(A)   (verb)   II(A)
1. Actors / live a hard life.

       I(A)   (verb) II(A)
2. Many students / envy actors.

 I(A) (verb)   II(A)
3. I / understand his actions.

    I(A)   I(a)   (verb)(adjective—completes job of verb)
4. The life of an actor / is hard.

I(A)   (verb)   (noun)   II(a)
5. I / understand the reason for his actions.

The Roman numerals indicate that the nouns are key words of one of the major parts of the sentences. Part I of a statement usually has only one key word. Part II of all statements focuses on the verb. Thus, Part II may have two key words—the verb, and the noun that helps the verb complete its meaning. The small *a* above the nouns in sentences 4 and 5 indicates that in these instances the nouns with the suffixes only explain key words in the part of the sentence where they occur and thus are of secondary importance in the basic structure of the sentences.

55

Noun Suffixes

EXERCISE 2A In the following groups of words, the first word is a verb, and the second and third words are nouns that have been produced by adding a suffix to the first word. Fill in the blanks in the sentences with a noun from the word groups. If the noun you supply is a key word, label it I(A) or II(A) as in the preceding example.

accept	depend	maintain
acceptance	dependence	maintenance
	dependent	
adopt	employ	offend
adoption	employee	offender
	employment	
allow	exclude	organize
allowance	exclusion	organization
annoy	guide	perform
annoyance	guidance	performance
contort	hypnotize	prefer
contortion	hypnotist	preference
contortionist		
correspond	interrupt	prosper
correspondence	interruption	prosperity
create	invent	refer
creation	invention	reference
creativity		

refer   1. _____ to several books on nutrition / produced no information on the values of eating raw vegetables.

allow   2. The _____ given to me by my parents / is enough to cover my expenses.

perform   3. I / enjoyed the _____ of the acrobatic team.

create   4. The _____ of a work of art / is an artists' gift to future generations.

hypnotize   5. We / were entertained by a _____.

maintain   6. Problems of _____ / are a consideration when buying a complicated piece of machinery.

employ   7. His continuous _____ / entitled him to many benefits.

annoy	8. Frequent telephone calls from solicitors / are an _____.
employ	9. One worker in the building / has been an _____ of the company for ten years.
exclude	10. _____ of any ethnic group from a public building / is not tolerated in this country.
correspond	11. Many famous people / carry on a large _____.
invent	12. Hundreds of new _____ / are patented each year.
contort	13. Performances of _____ / have always been attractions at circuses.
employ	14. _____ in a large industry / offers many fringe benefits.
guide	15. An informed and sympathetic counselor / can give helpful _____.
depend	16. He / has three _____.
prefer	17. Each child / stated his _____ in desserts.
accept	18. New ideas / must first gain _____.
create	19. Her _____ / was apparent in the beautiful things she had made.
organize	20. His talent for _____ / has helped his success.
offend	21. She / is a chronic _____ in the eyes of her supervisors.
adopt	22. Childless parents / find _____ of homeless children rewarding.
prosper	23. Citizens of a great country / expect _____.
interrupt	24. Frequent _____ / impeded the progress of the filming.
depend	25. His _____ on his notes / shows his insecurity about the subject matter.

EXERCISE 2B List as many noun suffixes as you can after scanning the words you have used to fill the blanks.

Common Noun Suffixes

_____   _____
_____   _____
_____   _____
_____   _____
_____   _____
_____

Another way to find nouns in sentences besides determining their function is to make note of the fact that some are preceded by short words like *a, an, the, some, no, any,* and a number of words like *my, his, her, your,* and *their.* Such words are often called *determiners.* Numbers also perform the same function as determiners. The determiner plus the noun and sometimes an adjective is called a *noun phrase.* Noun phrases are important parts of sentences, as we have already observed.

EXERCISE 2C Find noun phrases (determiners and the words that follow them) in the sentences in Exercise 2A. Write the noun phrases in the blanks below, placing all the noun phrases from one sentence in the same blank. If a sentence does not have any noun phrases, simply write "none" in the blank.
EXAMPLE:
  No information; the values (Sentence 1)

1. _____
2. _____
3. _____
4. _____
5. _____
6. _____
7. _____
8. _____
9. _____
10. _____
11. _____
12. _____
13. _____
14. _____

15. _____
16. _____
17. _____
18. _____
19. _____
20. _____
21. _____
22. _____
23. _____
24. _____

Verb Suffixes

A suffix can change a noun or an adjective to a verb. Some common verb suffixes are *ize, ate, fy,* and *en.* The second word in each of the following word pairs is a verb, formed by adding one of the above suffixes to the first word.

| short | terror | glory | origin |
| shorten | terrorize | glorify | originate |

Often writing style can be improved by replacing a word of one form class with another word from a different form class. Converting adjectives or nouns into verbs can rid our writing of overworked verbs such as *make* or *do* and can provide alternative ways of expression.

EXERCISE 3A Rewrite the underlined phrases in the following sentences by adding a suffix (*ize, ate, fy, en*) to the verb. Add *d* or *ed* to the new verb if it is needed to preserve the time element originally intended.

EXAMPLES:

A. Flexible scheduling has been introduced and has <u>made the school day shorter.</u>

<u>shortened the school day.</u>

B. The fact that there is a killer at large has <u>filled the community with terror.</u>

<u>terrorized the community.</u>

1. Just the thought of staying in the old deserted house all night <u>filled the boy with terror.</u>

   _____

2. The offer of a substantial reward <u>gave her a motive</u> to continue her search for the missing dog.

   _____

3. The undercover agent was required to <u>learn his instructions by memory</u> before undertaking the dangerous mission.

   _____

4. The arrival of settlers into the valley <u>was a threat to</u> the peaceful existence of the Indians.

5. When he was cross-examined, the witness <u>gave a false account of the incident</u> so that his friend would not be found guilty.

6. The visiting team was <u>given many penalties</u> for being offside.

7. The actress <u>held her audience captive</u> with her warm personality.

8. The attacks on the fort <u>became more intense</u> as darkness approached.

9. A committee was appointed <u>to make the parkway</u> in front of the school <u>beautiful.</u>

10. Much of the folk music of this country <u>had its origin</u> in the deep South.

11. As summer approaches the days gradually <u>become longer.</u>

12. The air in the plane was <u>kept under pressure</u> so that passengers could breathe normally at high altitudes.

13. News of the crash of the huge airliner <u>was received with horror by people</u> everywhere.

14. He decided to <u>make his stay at the lake longer</u> when the weather cleared up.

15. The driver <u>gripped the wheel tighter</u> when the fog made it impossible to see more than a few feet ahead.

EXERCISE 3B Complete the following exercise, using the same directions as in Exercise 3A.

1. The heavy snowstorm <u>made it necessary to use</u> chains to get to the ski lodge.

2. The teacher asked him to <u>arrange the books in categories</u> according to subject matter.

3. The motion <u>to add fluoride to the city water</u> supply was defeated by the council.

4. Attempts <u>to bring colonists into the new territory</u> failed because of the hostile natives.

5. As darkness approached, the efforts of the rescue party to find the missing boy <u>became more intense.</u>
   _____

6. The coach held extra practice sessions <u>to make the team's passing attack stronger.</u>
   _____

7. The committee was urged to <u>take a broader approach</u> to the problem of integrating minorities into the program.
   _____

8. The club leaders decided to <u>make the initiation a formal procedure.</u>
   _____

9. The instructor <u>made the problem clear</u> by drawing a simple diagram on the blackboard.
   _____

10. To save time and money, operations that formerly had been done manually <u>were now being processed by machines.</u>
    _____

EXERCISE 3C Below are more word groups. These groups consist of a verb, an adjective, and a noun—in that order; that is, three different form classes derived from the same base are grouped together. In one instance, no word is given in the verb class—*credible; credibility*. Occasionally, more than one example is given in one form class—*successor; succession*. Note that the different suffixes indicate different meanings. Select one of the words from the appropriate group and write it in the blank provided in the sentences that follow. The verb from the group is given in parentheses before each blank. Your familiarity with the language will help you to select the appropriate word. Add *d, ed,* or *s* where necessary.

act	*deduce*	*disturb*	*persist*
active	deductive	disturbing	persistent
action	deduction	disturbance	persistence
activity			
		enjoy	*predict*
		enjoyable	predictable
attract	*defend*	enjoyment	predictability
attractive	defensible		
attraction	defensive	*extend*	
	defense	extensive	*produce*
conclude		extension	productive
conclusive			production
conclusion	*delight*	*fascinate*	
	delightful	fascinating	*prosper*
conspire	delight	fascination	prosperous
conspiring			prosperity
conspirator		*imagine*	
	depend	imaginative	*relax*
credible	dependable	imaginary	relaxing
credibility	dependability	imagination	relaxation

61

rely	respect	solve	succeed
reliable	respectable	solvable	succeeding
reliance	respectability	soluble	successive
		solution	successful
repeat	*satisfy*		success
repetitious	satisfying	*stabilize*	succession
repetitive	satisfactory	stable	successor
repetition	satisfaction	stability	

The (*attract*) _____ of a good story is universal. Stories that many readers of all ages have (*enjoy*) _____ are those that center around one or two central characters whose (*act*) _____ are somewhat (*predict*) _____. It may be that when a reader selects a book for (*relax*) _____, he is looking for something (*rely*) _____ in an unreliable world.

For many generations readers have been entertained by the stories of Robin Hood. Robin was the leader of a band of outlaws who plied their trade of thievery in Sherwood Forest near Nottingham, England. It is not really known whether Robin Hood was a real person, but he lives in the stories of many writers and in the minds of millions of readers. He felt his deeds were (*defend*) _____ because he divided his spoils with the needy. Some people refer to Butch Cassidy as a modern-day (*succeed*) _____ to the legendary Robin Hood.

Readers with active (*imagine*) _____ have long enjoyed the many stories about Sherlock Holmes and his friend and confidant, Dr. Watson. To this astute private detective, every crime had a (*solve*) _____. His many (*deduce*) _____ led to (*conclude*) _____ that never taxed the (*cred-*) _____ of the armchair detectives who read them. The stories about Sherlock Holmes were created by the (*produce*) _____ mind of Sir Arthur Conan Doyle, who lived from 1859 to 1930 and was a physician as well as an author.

In the 1800s Horatio Alger was a very popular writer in the United States. All his novels were about young boys, who, at the outset of the stories, were penniless. In every story the youthful hero rose from tattered poverty to riches and (*prosper*) _____. This (*repeat*) _____ theme embodied the "American Dream," which fired so many people to think of the United States as a land of opportunity.

The heroes of the best childrens' books have had an enduring (*fascinate*) _____ for children of (*succeed*) _____ generations. Here again we find the element of being able to predict what the characters are going to do, and also the element of a happy ending. This (*rely*) _____ on (*predict*) _____ is often thought of as being a child-like characteristic. The fact that this characteristic may be (*persist*) _____ throughout life should not be (*disturb*) _____, since psychologists tell us that something of the child remains in all mature personalities.

No character out of children's literature is more beloved than Winnie the Pooh, who frolics through the stories of the English author, A. A. Milne. The antics of Pooh, a bear of the stuffed variety, and those of his fellow (*conspire*) _____ of the stuffed animal kingdom, are so (*delight*) _____ that parents enjoy reading them to their children as much as children enjoy hearing them.

Modern novels and stories do not provide such (*extend*) _____ resources for a reader to lose himself with a favorite character whose many problems are (*fascinate*) _____ because they come to such (*satisfy*) _____ (*conclude*) _____. Detective stories do provide this type of (*satisfy*) _____, and they continue to be a popular type of reading. We also have our favorite characters on television whom we can rely on to be (*depend*) _____ personalities whose lives are very (*stabilize*) _____ and who show us that all is right with the world. It seems very likely that Marshall Dillon in *Gunsmoke* will settle problems in Dodge City for at least two decades and that Kitty will continue to be his girlfriend.

EXERCISE 3D List the adjective suffixes used in Exercise 3C.

Common Adjective Suffixes

_____	_____
_____	_____
_____	_____
_____	_____
_____	

Improving Comprehension

EXERCISE 4 Read carefully each paragraph in the following article. From each paragraph whose *letter* is included in the outline form at the end of the article, select the sentence that best states the central idea of that paragraph and write the entire sentence in the blank following the letter. Following Roman numeral I write the sentence from the article that best states the article's central idea. Then complete the Fill-in-the-Blanks statements by inserting adjectives from the article.

What You Can Do Now with Inflatable Boats

[PARAGRAPH A]

In the past, running a rough whitewater river has been a sport for an expert or an impetuous fool. Riding raging rapids is like surfing a rock-strewn beach. A rough whitewater river can destroy a canoe in seconds. Then people began to run whitewater rivers in inflatable pontoon rafts. Today running whitewater rivers is one of the fastest growing sports in the country.

[PARAGRAPH B]

Until recently people were not aware of the features of

Adapted from "What You Can Do Now With Inflatable Boats" by Cecil Hoge, Jr., *Family Weekly,* May 23, 1971.

inflatable boats. Most people thought that they would instantly puncture and sink like a stone. They did not know that practically all of these boats have multiple, separately inflated compartments making them virtually unsinkable. And they were not aware of the great progress in the field of synthetic rubber materials. Then people began to learn about these improvements, and shed their prejudices about inflatable boats. Inflatable sales began to rise. People began to realize that these offspring of the old-style life raft, as well as being virtually unsinkable, were collapsible, maneuverable and cheap.

[PARAGRAPH C]

There are two types of materials used in making inflatables. The most expensive and toughest are made out of neoprene-treated nylon fabrics. The nylon fabric gives the boat its strength, and the neoprene provides a watertight seal. Any inflatable made out of this fabric is virtually impossible to puncture. The other type of material widely used is vinyl. This is far cheaper, but it is also easier to puncture. Still, provided that it is not of inferior quality, vinyl can withstand almost any treatment it receives, including whitewater. In addition, it is also easier to repair a vinyl inflatable.

[PARAGRAPH D]

Today, for the first time, the American public is realizing that the inflatable boat offers a cheap low-maintenance way to get in on the boating boom. More and more people, with limited space and money, are finding they can have full boating pleasure without the usual expense and bother. Inflatables have truly come of age.

I. _____

   A. _____

   B. _____

C. _____

Fill in the Blanks.
1. _____ boats are _____

2. In the article "What Camper Fits Your Family?" on pages 38–41, the author stated the central idea in the _____ paragraph. In the article above, the author stated the main idea in the _____ paragraph.

EXERCISE 5

Read the following article. In the exercise that follows it, complete the sentences as they correspond to the number beside each paragraph. Your sentence should summarize or restate the central idea of each paragraph. Then write a suitable title for the article in the space labeled *Title*. Try not to be catchy or cute in your title. The title should give the reader a good idea of what to expect from what he is about to read.

VOCABULARY:

prowess
biceps
physique
strenuous
prolonged
spectrum
puny
sustain

Be sure you know the meanings of these words before you read the article.

[PARAGRAPH I]

Doctors report that the already flabby American is getting softer, fatter, and more tired every day. Barely one-fifth of our adult population is in good physical condition, they say. Our basic physical condition is measured primarily by heart and lung performance. How the heart and lungs perform is far more important than any athletic prowess or the development of a muscular physique. No one ever died, after all, from scrawny thighs or flabby biceps. But weak hearts kill thousands of Americans every month. Millions more are more tired than they should be. A good way to avoid this fate is to achieve and maintain a good overall fitness program designed to enlarge the heart's capabilities.

[PARAGRAPH II]

Exercise is beneficial to overall fitness in proportion to the amount of steady exertion it demands. The best exercise is both strenuous and prolonged. Many people fool themselves into thinking they have a good exercise program. At one end of the spectrum is the golfer, who may walk all morning but get no real exercise. On the other hand, the athlete who makes an all-out effort in the interest of saving time and runs the hundred yard dash in ten seconds each morning gives his heart too little time to exert itself. The best sports are found somewhere near the center

Adapted from "Family Health," Gerald M. Knox, Editor, *Better Homes and Gardens*, May, 1971. © Meredith Corporation, 1971. All rights reserved.

of the spectrum. Such a sport would be long-distance running, where the heart must work steadily and hard. A track star may look puny beside a football player. But big muscles are not positive proof of overall fitness. Those muscles may have been developed to perfect a certain skill rather than to develop a general fitness.

[PARAGRAPH III]

A good yardstick by which most people can judge a sport is found in the number 130. Experts agree that exercise begins to be very useful when the heart is made to pump at a minimum rate of 130 times a minute. This rate is often called *pulse rate*. A healthy sport must not only provide a certain kind of activity but must be played with vigor. Many sports can be played in a strenuous manner. A busy governor played nine holes of golf every day, but with a difference. He played three balls at the same time over a distance of three holes. And instead of walking between shots—he ran!

[PARAGRAPH IV]

As with any fitness program, there are certain precautions. If you're over 35 or have not been very active in the past, get a medical checkup and your doctor's approval before you start. If your heart rate gets near 170, slow down. To sustain that fast a pace can be very risky. Don't expect too much of yourself too soon. And stop before you get too tired. A good indication that you might be overdoing it is if two minutes after you've stopped exercising, your heart rate is still more than 110.

Title: _____

   I. All Americans / _____
      A. should follow a fitness program to develop their physiques.
      B. should have regular physical examinations.
      C. should follow a fitness program that will produce good heart and lung performance.

  II. _____ / will make the heart work steadily and hard.
      A. Playing golf
      B. The most beneficial sport
      C. Participating in sports regularly

 III. _____ / _____
(*Supply both parts on your own.*)

 IV. In any fitness program take the following precautions:
      A. _____
      B. _____
      C. _____
      D. _____

Punctuation

You learn to respond to punctuation signals very early in your reading. When you come to a period, you know that you are reading an abbreviation or that a unit of thought has ended. Some other punctuation clues are almost as important as the period. If you ignore or misinterpret these clues, you can become confused—or, at the very least, lose reading power. The most common of these punctuation clues are the following:

1. PAIRS OF COMMAS

    Material included within a pair of commas explains a word or group of words that comes before it. Usually the material within the commas can be left out. However, this material can be quite interesting and informative.
    EXAMPLE:

Double knits, which have been made in West Germany for decades, did not come into popularity until English textile makers in the early 1960s found that they could produce the fabric with polyester.

You must admit that the information that double knits have been made in West Germany for decades is interesting, but the sentence has to do with what brought them into popularity.
    Sometimes the material contained within the commas identifies a name or place that comes before it.
    EXAMPLE:

Ralph Lazarus, chairman of the Nationwide Federated Department Stores chain, adds, "Men are buying knit slacks like there is no tomorrow."

2. PAIRS OF DASHES

    A pair of dashes serves much the same purpose as a pair of commas. The material between the dashes identifies or explains a word or words that come before it.
    EXAMPLE:

In the troubled textile industry, double knit clothes—apparel made of specially knitted material instead of woven cloth—stand out like a bright golden thread in a frayed gray shawl.

The dash is sometimes used to set off—for emphasis—material that is really part of the sentence.
    EXAMPLE:

Two helicopters hovered overhead to spot smoke and to dispatch every available inspector—with one exception.

The writer wants you to take special note of the fact that every available inspector was dispatched except one. Later on in the story, he states that one inspector went out on his own and made the only discoveries of smog-producing engines—two trains and a school bus.
    A dash can also be used to introduce a comment on what has just been said.
    EXAMPLE:

Officials conducted an early morning smog raid—it was delightfully unsuccessful.

3. PARENTHESES

Parentheses are very similar to pairs of commas or pairs of dashes in that they explain preceding material. The difference is that material included within the parentheses can definitely be left out without affecting the main idea of the rest of the sentence. It is *truly* supplementary.
   EXAMPLE:

Meanwhile, his colleagues searched in vain for a single industrial polluter among the 2,750 plants in their 135 square mile area (and they were out for three hours).

4. QUOTATION MARKS

You are probably familiar with the use of quotation marks to set off what is called a *direct quotation*—that is, a statement in which the speaker's exact words are used. You may not be so familiar, however, with the practice of enclosing words or phrases within a text in quotation marks. A writer may—when talking about a person—insert some of that person's own words into his description of that person in order to communicate more clearly something of the person's style or personality.
   EXAMPLE:

The brawny tailback, who lifts weights before each game to "get my blood going," needs all the muscle he can muster.

5. A SERIES OF DOTS (*ellipses*) . . . .

These are used in a quoted passage when a word or words have been left out.

6. ITALICS, a slanted kind of print, are used for a number of reasons. They are indicated in handwriting by underlining. The most common uses for italics are these:
   a. For emphasis
      EXAMPLE:

   The papers are due on Thursday. *No late papers will be accepted.*

   b. To indicate the title of a book, play, movie, popular song, etc.
   c. To refer to a word as a word or a letter as a letter.
      EXAMPLE:

   Double the final *g* in *clog* when you add *ed*.

   d. When a word from a foreign language is used along with the English text.
      EXAMPLE:

   The author of the book was no longer welcome in his home town—he was *persona non grata*.

EXERCISE 6 Read the following selection from a popular news weekly. Note the use of the many punctuation signals. Does the use of these signals add to your reading power? Are Craig, his counselor, and the students of the private school more vivid to you because of the use of quotations?

Craig's Message

"I'll tell you one thing, Dave, and anybody else who's listening: you can really get messed up on that stuff." The "stuff" was LSD, and the words were spoken into a tape recorder last year by Craig Gardner, a University of Utah honor student, just a few hours before he drove into the Wyoming countryside and shot himself between the eyes. Craig's warning about the hazards of LSD, addressed chiefly to his roommate Dave Bizak, is beginning to reach a far wider audience. It is incorporated into the sound track of a new educational film that shuns the usual dull recital of facts about drugs in favor of a firsthand story about one addict's innermost feelings.

The film, titled *...And Anybody Else Who's Listening,* is the work of Producers Maynard Clark and Arthur Miller of Princeton, N.J. They acquired the tape by chance and set out to learn more about Craig by interviewing his relatives and friends. Then they filmed the apartment he had shared with Dave (and where he had begun experimenting with marijuana before moving to LSD). They also worked in some of the Gardner family snapshots and home movies and added some moving comments by Craig's younger sister Gayle.

Craig's own final comment on his life begins with a kind of oral will: "Larry, you can have my shaver. Big deal. Oh brother, this is terrible... I give Dave my stereo and tapes." Then he settles his debts: "I got Dick's money on the table, ten bucks that I owe him, and got my settlement with Dave here on the table." Then he tries in vain to explain his imminent suicide: "Well, actually, the real reason is that I really don't know."

All he is sure of is that he should not have taken LSD: "It's bad news; it really is... I think what acid does is it intensifies everything, my feelings about myself. I was screwed up enough without taking acid. Probably just buried me deeper in my hole than I was before I started tripping out."

One feeling magnified by Craig's addiction was his sense of physical inferiority: a bout with polio at age two had left him with a shortened arm. The defect was so slight that most of his friends were not aware of it, and it did not keep him from becoming expert at tennis and skiing. Yet on the tape he said, "I've lived with my physical condition, but I really can't cope with it." In the end he even doubted his sanity: "After you've taken so much of that stuff, you just really don't know where you're at. You don't know if your reasoning is correct. It's hard to distinguish between real and unreal, and you're lost. I really don't know if I'm nuts or what."

To Yosh Kawano of the New Jersey division of narcotic and drug abuse control, Craig's indictment of drugs is an effective form of "feeling communication." Students at Peddie, a Hightstown, N.J. private school where the film was shown, emphatically agree. Says one: "You walk out and the film hasn't ended. That picture really doesn't end for a long time."

Reprinted by permission from *Time, The Weekly Newsmagazine;* © Time, Inc., 1971.

EXERCISE 7 Read the following selection and take careful note of all punctuation signals; then answer the questions that follow the selection.

Mountain to Molehill

BE THERE WHEN THE MOUNTAIN COMES TO MUHAMMAD declared the billboards in Houston. The come-on was as flabby as the contenders. Muhammad Ali, the walking billboard, was so uninterested in his twelve round bout with bulky (256 lbs.) Buster Mathis that he trained seriously only for nine days.† Ali divested himself of a bit of doggerel ("I'll do to Buster what the Indians did to Custer"), but his heart was clearly not in it.† Buster, whose last fight was a humbling loss to Jerry Quarry in 1969, was out to prove that "I'm no dog."† As expected, when the Mountain finally came to Muhammad last week in the Houston Astrodome the result was a molehill of a fight.

Ali, who weighed in at 227 lbs., his heaviest ever, peppered away during the first 10 rounds with his rat-a-tat-tat left jabs and a supposedly merciful "new" punch he calls the "linger on," a light chopping right designed to daze but not drop a lesser opponent. Mathis, surprisingly agile for a big man, suggested a pachyderm on *pointe*, dancing, dipping and doing no damage whatsoever.† In the final two rounds Ali decked Mathis four times—twice with punches that were little more than taps.†

Ignoring cries from the crowd, Ali refused to finish off his defenseless opponent. "Yes, I deliberately held up," explained Muhammad, who won a unanimous decision. "I don't believe in killing a man just to satisfy a crowd."

Ali picked up $300,000 for the light workout (Mathis' cut was $60,000), which was designed as a promotional prelude to the expected multi-million dollar rematch with Champion Joe Frazier.† Trouble is, Ali and Frazier both so outclass the other contenders that in tuning up for their second "fight of the century" (Muhammad meets Germany's Jurgen Blin next month, Joe fights Texan Terry Daniels in January), they seem to be reviving the old bum-of-the-month club.†

Reprinted by permission from *Time, The Weekly Newsmagazine;* © Time, Inc., 1971.

Fred Kaplan from Black Star

Muhammad Ali

Note: The title is a reference to a saying about "making mountains out of molehills;" i.e., making a big issue out of a small complaint. Mathis is compared to a mountain. The message on the billboards mentioned in the first line refers to an old saying, "If the mountain will not come to Mohammed, Mohammed will come to the mountain."

1. Rewrite the sentences marked with a dagger (†), deleting all material that can be eliminated without affecting the meaning of the sentence. Be prepared to tell what punctuation marks gave you the signal that material could be eliminated.

   A. _____
   B. _____
   C. _____
   D. _____
   E. _____
   F. _____
   G. _____

2. Select quotations that you believe contributed to the description of the style or personality of the people mentioned in the article. Write these quotations in the spaces provided below.

   A. Muhammad Ali _____
   B. Buster Mathis _____
   C. Newswriters or promoters _____

3. Why is the word *pointe* in italics?
   _____

Two abbreviations of Latin terms are used frequently in writing exactly as if they were words. The meanings of each of these abbreviations should be memorized and you should recite that meaning to yourself each time you see one of them. They are:

1. *i.e. that is*
   EXAMPLE:

The machinery had broken down; i.e., it did not work well enough to be of any practical use.

2. *e.g. for example*
   EXAMPLE:

People with allergies can be severely affected by many turf grasses, e.g., non-hybrid-type Bermuda grass, perennial ryegrass, Kentucky bluegrass, and redtop.

EXERCISE 8

Read the following selection. As you come to one of the above abbreviations, write the meaning of the abbreviation in the blank provided.

Osmosis is the passage of one fluid into another through a membrane. It occurs with both liquids and gases. This transfusion, i.e. _____, passage of one fluid into another, results in a mixture of the two fluids. Osmosis takes place through a *semipermeable* membrane, i.e. _____, a membrane that is partially porous.

Osmosis affects many things in our daily life; e.g. _____, meats shrink when they are packed in a salt solution. Osmosis takes place when some of the water from the meat passes into the salt solution. The principle of osmosis is used in preserving foods such as fish or pickles in *brine*, i.e. _____, a salt solution. The salt solution passes into the food being preserved and kills the organisms that might cause decay. Some substances have greater osmotic pressure than others; i.e. _____, the two substances will not pass into each other at an equal rate. This osmotic pressure is an important factor in nature; e.g. _____, it helps raise the sap to the high branches of trees.

Use of Context Clues to Increase Vocabulary

The dictionary should always be considered the final source for accurate word meanings, but the busy reader must use many methods for increasing his vocabulary. The most common method used by skilled readers is that of using *context* clues. *Context* is the text that surrounds a particular word. It may be a single sentence, or a series of words, phrases, or sentences that come before or after the word in question. The use of context clues is a form of guessing, and should be considered as such, but a guess can be an *educated* guess. Using context clues sometimes involves pressing on without understanding fully what you have read, but it also involves having the judgment to know when you should not press on any further or when a second reading is necessary.
Read the newspaper item below:

Oregon Prison Style

Colorful Garb Cuts the Jailhouse Blues

STATELINE, Nev. (UPI)—Prisons are usually considered grim and dreary but at least one state, Oregon, is making an effort to give them some color.

Inmates wear multicolored shirts and are allowed neatly trimmed beards, mustaches and hair down to the shirt collar. Prison guards dress in sport coats and slacks.

Copyright 1971, *Los Angeles Times*. Reprinted by permission.

Let's assume that the word *garb* in the larger headline is unfamiliar to you. In the smaller headline above, note the word *style*. In the second paragraph of the item itself note the mention of what the prison inmates *wear* and how they *dress*. Of course, you also see reference to styles of hair, beards and mustaches, but if you take into consideration that the headline describes *garb* as being *colorful,* you can quite logically guess that *garb* has something to do with clothes. Thus, by using context clues you fully comprehend the news item and you add another word to your vocabulary. Further exposure to the word *garb* will add to your depth of understanding of the word and will make you familiar with the various ways it can be used.

Types of Context Clues

1. Context clues are present in many forms, or combinations of forms. The easiest clue is very direct—the writer tells us what the word means.
   EXAMPLE:

   DeGaulle, who would have been 80 on his next birthday, died of a ruptured aneurysm—burst blood vessel—shortly before 8:00 P.M. Monday night.

   The writer follows the unfamiliar phrase *ruptured aneurysm* with an explanation. He tells us that the phrase means *burst blood vessel*. It is logical to conclude that *aneurysm* means *blood vessel* and *ruptured* means *burst*.

2. Sometimes the meaning of an unfamiliar word will be clear because something in the context will show that the unfamiliar word means the opposite of another word or idea in the sentence.
   EXAMPLE:

   The citizens of the community expected that the vandals would be *contrite* when they viewed the damage they had done to the civic buildings of their own community. But instead, the boys said that they were glad to see the buildings destroyed.

   The use of the phrase *but instead* tells us to look for opposing or sharply contrasting ideas on either side of it. Thus, the word *glad* must be the opposite of *contrite,* and *contrite* must therefore mean sad or sorry.

3. Sometimes the clue is a general one coming from several words or ideas found throughout the surrounding context.
   EXAMPLE:

   My mother was one of the most *intrepid* women who ever lived. I never heard her complain or express fear. She accepted every burden that life imposed upon her. No illness or pain drew a murmur from her.

   From the general context you can gather that *intrepid* must mean something like *fearless, courageous,* or *having strength to endure hardship.*

Getting Word Meanings from Context

EXERCISE 9   Read the following selections. Using clues from the context, write a definition for the words listed below the selections. Explain the clues that led you to your decision.

Louis Armstrong Dies at 71— Set World to the Beat of Jazz

Onetime Waif on Streets of New Orleans Who Blew Horn and Sang Way to Fame Succumbs in Sleep in New York

1. waif _____

   succumbs _____

At about the age of 11, Armstrong began to study the trumpet. The identities of his first teachers are <u>shrouded</u> in mystery. One story has it that he was tutored by Bunk Johnson, himself the center of a New Orleans jazz revival in the 1930's and 1940's. But Armstrong himself denied this, saying his only <u>mentor</u> was New Orleans trumpeter and band-leader King Oliver.

2. shrouded _____

   mentor _____

From the nation's beginnings, in fact and fiction, the gun has been provider and protector. The Pilgrim gained a foothold with his <u>harquebus</u>.*

3. harquebus _____

Context clues provide us with partial and possibly temporary understanding of words. But they enable us to proceed with our reading with reasonably good comprehension. Many more experiences with a word and checking with a dictionary may be necessary for accurate, precise, and complete definitions. For example, can you describe a harquebus in detail?

EXERCISE 10

There are strong context clues to all of the underlined words in the following sentences. In the first blank space opposite each selection, write what you think the underlined word means. You need not define the word with a synonym (one word), but may use a group of words or a phrase to get your idea across. If your clues were *specific words,* write the word or words that served as clues in the second space. If your clue was an accumulation of ideas found throughout the text, write *general* in the second space, and jot down the ideas that gave you the clues below the lines.

EXAMPLES:

Definition	*Clue*	
Some kind of bird	flock	a. The hikers were attracted by a flock of <u>ptarmigans</u> in a nearby tree.
A put-on is a trick or joke. The story tells us he played a practical joke on his friends. So jovial could mean jolly, good natured.	general	b. Rosie Grier, a <u>jovial</u> mountain of a man, explains that the whole needlepoint thing started as a put-on. Friends of his manage a needlepoint shop in Beverly Hills and he often dropped in to visit. He'd pretend that he was there to buy supplies for his own stitchery. After just so much of this deception, he decided he'd better learn to do needlepoint.

* Reprinted from "The Gun Under Fire," by permission from *Time, The Weekly Newsmagazine;* © Time Inc. 1968.

_____ _____ 1. He had come to accept a job at the castle—a drab, sprawling, prison-like <u>edifice</u> on top of a distant hill.

_____ _____ 2. The royal gardens are known for their beds of scarlet <u>pimpernel</u>, which are ablaze with color during the tourist season.

_____ _____ 3. It was an age when everyone was looking for relief from boredom, restlessness, or impatience with a war that had gone on too long; but drugs were a poor <u>palliative</u>.

_____ _____ 4. The protesters thought that the administration would <u>concede</u> after a suitable amount of discussion. They were all very much surprised when all administrators present voted to tighten regulations regarding open meetings.

_____ _____ 5. *The Search for Bridey Murphy,* a world-wide best seller, is the strange <u>saga</u> of an American woman who claimed, under hypnosis, to have lived another life in Ireland over 100 years ago.

_____ _____ 6. The principal character in the book, whose story of another life as another person was checked with records in Ireland, talked to the hypnotist about many people and events from Ireland's past. The book aroused much interest in the theory of <u>reincarnation</u>.

_____ _____ 7. After publication of the book, scores of articles appeared claiming to disprove the story, but nobody has been able to <u>refute</u> it.

_____	_____	8. The clean-shaven college man of the '60s is in direct contrast to the <u>hirsute</u> student of the '70s.
_____	_____	9. It was senseless to accuse the salesman of <u>chicanery</u>. It was apparent that his method of selling through trickery had become a way of life.
_____	_____	10. He was <u>surfeited</u> with advice and admonitions, but he was starved for affection.

Bonus question:
What do you think <u>admonitions</u> means in sentence 10?

_____

EXERCISE 11

It is very important to be aware of context clues when reading books written by English authors or in earlier times. Styles in language change just as styles in anything else do, so writers of another time use words that are unfamiliar to many people today or use words in a way that differs from modern usage.

Using the directions from Exercise 10, do the following exercise. All the sentences in this exercise have been selected from books written by English authors about 100 years ago. After you have discussed with others in your class what you think each word means and why, check a dictionary for accuracy.

Definition	*Clue*	
_____	_____	1. With that he blew out his candle, put on his <u>greatcoat</u>, and set forth in the direction of Cavendish Square.
_____	_____	2. You are to go in alone; to open the glazed <u>press</u>, breaking the lock if it be shut; and to draw out, with all its contents as they stand, the fourth drawer from the top.
_____	_____	3. "You know the doctor's ways, sir," replied Poole, "and how he shuts himself up. Well he's shut up again in the <u>cabinet</u>."
_____	_____	4. He thanked me and measured out a few <u>minims</u> of the mixture.

_____   _____   5. I sent out for a fresh supply and mixed the <u>draught</u>. I drank it.

_____   _____   6. There was a policeman not far off, advancing with his <u>bull's eye</u> open.

_____   _____   7. It was a bitter night, so we drew our <u>ulsters</u> and <u>cravats</u> around our throats.

_____   _____   8. There stood a large woman with a heavy fur <u>boa</u> around her neck and a large, curling red feather in a broad brimmed hat, which was tilted in a "Duchess of Devonshire" fashion over her ear.

_____   _____   9. Homer came for us in a <u>hansom</u>, but as there were two of us, he put us both into it, and
_____   _____   stepped himself into a <u>four-wheeler</u>, which happened to be the only other cab in the street.

_____   _____   10. The dress which I found waiting for me was of a peculiar shade of blue. It was of excellent material, a sort of <u>beige</u>, but it bore unmistakable signs of having been worn before.

Note: Sentence 10 illustrates a word meaning that is markedly different from its meaning in modern usage. With the aid of the dictionary entry on *beige,* can you trace the probable shifts or change in usage that brought about today's meaning?

EXERCISE 12

The context can involve material that precedes the material being read by considerable space, and it can also involve knowledge that the reader brings with him to his reading. The following news report followed a racial disturbance. The reader, to get the full meaning of this item, should be aware that, historically, many such disturbances have occurred in the summer. He should also have the ability to visualize the scene described by recalling similar items he may have read or television reports he may have seen.

Read the item through quickly to get the general meaning. Then reread it more carefully, and, with the aid of context clues, try to attach a meaning to the underlined words. Write what you think the words mean in the blanks provided below the paragraph. Do not be afraid of making incorrect answers. The fact that you think about the word and can make a guess about its meaning indicates that you are becoming an active reader.

> Outside New York, there were other harbingers of what may be a difficult summer. The mayor called in the National Guard in Chattanooga, Tenn., after a cancelled soul concert touched off five nights of sporadic arson and rioting. A wild racial melee erupted at California's Travis Air Force Base, which had been cited less than a year ago as a model of good racial relations in the service. And in the delta town of Drew, Miss., three young whites who had been drinking were charged with gunning down a 19-year-old black girl after her high school graduation, touching off rock-tossing protests by black youths and drawing a message of condolence (and help of the FBI in the investigation) from President Nixon.*

1. harbinger _____
2. sporadic _____
3. melee _____
4. cited _____
5. condolence _____

* From "Suddenly, This Summer," Copyright *Newsweek,* Inc., June 7, 1971.

EXERCISE 13

Before you read the following selections from *The Population Bomb,* look at the vocabulary list that precedes them. In the blanks write a meaning for any words that you think you know. If you don't know any of the words, don't be disturbed. This reading selection, though written for the general public, is scientific in nature and contains a more specialized vocabulary than would be found in a nonscientific selection. This is true in much textbook reading. Read the selection carefully, and, when you finish reading it, see how many word meanings you can fill in with the help you get from the context. Write in any meanings you feel fairly sure of. You can use more than one word to explain a meaning. Then study the vocabulary words and the meanings you have given them. Read the selection again and do the exercise at the end of the selection. Play fair in this exercise and do not consult a dictionary!

1. extinct _____
2. ecologist _____
3. ecosystem _____
4. salinization _____
5. population biology _____
6. deterioration _____
7. accelerate _____
8. intensify _____
9. predator _____
10. role _____
11. compensation _____
12. carnivorous _____
13. herbivorous _____
14. carnivore _____
15. escalated _____
16. potent _____
17. miticides _____
18. carcinogens _____

The Population Bomb

[PARAGRAPH I]

It is fair to say that the environment of every organization, human and nonhuman, on the face of the Earth has been influenced by the population explosion. As direct or indirect results of this explosion, some organisms, such as the passenger pigeon, are now extinct. Many others, such as the larger wild animals of all continents, have been greatly reduced in numbers. Still others, such as sewer rats and house flies, enjoy much enlarged populations. But these are obvious results and probably less important than more subtle changes in the complex web of life and in delicately balanced natural chemical cycles. Ecologists—those biologists who study the relationships of plants and animals with their environments—are especially concerned about these changes. They realize how easily disrupted are ecological systems (called eco-systems). They also are afraid of both the short- and long-range consequences of mankind's activities.

[PARAGRAPH II]

Environmental changes connected with agriculture

*Adapted from *The Population Bomb* by Dr. Paul R. Ehrlich. Copyright © 1968 by Paul R. Ehrlich. Reprinted by permission of Ballantine Books, Inc. and the author. All rights reserved.

are often striking. For instance, in the United States we are paying a price for maintaining our high level of food production. We have lost many thousands of acres to erosion and gullying, and many thousands more to strip mining. It has been estimated that the agricultural value of Iowa farmland, which is about as good as we have, is declining by 1% per year. In the rich but naturally arid lands of the West, there is the constant danger of salinization, as salts rise to the surface as the result of constant surface irrigation. Along the coastlines of both the Atlantic and the Pacific we have drawn on underground water supplies to such an extent that good land is being endangered by seepage of salt water from the ocean.

[PARAGRAPH III]

The history of similar deterioration in other parts of the world is clear for those who know how to read it. In the Middle East, deserts now occupy what were once rich and productive farmlands. And the process of destruction still goes on. Water resources are being used and redirected with no consideration of the ecological effects. A good example is the building of dams on the Nile, preventing deposit of nutrient-rich silt that used to accompany annual floods of the river. As almost anyone who remembers his high school geography could have predicted, the result has been a continuing decrease in the productivity of soils in the Nile Delta. The proposed damming of the Mekong River could produce the same results for Vietnam and her neighbors.

[PARAGRAPH IV]

Plans for increasing food production invariably involve large-scale efforts at environmental modification. Such efforts almost always involve the increased use of fertilizers and insecticides. Growing more food also may involve the clearing of forests from additional land and the provision of irrigation water. I predict that the rate of soil deterioration will accelerate as the food crisis intensifies. Ecology will be ignored more and more as things get tough.

[PARAGRAPH V]

One of the basic facts of population biology—that branch of biology that deals with groups of organisms—is that the simpler an ecosystem is, the more unstable it is. A complex forest, consisting of a great variety of plants and animals, will persist year in and year out with no interference from man. The system contains many elements, and changes in different elements often cancel each other out. Suppose one kind of predator eating mice and rabbits suffers a population decline. For instance, suppose most of the foxes in the forest die of disease? The role of that predator will probably be assumed by another animal, perhaps weasels or owls. Then there will be no population explosion of mice or rabbits. Such compensation may not be possible in simpler ecosystems.

[PARAGRAPH VI]

Man, however, is a simplifier of complex ecosystems. Or in other words, man is a creator of simple ecosystems. Synthetic pesticides, for instance, are one of man's powerful tools for reducing the complexity of ecosystems. What happens when a complex ecosystem is treated with a synthetic pesticide? Some of the carnivorous (animal-eating) species are exterminated, and the herbivorous (plant-eating) species or pests become resistant. The ecosystem is simplified by the removal of the carnivores and becomes less stable. Since carnivores can no longer help control the size of the pest population, the pesticide treatments must be escalated to more and more dangerous levels. Ads for insecticides sometimes imply that there is some absolute number of pests—that if we could just eliminate all the "public enemies" things would be dandy. In fact, pesticides often create pests. Careless overuse of DDT has promoted to "pest" category many species of mites, little insectlike relatives of spiders. The insects which ate the mites were killed by the DDT, and the mites were resistant to DDT. There you have it—instant pests! What's more, some of the more potent miticides the chemists have developed with which to do battle seem to be powerful carcinogens—cancer - producing substances.

EXERCISE 14

The following paragraph sums up the principle ideas contained in the preceding selections from *The Population Bomb*. Fill in the blanks. You may refer to the text as much as you feel is necessary, but the most precise word for the blank may or may not be one used in the text, as this is a summary—not an excerpt.

All forms of life have been affected by the _____ _____. _____ are concerned about the fact that some organisms are _____ _____, many others are greatly reduced in numbers, while others are greatly _____ in numbers. These are _____ results of man's attempt to deal with the population explosion. However, ecologists are much more concerned about changes in the complex _____ of life and the _____ that must exist among many natural chemical cycles.

_____ changes connected with agriculture can be quite striking. Attempts to increase productivity of the soil have resulted in soil _____. Attempts to _____ water resources are robbing valuable agricultural land of nutrient-rich soil. Persistent use of insecticides has interfered with the basic facts of _____ _____. Dr. Ehrlich implies that the trend to meet the population explosion by these methods will _____ and predicts that the concerns of ecologists will be increasingly more justified.

One of Dr. Ehrlich's most interesting points is made about population biology. He states that the simpler an ecosystem is the more _____ it is. Man, he says, tends to _____ ecosystems. An ecosystem becomes simplified when carnivores are _____ and pests become resistant to attempts to control them. Such attempts involve an _____ in the use of pesticide treatments. Such _____ actually _____ pests, he says, as the _____ kill some pests that kill other pests. He introduces the frightening idea of _____ pests along with _____ ecosystems.

82

Section Three

Power Through Seeing Relationships

Sentences

Many English sentences contain two or more thought-bearing units woven together. As they mature, all speakers begin to weave ideas together in their speech more or less unconsciously. However, the process of interpreting written English is more difficult than interpreting spoken English. There are many reasons for this. The listener is face-to-face with a speaker and can observe his gestures and facial expressions, which give many clues to meaning. And, except in very formal situations, there are opportunities for interaction between listener and speaker that can produce questions, explanations, and repetition. Most important of all, written English in almost all forms tends to be more tightly woven—more concise and concentrated—than spoken English. Therefore, it is worth a little time to examine how ideas are combined in English sentences.

Thought-bearing units are linked by *structure words*. These words have no meaning in themselves but do indicate a specific relationship between the ideas they tie together. Some structure words are used only to indicate a relationship between ideas within the same sentence. Others can show a relationship between ideas in two separate sentences and can serve as a guide for the reader to work his way through a paragraph.

Some Common Structure Words

Extenders	Contrasters	Qualifiers	Summarizers	Emphasizers
and	but	if	so	in fact
who	although	when	thus	in other words
which	yet	after	therefore	
moreover	however	because		
that	nevertheless			

EXERCISE 1

With the aid of structure words, rewrite the following pairs of sentences to form one sentence. You may have to omit a word or insert a word in addition to the structure word. Write the structure word you have used and its classification in the blank at the right of your new sentence.

EXAMPLE:

A. A baby gray whale was captured off the coast of Mexico.
B. The baby whale was later named Gigi.

A baby gray whale, which was later named Gigi,	which
was captured off the coast of Mexico.	extender

1. A. She lived in a tank at San Diego's Sea World for a period of a year.
   B. She weighed fourteen hundred pounds and measured twenty-seven feet.

   _____ _____

   _____ _____

2. A. The purpose of taking her into captivity was to provide a specimen for zoologists and ocean mammal specialists to study.

B. She also provided much amusement for visitors at the oceanarium.

3. A. She was released in the Spring of 1972.
   B. Tracking gear was affixed to her back.

4. A. She was free to go wherever she wished.
   B. First signals revealed that she was swimming in circles just as she had in the huge tank at Sea World.

5. A. A month after her release trackers could not pick up the trace.
   B. Many scientists feel that she followed the pattern of other gray whales in their yearly migration to the Bering Sea.

EXERCISE 2

Read the following pairs of sentences. Determine the relationship between the ideas in the two sentences. In the blank, write a structure word that could be used to combine the two sentences. Test your choice of structure word by saying aloud the new sentence you propose to build.

1. A. In 1850 a young New Yorker named Levi Strauss landed in San Francisco with a roll of canvas under his arm.
   B. He ran into a miner with torn pants.
2. A. He made the miner some trousers from the canvas.
   B. This was the beginning of Levi Strauss & Company and the origin of your favorite pair of pants.
3. A. Levi's almost immediately became a success in the mining camps.
   B. They might have disappeared with the goldrush and the cowboy except for their popularity among Easterners taking dude ranch vacations in the West in the early 1900s.
4. A. The tough pants with the famous advertising slogan "copper riveted" soon became known in the East as well as the West.
   B. Levi Strauss had a million dollar business on his hands.
5. A. Levi's (often made in a coverall style) became the standard uniform for working men on the farm and in the factory.
   B. They still might have bowed to the competition except for the college student.

Courtesy of Levi Strauss & Co.

6. A. In the fifties white Levi's (actually light beige) became a status symbol for college men throughout the country.
   B. Whatever social stigma might have been attached to wearing a pair of jeans disappeared.
7. A. The original Levi's carried a tag above the rear pocket.
   B. This tag announced to all the world the waistline size of the garment.
8. A. It was traditional to buy Levi's in a slightly larger size to allow for shrinkage.
   B. The sensitivity of some of their customers led Levi Strauss & Company to experiment with shrink-proof fabrics.
9. A. In the sixties young British fashion-mongers came to the United States and found every great-looking young kid—male and female—in Levi's.
   B. A world fashion was raging.
10. A. Levi's can now be bought in colors and stripes, with flare and bell bottoms and in Sta-Prest fabrics.
    B. The largest seller in the line is still the old blue jeans—button-fly and shrink-to-fit.

EXERCISE 3   The following article contains many structure words. Some relate two thought units within the same sentence. Others relate thought units that are each entire sentences. Find the structure words and write them in the margin beside the line in which they occur. Be prepared to explain what thought units the structure word links and what relationship it establishes.

EXAMPLE:

If you can break through the fierce competition in modeling, the rewards in this field can be unbelievable.

Explanation:

The thought unit, "If you can break through the fierce competition in modeling" *qualifies* the thought unit, "the rewards in this field (modeling) can be unbelievable."

EXAMPLE:

A male model can earn as much as $50,000 a year, and he usually will have a longer career than a girl.

Explanation:

The thought unit, "he usually will have a longer career than a girl" *extends* the thought unit, "A male model can earn as much as $50,000 a year."

They Never Shout "Mush"

Dogs have pulled sleds since prehistoric times, but putting them into racing is a recent development. In 1914 Leonard Seppala organized a "race against death" when he and other drivers rushed diphtheria serum to Nome. As a popular sport sled-dog racing was centered in New England for a long time, but it eventually and inevitably spread across the northern reaches of the country.

Although there are many hard and fast rules connected with sled-dog racing, there is none that specifies what type of dog may be used. Many teams are made up of the expected northern breeds—the Eskimo dog, Alaskan Husky, Indian dog, Samoyed, Alaskan Malamute. But other breeds have proved themselves excellent competitors in the field. Moreover, some teams are made up of a variety of breeds—setters, retrievers, coon-hounds and just plain dogs in the mongrel category. If your dog can and will run, he's a sled dog.

There are several classes of teams in each race, depending on speed, number of dogs, ability to handle the team, etc. Teams in the senior class must enter with at least seven dogs on the first day, but in other classes there is an Open Five Dog Class. And Juniors are offered Five Dog Amateur and Regular Amateur Classes.

The dogs love to race. After they have run a few vigorous laps they quite naturally pant and may look tired, but they're intensely happy about the whole thing. In fact, we are told that the only time a sled dog is not happy is when he's not with his team.

Adapted from *Yankee,* February, 1972.

Most important is the lead dog, who controls the entire team with his strength, determination and intelligence. It's up to him to maintain the pace, to understand the driver's commands, and to inspire the other dogs to keep at it when they might feel inclined to take a breather somewhere along the line.

Commands are verbal, and beamed right at the lead dog. The horse-y directions of "gee" and "haw" are most frequently used, although now and then a purist uses Eskimo and Indian dialect. However, one command they never shout is "Mush." "Mush" is a widely-known sled-dog command meaning to go faster, coming from the Canadian-French word *mouche* meaning *run*. The excited onlookers yell "Mush, Mush," and it is vital that the dogs not be confused about their commands.

The rules of the Club, which are aimed at protecting the animals as well as maintaining order, are strict. Race courses are frequently-used country roads. However, roads must not be plowed and sanded. Because more and more automobile travelers are taking alternate routes to avoid traffic, finding suitable race courses becomes a greater problem.

Sled dog racing is a race against time and the best total time for two days determines the winner. Therefore, unlike many other forms of racing, the race is not a matter of a number of teams plowing along side by side. Because the teams leave at two-minute intervals, the people standing along the course have a good chance to see each team in action. Thus, spectators have their favorite team chosen by the time the dogs come roaring back down the home stretch. Many races are composed of a number of laps presenting all the more opportunities to observe the dogs.

You would think cold weather, the location of the race courses and the lure of football games on television would limit the attraction of sled-dog racing, yet more races are scheduled every year. In fact, the latest wrinkle is the International Border Race, which takes teams across the border between the United States and Canada six times in each lap. So next winter check the calendar of events for a sled-dog race and join the fun.

EXERCISE 4

Look at the structure words you have listed in Exercise 3. Reread the thought units that they connect. Which classification of structure word

A. Repeats in another way something that has already been said?

B. Adds two thoughts together?

C. Suggests that the information in one thought-bearing unit places a condition on the information in the other thought-bearing unit?

D. Suggests that the two ideas more or less cancel each other out?

E. Pulls many ideas together or suggests a conclusion?

Dog sled Denver Public Library, Western History Department

Paragraphs

You have observed that the parts of sentences can be knit together in a manner that shows how one part is related to another. The structure of a paragraph does not always reveal the relationship of ideas in such a clearly defined manner. A writer *may* state his subject at or near the beginning of a paragraph: however, most writers do not write according to formulas. Good writers do write with organization, and the good reader is aware of that organization. In other words, the good reader thinks in the pattern established by the writer.

All relationships of ideas in paragraphs revolve around a particular idea the writer is stressing. In this section we will refer to that idea as the *primary idea*. Other ideas must be evaluated as to how they relate to the primary idea and how they relate to each other. If an idea explains or illustrates the primary idea or makes the primary idea more convincing, it is important to the organization of the paragraph. We will refer to such ideas as *secondary ideas*. In many instances secondary ideas need to be noted or remembered, particularly in the reading of textbooks, from which you are expected to retain a great deal of information. It is especially important to be able to recall secondary ideas when writing an essay-type examination in which you are asked to explain or support your answers.

Let's look at the simplest type of paragraph—one in which the writer states the primary idea at the beginning.

> Schools across the country are recognizing the usefulness of the guitar in teaching music fundamentals. In some schools, pupils in the fourth and fifth grades are plunking tunes after a few lessons. In a school in New York, guitar instruction has been going on for several years in the seventh through twelfth grades. The program was initiated to teach music fundamentals, not necessarily guitar. A class in folk guitar is also very popular. On the West Coast, the same kind of guitar programs are under way. The guitar scene is equally bright at the college level. Today several colleges and universities offer majors in classical guitar, which is becoming increasingly popular. Graduates often go into school music programs or teaching in studio operations.*

The principal ideas in this paragraph have been placed in a diagram that designates the primary idea and the secondary ideas. Not all the statements are included in the diagram. Some statements may state in another way what has already been said or they may merely serve as interesting "filler" of relatively unimportant points. In this paragraph, the last sentence is "filler." Some writers use the last sentence in one paragraph to lead the reader to the subject covered in the next paragraph.

Primary Idea

Schools across the country are recognizing the usefulness of the guitar in teaching music fundamentals.

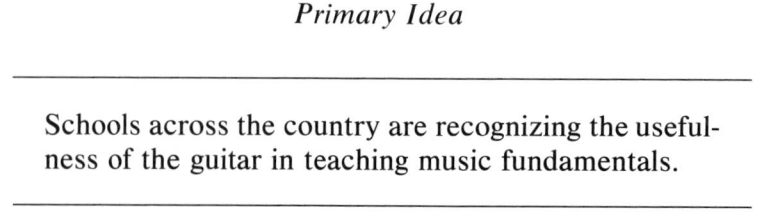

* Adapted from "Try the Guitar for an Icebreaker," *Better Homes and Gardens,* March 1971. © Meredith Corporation, 1971. All rights reserved.

Secondary Ideas

In some schools, pupils in the fourth and fifth grades are plunking tunes after a few lessons.

In a school in New York, guitar instruction has been going on for several years in the seventh through twelfth grades.

On the West Coast, the same kind of guitar programs are under way.

The guitar scene is equally bright at the college level.

The first sentence in any paragraph is an important sentence. It may or may not state the primary idea. However, it should always be considered carefully in determining what the writer is stressing and in evaluating the importance of other sentences.

EXERCISE 5 Read the following paragraph. Select three sentences that best express the primary and secondary ideas and write them in the appropriate frames. In what ways do the remaining sentences lead up to or provide important or interesting commentary on the sentences you have selected?

A great drawing card for the guitar is the social aspect of this versatile instrument. Teens and subteens find that guitar playing is an easy route to enhancing and increasing friendships. Whereas ten to fifteen years ago teens at a party or get-together turned on the phonograph, nowadays doing your own thing involves making your own music. And the guitar provides the music today in the teen world. More often than not, the guitar player has learned to play in a group class rather than with individual instruction. Group instruction offers many advantages. Students can learn to play at little or no cost (if they take a class in a public school). And more important, they learn to profit from other people's accomplishments and get experience in overcoming shyness. Instructors of group guitar classes report that very few students drop out of group guitar classes and that students tend to practice more than for individual instruction. Instead of approaching lessons with grim resignation, students seem to look forward to a challenging and rewarding experience. In music—that's more than half the battle.*

* Adapted from "Try the Guitar for an Icebreaker," *Better Homes and Gardens,* March 1971. © Meredith Corporation, 1971. All rights reserved.

Primary Idea

Secondary Ideas

The structure of many paragraphs—even though they are well written and well organized—may not be easy to analyze. To place the ideas in frames such as were used in Exercise 5, you must combine ideas from different sentences and restate them in your own words. Of course, you may borrow words or phrases from the writer to do this.

EXERCISE 6

Read the following paragraph written by Stirling Moss, a world-renowned professional race driver. Then fill in the diagram below. Build the primary idea by choosing words or phrases for the numbered blanks from the corresponding lists of words. For the secondary ideas select the two statements from List 5 that, in your opinion, support the primary idea most accurately.

It took me eight years of intense effort to learn to concentrate so thoroughly while I was driving that in a three-hour race I would not have to tell myself to concentrate. I have never done anything that was so hard. Try it. You'll see. Within the first 60 seconds you'll lose your concentration. You'll see a red station wagon; it will remind you of a friend who had a red station wagon; you went fishing with him . . . . and there you are. You've lost your concentration. This loss of concentration will kill a professional driver in short order. A layman can get away with it for a time . . . . a long time or a short time as the case may be. One day, when you have a second-and-a-half in which to *do* something about an emergency, and you need a full half-second to come out of your daydream—too bad chum!*

Primary Idea

(1) _____ / is (2) _____
for both the (3) _____ and the
(4) _____

1. concentration 2. difficult   3. beginning driver   4. beginning driver
   intense effort   important   fast driver   layman
                     vital   professional driver   slow driver

Secondary Ideas

5. A. It is very difficult to concentrate while driving.
   B. It takes at least a half second to pull yourself out of a daydream.
   C. The average driver does not need to concentrate as much as a racing driver.
   D. Any driver who has not learned to concentrate while driving will eventually meet an emergency situation that he cannot handle because of lack of time.

* Reprinted from "How to Drive and Survive" by Stirling Moss as told to Ken Purdy. *Better Homes and Gardens,* June 1964. © Meredith Corporation, 1964. All rights reserved.

All of the ideas in the following selection are important and thought-provoking. One or more paragraphs could be written on the idea presented in each sentence. However, the ideas can be evaluated within the structure of the paragraph as either primary or secondary.

EXERCISE 7A

Read the paragraph and then read the principal ideas as they have been restated for you below the paragraph. Select the statement that communicates the primary idea and write it in the frame.

One of the reasons why life today seems more complex than it did half a century ago is the speed with which bad news communicates. A major factor in the Vietnam War has been the presence of television, which makes the actuality of war insupportable. This raises certain interesting speculations. Abraham Lincoln would not have been able to prosecute the Civil War to a successful conclusion had television been flooding the contemporary scene with daily pictures of the northern Copperheads who opposed the war, of the draft riots that rocketed through northern cities, and especially of the stark horror of Vicksburg. Sometime in late 1863 he would have been forced to capitulate, with the probability that slavery would have continued in the southern states till the early years of this century.*

Primary Idea

1. If television had existed during the Civil War, slavery would have continued in the South until the 1900s.
2. Television brings the realities of war into everyone's living room.
3. Life in the United States today seems more complex than it used to be because bad news travels so fast.
4. The Civil War would have ended in 1863 with defeat for Lincoln and the North if pictures of the horrors of the war could have been flashed to the nation by television.
5. A major factor in the Vietnam War has been the presence of television.

Sometimes the ideas in a paragraph fall into a step-type pattern with some ideas being more directly related to the secondary ideas than to the primary idea. Although it is not always necessary to diagram in great detail the structure of a paragraph on paper—or even in our minds—it is good practice. Such practice can be very helpful in understanding the logic of an opinion or theory.

* From the book *The Quality of Life* by James Michener. Copyright © 1970 by James Michener. Reprinted by permission of J. B. Lippincott Company.

EXERCISE 7B Rearrange the five statements in Exercise 7A, placing only the number of the statement in the frames below. In the place provided after the first three frames write the sentence *from the paragraph* (not one of the restatements) that signals that the writer is proceeding to a new step.

Primary Idea

Secondary Ideas

Sentence from paragraph that signals a new step:

_____

_____

95

EXERCISE 8

In this paragraph all the sentences or sentence units have been numbered. The logic of this thought-provoking selection can best be grasped by arranging the ideas in a step-type pattern. Place the number of the sentences in the appropriate frames. You may want to write out the sentences in similarly arranged frames on a piece of scratch paper to test your logic.

[1] In U.S. folklore, nothing has been more romanticized than guns and the larger-than-life men who wielded them. [2] From the nation's beginnings, in fact and fiction, the gun has been provider and protector. [3] The Pilgrim gained a foothold with his harquebus. [4] A legion of loners won the West with Colt .45 Peacemakers holstered at their hips or Winchester 73 repeaters cradled in their arms. [5] Often as not, the frontiersman was an antisocial misfit who helped create a climate of barbaric lawlessness. No matter. [6] Daniel Boone and Buffalo Bill, Jesse James and Billy the Kid, hero and villain alike, all were men of the gun and all were idolized. [7] "Have gun, will travel" was more than a catch phrase. It was a way of life. [8] Even after the frontier reached its limits, the myths lingered and the legends multiplied, first in dime novels, later in movies and on TV.*

Primary Idea

☐

Secondary Ideas

☐

☐

☐

---

* Reprinted from "Gun Under Fire," by permission from *Time, The Weekly Newsmagazine;* © Time, Inc., 1968.

Secondary Ideas

Secondary Ideas

Sometimes a writer seems to develop two ideas of equal importance in a paragraph. Although these two ideas can be woven together into a generalization that includes both of them, it is often valuable to first consider each one separately in order to see the logical development of the two ideas.

EXERCISE 9A The sentences in the following paragraph have been numbered. Read the paragraph carefully and place the numbers of the sentences in the appropriate frames below the paragraph. Note that there are two frames for primary ideas and that each one is developed with the aid of secondary ideas.

¹There is probably no older more romantic stereotype in our national consciousness than the cowboy on his horse. ²The Indian, the mountain man, and ultimately the cowboy, all pursued their destiny on horseback. ³The folklore of a nation is inextricably bound up with the image of the lone rider on his steed, free to go anywhere over the face of a great land, his body and his mind attuned to sharper awareness by exposure to the elements. ⁴This element in our heritage may explain in part the phenomenal growth of the motorcycle industry in the last decade. ⁵This iron steed is perhaps the logical culmination of the abiding romance of the horse coupled with the vastly increased speed and range of the motorized vehicle. ⁶The motorcycle rider in the wind knows he is alive in a way that the car driver, insulated from the world by two tons of steel and glass and gimmicks, can never appreciate. ⁷And if he chooses, the motorcycle rider can thumb his nose at the automobile's slavish dependence on graded surfaces. ⁸The iron steed can cross streams and deserts and climb mountains in the rider's quest for life.*

Primary Idea

Secondary Ideas

---

* Adapted from "The Iron Steeds" by Swede Carlson. Reprinted by permission of the author.

EXERCISE 9B   Identifying the principal strains of thought in a paragraph helps the reader to generalize about the paragraph as a whole. You recall from Section I that a generalization *weaves* together ideas from a series of statements and must be broad enough to touch upon the most important ideas. In the paragraph in Exercise 9A many more sentences are devoted to secondary ideas than to primary ideas. Reread the paragraph and take particular note of any ideas among the secondary ideas that gain strength through repetition. You may want to write out each sentence completely in a pattern like the one in Exercise 9A so that you will be more aware of all the ideas presented. Then complete the following generalization about the paragraph by choosing one of the phrases listed. Circle.

The phenomenal growth of the motorcycle industry in the United States can be traced _____

A. to the fact that Americans are getting tired of all the glass and gimmicks in automobiles.
B. to the fact that the motorcycle in the motorized twentieth century helps to perpetuate historical images and drives that are strong in the national consciousness.
C. to the fact that Americans basically don't like to be confined and are rebelling against the constraints of closed cars and paved roads.
D. to the fact that the stereotype of the lone rider on his steed is strong in the national consciousness and that many Americans would like to live the life of earlier times.

A motorcyclist charging up a sandy slope near Dallas, Texas

Ralph Krubner from Black Star

EXERCISE 10

In this selection the writer emphasizes his main ideas in the first four sentences. Following the paragraph are two phrases, each of which is a good beginning for a single statement of the primary idea. Using one of the phrases labeled *Part II, Primary Idea,* complete the two statements so that each one contributes a satisfactory primary idea for a diagram of this paragraph. In your own words write two secondary ideas that logically support the primary ideas. Read sentences 5–8 carefully and think through what is said before you write the secondary ideas.

[1] Kids who were too small to ride motorcycles weren't willing to wait to grow up. [2] The mini-bike, which had originally come on the scene with the Go-Kart, now found its place, and the two-wheeled motorized market was down to age 5 or 6. [3] The importance of the mini-bike is too little understood. [4] The enthusiasm of youngsters for motorized vehicles is in keeping with the American love affair with wheels. [5] This passion is more universal than, say, the commitment to Little League baseball or Pop Warner football. [6] In a pilot program in one major U.S. city, the Y.M.C.A. found that previously incorrigible youngsters would attend school and obey rules for the reward of mini-bike riding in supervised events. [7] So striking is the success of this project that a national Y.M.C.A. program is being organized, with one of the leading motor-bike manufacturers pledging 10,000 mini-bikes to the cause. [8] Small wonder that annual sales of more than a half-million mini-bikes are already a reality, creating millions of future motorcycle riders.*

Primary Idea

Part I   *Part II*

1. American youngsters / _____

   _____

2. The importance of the mini-bike / _____

   _____.

Part II
- A. weren't willing to wait to grow up.
- B. goes back to the Go-Kart.
- C. is directly related to the enthusiasm of American youngsters for anything with wheels.
- D. fell in love with the mini-bike as soon as it came on the market.
- E. is too little understood.
- F. found in the mini-bike another outlet for the American love affair with wheels.

* Adapted from "Boots and Saddles" by Swede Carlson. First published in *West Magazine.* Reprinted by permission of the author.

Secondary Ideas

Many paragraphs are developed by relating a sequence of events. That is, facts or observations are stated in the order in which they happened or should happen. This type of paragraph is very common in history texts, how-to manuals, or any writing that has to do with an account of a particular incident. Of course, this pattern is easy to recognize when it contains words like first, second, finally, etc., but a writer often expects you to sense that he is writing in logical sequence. He may even assume that you are quite good at visualizing what he is talking about.

EXERCISE 11A Read the following selection from a recent book in which the author deals with the physical signals that he says we all send out. These signals, he says, telegraph our thoughts to all who observe them. In the spaces provided, list the acts of the listener in the same order that the author has recorded them. Two moves can make up one act. Opposite the acts write what the act means—an interpretation of the physical signal. If one act is an alternative to another, connect the two with *or*.

To illustrate the use of positions, imagine a situation in which one man is holding forth on a particular subject. The listener leans back in his chair, arms and legs crossed, as he listens to the speaker's ideas. When the listener reaches a point where he disagrees with the speaker, he shifts his position in preparation for delivering his protest. He may lean forward and uncross his arms and legs. Perhaps he will raise one hand with the forefinger pointed as he begins to launch a rebuttal. When he is finished he will again lean back into his first position, arms and legs crossed—or perhaps move into a more receptive position where his arms and legs are uncrossed as he leans back, signaling that he is open to suggestion.*

Acts   *Interpretation*

_____

_____

_____

* From *Body Language,* by Julius Fast. Copyright © 1970 by Julius Fast. Reprinted by permission of the publisher, M. Evans and Company, Inc.

EXERCISE 11B   In the preceding paragraph, the primary idea is not stated. Furthermore, if you try to summarize the several sentences or combine them by borrowing phrases from them, you cannot produce the primary idea. You are expected to generalize about what the author has said and in your own mind develop the primary idea. In your reading you will find many paragraphs that resemble this one. Reread the paragraph. Then, using the opening phrase, in the following frame write a good primary idea for the paragraph.

Primary Idea

In a conversation between two people
_____
_____
_____

EXERCISE 12A   Mr. Fast explores another aspect of human behavior in the following paragraph from the same book. He states his primary idea in the first sentence. In order to convince his readers of what may be a new and startling idea, he illustrates his statement with a series of cause-and-effect situations. The use of a cause-and-effect situation is also an effective device to explain the logic of an idea. From the list below the paragraph supply the effects of the two causative situations that are given to you.

    A man driving a car often loses an essential part of his own humanity and is, by virtue of the machine around him, once removed from a human being. The body language communication that works so well for him outside the car often will not work at all when he is driving. We have all been annoyed by drivers who cut in front of us, and we all know the completely irrational rage that can sometimes fill the driver who has had his space invaded. The police will cite statistics to show that dozens of accidents are caused by this cutting in, by the dangerous reaction of the man who has been cut off. In a social situation few men would dream of acting or reacting in this fashion. Stripped of the machine, we adopt a civilized attitude and allow people to cut in front of us, indeed we step aside quite often to permit people to board a bus or elevator ahead of us.*

Cause
1. Man surrounds self with car

2. Man is stripped of car

Effect
_____
_____
_____

_____
_____
_____

* From *Body Language,* by Julius Fast.

Effects
A. Man cuts in front of others
B. Conventional body language works
C. Conventional body language does not work
D. Man responds with rage when space invaded
E. Man adopts civilized attitude
F. Man steps aside in favor of other people

Question: Do you agree with the primary idea of this paragraph? Explain.

_____

_____

_____

EXERCISE 12B In Exercise 12A the causes were *general* in nature. The effects that they produced are both *general* and *specific*. Label the effects in your answers as general or specific by writing G or S after each of them.

EXERCISE 13 The following paragraph, when carefully analyzed, is made up of a series of cause-and-effect statements. That is, the writer tells that people do or do not do certain things (causes) and this action or lack of action produces certain results (effects). Read the paragraph. From the statements below it, separate the causes from the effects and list them. In the opposite column record what is, in the author's opinion, the effect of each cause. Several causes can have the same effect, and an effect can be expressed in more than one way.

> The most important technique of eye management is the look, or the stare. With it we can often make or break another person. How? By giving him human or non-human status. Simply, eye management in our society boils down to two facts. One, we do not stare at another human being. Two, staring is reserved for a non-person. We stare at art, at sculpture, at scenery. We go to the zoo and stare at the animals, the lions, the monkeys, the gorillas. We stare at them as long as we please, as intimately as we please, but we do not stare at humans if we want to accord them human treatment.*

a. We classify as human and/or non-human
b. We stare at scenery
c. We stare at people
d. We make or break a person
e. We manage our eyes
f. We stare at art
g. We give human status
h. We stare at animals
i. We do not stare at people
j. We give non-human status

* From *Body Language* by Julius Fast.

Causes   Effects

1. _____   _____
2. _____   _____
3. _____   _____
4. _____   _____
5. _____   _____
6. _____   _____

From the lists you have made, select the cause and effect that you think contains the logic of the writer's primary idea in the paragraph and write them in the frame below.

Primary Idea

Cause: _____
Effect: _____

Section Four

Power Through Reference

We read for many reasons. Probably the two most common reasons are to provide pleasure and to gain information. Reading often arouses interest in reading further in a subject or finding the answer to some question arising from what you have read, but you may not know where to look for the information. The purpose of this section is to acquaint you with the three most readily available reference sources—the dictionary, the daily newspaper, and the encyclopedia. The use of these reference sources requires only a minimum of instruction if you already have good reading ability. They provide a wealth of interesting and valuable reading material. Such reading can bring a greater depth of understanding to what you hear, read, learn, or become interested in from other sources.

The Dictionary

A dictionary is the most valuable and least expensive reference book a person can own. It can be a source of information on a wide range of subjects. It is really a miniature encyclopedia. A dictionary is most frequently consulted to find the meaning or pronunciation of a word. It takes some skill to use the dictionary for either of these purposes, but any person can develop these skills and greatly increase his word power by doing so. In this section you will become acquainted with all the information that is available to you in a complete dictionary entry. However, the emphasis will be on helping you to develop skill in using a dictionary as an aid to pronouncing unfamiliar or hard-to-pronounce words. Frequent use of your dictionary will soon make you aware of all the other information that it contains.

This work on the use of a dictionary for word pronunciation can be thought of as a supplement to the Word Recognition portion of Section I. If the spelling pattern approach does not produce a satisfactory pronunciation of a word, or if you feel unsure of the pronunciation it produces, you must consult a dictionary. What you may discover is that the spelling pattern technique has made it possible for you to respond quite accurately to some parts of the word, but you may need further help with the response to one part, or you may have a question as to what syllable to stress. A dictionary can resolve these uncertainties. The way a word is pronounced can be the result of a long language history for that word involving the influence of many languages and many speakers. Even the most educated scholar does not possess built-in programming to predict pronunciation of all words with certainty. Familiarity with the language gives all native speakers a basic "feel" for appropriate pronunciations, but history and custom have in some instances produced unpredictable variations to what might be considered expected responses or a natural rhythm.

Use of the Dictionary—Pronunciation

In order to use the dictionary to pronounce words, you must be able to use the pronunciation key. In most dictionaries, the most frequently used symbols are printed in a pronunciation key at the bottom of each right-hand page. Less frequently used symbols may be in the front or back of the dictionary. It is not necessary to memorize pronunciation symbols (diacritical marks), because they differ from one dictionary to another. However, you should become thoroughly familiar with the symbols in your own dictionary. You will find that there are only minor differences between these and the symbols used in other dictionaries, so thorough familiarity with one will help you to make quick and effective use of another. Making use of diacritical marks involves transferring the sound in a reference word in the key to the word that you want to pronounce. You have already acquired skill in transferring sounds from one word to another in Section I (Word Recognition).

EXERCISE 1A

Study carefully the pronunciation key printed across the bottom of the next several pages. The dictionary gives a reference word for every letter and symbol. Write the reference word for each of the following symbols in the first blank. In the second blank write another word that contains the same sound that the symbol illustrates. The second word may or may not have the same spelling pattern as the reference word.

	Symbol	Reference Word	Additional Word
EXAMPLE:	ä	father	harm
	ô		

th	_____	_____
ir	_____	_____
zh	_____	_____
oŏ	_____	_____
ōo	_____	_____
ə	_____	_____

INTERPRETATION OF DIACRITICAL MARKS

The writer of a dictionary tells you how to pronounce a word by respelling that word in such a way that there can be no confusion about its pronunciation. The respelling is done with a combination of letters and symbols. Letters are used to which there is only one response; for example, we all know how to respond to *k*. However, when *c* is pronounced like *k*, in the dictionary it is respelled with *k;* when *c* is pronounced like *s*, it is respelled with *s*. Symbols are used in combination with letters when the letter might call for many responses. Symbols are used mainly with vowels, because the same vowel can—as you already know—call for several responses.

The respelling can be quite different from conventional spelling. In using a pronunciation key, therefore, you are actually responding to a new language. Use this new language calmly and with confidence. The respelling of *quick* for the purpose of pronunciation is *kwĭk*. If the second spelling does not look like English, it's because it is not English. But it should make the pronunciation of *quick* clear to anyone consulting a dictionary if he uses the appropriate key.

EXERCISE 1B   In the blanks next to each of these hard-to-pronounce words write the word as it is respelled for the purpose of pronunciation in a good dictionary. Pronounce the words. Be prepared to explain how the key in the dictionary you used differs from the key at the bottom of this page.

1. mauve   _____
2. sauve   _____
3. taupe   _____
4. corps   _____
5. chic   _____

EXERCISE 2   Identify the television personalities whose names have been respelled with the letters and symbols of the key at the bottom of the page. Try to spell the names correctly.

1. dĭk văn dīk _____
2. flĭp wĭl sən _____
3. mīk dŭg ləs _____
4. jŏn chăn sə lər _____

ă pat/ā pay/är care/ä father/b bib/ch church/d deed/ĕ pet/ē be/f fife/g gag/h hat/hw which/ĭ pit/ī pie/îr pier/j judge/k kick/l lid, needle/m mum/n no, sudden/ ng thing/ŏ pot/ō toe/ô paw, for/oi noise/ou out/oo took/ōo boot/p pop/r roar/s sauce/sh ship, dish/

108

5. hou ərd kā smĭth _____

6. săn dē dŭn kən _____

7. lôrn grēn _____

8. kăr əl bûr nĕt _____

9. mīk kŏn ərs _____

10. ē frəm zĭm bə lĭst _____

11. lo͞o sēl bŏl _____

12. dăn rō ən _____

13. ĕng̑ əl bûrt hŭm pər dĭngk _____

14. rŏb rī nər _____

15. hou ərd kō· sĕl _____

16. mē yō shē ū mĕk ē _____

17. wŏl tər krŏn kīt _____

18. zhäk ko͝o stō _____

19. bĭl kŏz bē _____

20. klôr əs lēch mən _____

In addition to developing your skill in interpreting diacritical marks, you must learn to understand and apply the accent mark. This short diagonal mark is usually placed above and to the right of a syllable to be stressed. Its proper use often represents the difference between an acceptable and a nonacceptable pronunciation. Most students understand what is meant by the accent mark, but many find difficulty in doing what the mark dictates, especially if they have been unsuccessful in their first attempt. The best way to conquer this difficulty is through much practice and concentration on maintaining a flexible approach. To be flexible you must discard completely the results of a first attempt and make a new and fresh approach to the word.

EXERCISE 3

All of the words listed below shift the accent from one syllable to another when a suffix is added. By interpreting the diacritical marks (see key below) and the accent marks, pronounce each word in the left-hand column. Then pronounce that same word with the addition of a suffix. Note the different placement of the accent mark and the difference in your responses to specific syllables as the accent shifts. In some instances you will notice two accent marks—a heavy mark and a light mark. These indicate primary (more) stress and secondary (less) stress. Concern yourself mainly with primary stress in this exercise.

1. vulgar   vŭl′gər   vulgarity   vŭl găr′ ə tē′
2. minor   mīn′ ər   minority   mə nôr′ ə tē′
3. Japan   Jə păn′   Japanese   Jăp′ ə nēs′
4. frugal   fro͞o′gəl   frugality   fro͞o găl′ ə tē′
5. acid   ăs′ ĭd   acidity   ə sĭd′ ə tē′

t tight/th thin, path/ṯh this, bathe/ŭ cut/ûr urge/v valve/w with/y yes/z zebra, size/zh vision/ə about, item, edible, gallop, circus/à Fr. ami/œ Fr. feu, Ger. schön/ ü Fr. tu, Ger. über/ᴋʜ Ger. ich, Scot. loch/ɴ Fr. bon. *Follows main vocabulary. †Of obscure origin.

Fill in the blanks in the following generalizations:
1. Often the addition of a suffix to a word will mean that the _____ will be shifted from one syllable to another.
2. This shift may mean that a _____ in the new word will be pronounced differently from the way it was pronounced in the base word before the suffix was added.

EXERCISE 4

Your ability to respond to different but similar pronunciations is a good way to find out how well you have learned to make use of a pronunciation key. The pronunciation of many of the following words is different from what might be expected because of the history of the word. The history of a word (derivation) is located in different places in the entries of different dictionaries, but it is always enclosed in brackets. Look up the pronunciation of the following words in a good dictionary. Copy the word as it is respelled. Be sure to include all diacritical marks and accent marks. If more than one pronunciation appears, write down all pronunciations.

1. dogged _____
2. reprise _____
3. fetish _____
4. quay _____
5. harass _____
6. infamous _____
7. acumen _____
8. realtor _____
9. quasi _____
10. gauche _____
11. victual _____
12. melee _____
13. anomaly _____
14. mores _____
15. liaison _____
16. subtle _____
17. boatswain _____
18. denouement _____
19. charade _____
20. charisma _____

ă pat/ā pay/âr care/ä father/b bib/ch church/d deed/ĕ pet/ē be/f fife/g gag/h hat/hw which/ĭ pit/ī pie/îr pier/j judge/k kick/l lid, needle/m mum/n no, sudden/ng thing/ŏ pot/ō toe/ô paw, for/oi noise/ou out/oo took/ōō boot/p pop/r roar/s sauce/sh ship, dish/

EXERCISE 5

Almost everybody needs to consult a dictionary for the pronunciation of the names of many geographical locations such as cities or rivers. The spelling of such names often reflects borrowings from earlier periods or from languages in which spelling does not predict pronunciation. You should pronounce names of people and places as they are pronounced in their native country, in so far as you can without having a speaking knowledge of the language.

Find the pronunciation of the following names of cities in a good dictionary and fill in the required information. Be prepared to pronounce the name of each city. Some dictionaries include special sections for entries of proper nouns (names). Other dictionaries include these entries in their regular listings.

City	Pronunciation	Location
EXAMPLE: Worcester	wŏŏs′tər	England; Massachusetts
1. Meissen		
2. Tientsin		
3. Pago Pago		
4. Versailles		
5. Butte		
6. Junin		
7. Kauai		
8. Leixoes		
9. Kuala Lumpur		
10. La Jolla		

EXERCISE 6A

From one of your textbooks or from another book or magazine article, select ten words that you would not want to read aloud to the class without first checking pronunciation. Write these words in the left-hand column and the pronunciation (with diacritical markings) in the right hand column. You may find the pronunciation in the glossary of a textbook. Otherwise, get the pronunciation from a good dictionary.

Word	Pronunciation
1.	
2.	
3.	
4.	
5.	
6.	
7.	
8.	
9.	
10.	

t tight/th thin, path/*th* this, bathe/ū cut/ûr urge/v valve/w with/y yes/z zebra, size/zh vision/ə about, item, edible, gallop, circus/à *Fr.* ami/œ *Fr.* feu, *Ger.* schön/ü *Fr.* tu, *Ger.* über/ᴋʜ *Ger.* ich, *Scot.* loch/ɴ *Fr.* bon. *Follows main vocabulary. †Of obscure origin.

EXERCISE 6B Many words are not pronounced as their spellings indicate they should be. This may be because they have come to the English language directly from another language and retain the pronunciation of the language of their origin. Find the information requested for the following words:

Word or Phrase	Language from which it is borrowed	Pronunciation	Meaning
EXAMPLE: coup	French	ko͞o	a blow
subpoena			
vigilante			
cum laude			
nee			
verboten			
debut			
couture			
per se			
geisha			
alma mater			
ingenue			
bourgeois			
smorgasbord			
hors d'oeuvre			
gourmet			
bravo			
ennui			
de jure			
faux pax			

QUESTION:

How can the history of a word be reflected in its pronunciation and in its present meaning? Find the derivation of *lieu* as seen in the phrase *in lieu of* and copy it.

_____

_____

_____

ă pat/ā pay/âr care/ä father/b bib/ch church/d deed/ĕ pet/ē be/f fife/g gag/h hat/hw which/ĭ pit/ī pie/îr pier/j judge/k kick/l lid, needle/m mum/n no, sudden/ng thing/ŏ pot/ō toe/ô paw, for/oi noise/ou out/oo took/o͞o boot/p pop/r roar/s sauce/sh ship, dish/

The Dictionary Entry

Careful examination of an entry in any good dictionary will show that an entry can be the source of an amazing amount of information about a word. Below is a list of the information about the word *score* found in the *American Heritage Dictionary of the English Language*.

EXERCISE 7A Draw a line from the description of the information to the information in the entry.

1. Spelling
2. History of the word
3. Pronunciation
4. A special meaning when used in a particular art or skill
5. Informal expression (some dictionaries label such expressions as *slang*)
6. Abbreviation for form class (part of speech)
7. A meaning that would not be used in a formal situation

score (skôr, skōr) *n.* 1. A notch or incision, especially one made to keep a tally. 2. An evaluative record, usually numerical, of any competitive event: *keeping score.* 3. a. The total number of points made by each competitor or side in a contest, either final or at a given stage. b. The number of points attributed to any one competitor or team. 4. A result, usually expressed numerically, of a test or examination. 5. a. An amount due; a debt. b. A harbored grievance; a grudge demanding satisfaction. 6. A ground; reason; account. 7. A group of 20 items. 8. *Plural.* Large numbers. 9. The written form of a musical composition for orchestral or vocal parts, either complete or for a particular instrument or voice. 10. The music composed for a stage show or film. —**know the score.** *Informal.* To be aware of the realities of a situation. —*v.* **scored, scoring, scores.** —*tr.* 1. To mark with lines or notches, especially for the purpose of keeping a record. 2. To cancel or eliminate by or as if by superimposing lines. Used with *out* or *off.* 3. *Cooking.* To mark the surface of (meat, for example) with usually parallel cuts. 4. a. To gain (a point) in a game or contest. b. To count or be worth as points. 5. To achieve; win. 6. To evaluate and assign a grade to. 7. *Music.* a. To orchestrate. b. To arrange for a specific instrument. 8. To criticize cuttingly; berate. —*intr.* 1. To make a point in a game or contest. 2. To keep the score of a game or contest. 3. a. To achieve a purpose or advantage; succeed. b. *Informal.* To make a surprising gain or coup. [Middle English *scor,* Old English *scoru* (attested only in plural *scora*), twenty, from Old Norse *skor,* notch, twenty. See sker-¹ in Appendix.*] —**scor′er** *n.*

Question: How many different meanings for *score* are listed? _____

EXERCISE 7B Consult the dictionary entry for *score* and select the appropriate meaning for the word as it is used in the following sentences. In the blanks following the sentences write the part of speech under which you found the definition and also the number of that definition.

1. The pavement was <u>scored</u> to reduce the number of accidents on the freeway during the wet weather. _____
2. A <u>score</u> of years passed before he had enough money for the long trip home. _____
3. A roar went up from the stands when the home team evened the <u>score</u> in the last few seconds of the game. _____
4. Casey bided his time to settle the <u>score</u> with the man who fired him from his job without letting him tell his side of the story. _____
5. The recording of the original <u>score</u> of the hit show was sold out within a few days. _____
6. He finally <u>scored</u> in his efforts to get the order for all the lumber required for the huge tract of new homes. _____
7. Tom was especially pleased with his <u>score</u> on the history test because he had worked so hard preparing for it. _____
8. Marie got a very high <u>score</u> in the college entrance examinations. _____

t tight/th thin, path/*th* this, bathe/ü cut/ûr urge/v valve/w with/y yes/z zebra, size/zh vision/ə about, item, edible, gallop, circus/ä *Fr.* ami/œ *Fr.* feu, *Ger.* schön/ ü *Fr.* tu, *Ger.* über/KH *Ger.* ich, *Scot.* loch/N *Fr.* bon. *Follows main vocabulary. †Of obscure origin.

EXERCISE 7C

Write two sentences that illustrate the use of *score*—one that illustrates definition 7, using *score* as a noun—and one that illustrates definition 3, using *score* as a transitive verb.

7. (*n.*) _____

_____

3. (*v.—tr.*) _____

_____

Examination of a shorter entry from the same dictionary illustrates how interesting the history of a word can be. Notice that *denouement* is borrowed directly from another language—French. This, of course, accounts for the fact that it is not pronounced in the way its spelling patterns would predict. Further reading in the bracketed historical information shows that the history of the word in Old French is quite interesting. In this instance the meanings of the words from other languages that produced the English word *denouement* are very directly related to its present-day meaning. The present-day meanings of many English words whose derivation can be traced to words from other languages have drifted considerably from the meanings of the words that contributed to their history.

de′·noue·ment (dā-nōō-män′) *n.* Also **de-noue-ment.** 1. The solution, clarification, or unraveling of the plot of a play or novel. 2. Any outcome or final solution. [French, "an untying," from Old French *desnouement,* from *desno(u)er,* undo: *des-, de-,* reversing + *no(u)er,* to tie, from Latin *nōdāre,* from *nodus,* knot (see **ned** in Appendix*).]

EXERCISE 8

Leaf through a dictionary, taking note of the derivations of several words. Select three that you find interesting and copy the historical information given in the entry. Be prepared to interpret all abbreviations used in the information you have copied.

Word _____
1. History [_____

_____

_____].

Word _____
2. History [_____

_____

_____].

Word _____
3. History [_____

_____

_____].

* Follows main vocabulary [in *The American Heritage Dictionary of the English Language*].

ă pat/ā pay/âr care/ä father/b bib/ch church/d deed/ĕ pet/ē be/f fife/g gag/h hat/hw which/ĭ pit/ī pie/îr pier/j judge/k kick/l lid, needle/m mum/n no, sudden/ ng thing/ŏ pot/ō toe/ô paw, for/oi noise/ou out/oo took/ōō boot/p pop/r roar/s sauce/sh ship, dish/

The Newspaper

Many people interpret the word *newspaper* literally and think of it as merely a record of the day's news. Some people almost seem to take pride in saying that they get all their information about the news from television and cannot be bothered with reading a newspaper. A noted television newscaster has said that, at best, television reporting can give only an overview of the news. Those who overlook the newspaper as a source of news are also overlooking the most inexpensive and varied source of reading material available. Although it is difficult to use the newspaper as a reference source in an organized manner, regular reading of a good daily paper can expand your knowledge of many subjects. A good newspaper contains many articles of general interest that may be only indirectly related to the news.

The Feature Article

A good editor puts himself in his reader's place and asks his staff to write articles on subjects that his readers would be interested in. Such articles are called *feature articles* and, unlike general news items, they often carry the name, or *byline*, of the author. The writer of the feature article has to write under pressure of time, but he is often an efficient researcher and has access to good research sources.

EXERCISE 9

The film *Butch Cassidy and the Sundance Kid* will probably be talked about for years to come as one of the most popular films of all times. Read this feature article published in a large daily newspaper about the real Butch Cassidy and answer the questions that follow it.

Butch Cassidy's Sister Tells All

By Charles Hillinger
Times Staff Writer

CIRCLEVILLE, Utah—"Butch Cassidy wasn't killed by the Bolivian army," declared the sister of the Old West's last great outlaw.

"He lived to be 69 and died a natural death in 1936 in this country."

The current film "Butch

Copyright, 1970, *Los Angeles Times*. Reprinted by permission.

George Leroy Parker (Butch Cassidy)

Denver Public Library, Western History Department

Cassidy and the Sundance Kid" ends with the two desperados being riddled with bullets in a gunbattle with 200 Bolivian soldiers in the year 1909.

"That's the story the Pinkerton detective agency and the Bolivian government was supposed to have given out," explained Mrs. Lula Parker Betenson, Butch Cassidy's sister.

Death Not as Reported

"But everyone in the family and a few others have always known my brother was not shot down and left for dead in South America.

"He visited me years after his reputed death. We heard from him from time to time through the years until he died. It's my secret where he's buried."

Wyoming, Utah and Colorado newspapers carried stories of reports from time to time during the 20s and 30s that Butch Cassidy had been seen alive in various places.

Mrs. Betenson said there is "no end" to what she knows about the true story of her brother, whose real name was Robert LeRoy Parker.

Now 86, a widow of 22 years living in a modest home in this small southern Utah cowtown, Butch Cassidy's sister is the last survivor of 13 children of a pioneering Mormon family.

"We never talked about my brother outside the family. We were ashamed and embarrassed about the things he did," she said.

"But within the family, seems like it's all we ever talked about. He broke my folks' hearts.

"I can still hear my mother praying every night of her life that Butch would come home and lead a good life again."

Her mother died at 58 in 1905. Butch Cassidy had been holding up trains and banks for 15 years by that time and had already left the United States for a career of crime that spanned two continents.

Shortly after the death of an older sister in 1961—when Mrs. Betenson became the sole survivor of a family of seven boys and six girls—she decided the true story of her brother's life should be told.

Decides to Tell Story

"I decided while there was still someone alive that could tell it, I should do it."

She has just completed a book about her brother's life and is seeking a publisher.

"A lot of things have been written over the years —way back since before the turn of the century about my brother, in books, magazines and dime novels," she said.

"Some of it is factual, much of it made-up stuff without an ounce of truth. His life was colorful enough without dressing it up with untruths. Some of the drivel written about my brother makes me mad enough to want to kick the writers in the britches."

Butch Cassidy was born in Beaver, Utah, a few miles from Circleville. A log cabin British immigrant Maximillian Parker built for his wife and brood still stands there.

"Butch and the whole bunch of us Parkers lived in this small place Dad built," explained Mrs. Betenson. A corral nearby the cabin was put up by the outlaw, his brothers and father.

Robbery Recalled

Some of the oldtimers in Baggs, Wyo., who were youngsters at the time recall when Butch and his boys rode into the isolated community in the late 90s following a $35,000 bank robbery in Winnemucca, Nev.

Cassidy's gang stayed in Baggs raising hell for a week, spending and giving away all of the $35,000 in the tiny town noted in those days as a rendezvous for badmen.

Through the years Cassidy and his cronies were known by various names. They were called the Hole in the Wall Gang when they operated from a hideout near Kaycee, Wyo.

At other times they were the Powder Springs Gang, the Robbers Roost Gang, Butch Cassidy and the Wild Bunch.

In newspaper stories of that period, Cassidy was described as a good natured fellow with a ready smile, a western Robin Hood, a man never known to kill.

"Anyone in hard luck could go to him for help. If he didn't have cash he'd go out and get it for those that needed it," notes a government publication of the day.

"He was a good looker but not handsome like Paul Newman in the movie," says Mrs. Betenson. "He wasn't tall. He had a tendency to be on the heavy side. Never did any of us in the family hear of anyone—even those he robbed—say they didn't like my brother. Even the officers that had contact with him. He had an easy going, friendly way about him. He was good hearted. He was always for the underdog. A woman in Helena, Mont., remembers his coming to her folks' place and helping them out. She said her mother could never believe Robert LeRoy Parker could ever do anything wrong. And everybody always emphasized one point about Butch Cassidy—that he never killed a man."

Wrong Companions

Mrs. Betenson said her brother "fell into the wrong company when a young man."

"My mother would go up the Sevier River to make butter and cheese to sell to help keep the family going. She would take Butch along. There were some tough fellows up in that country at the time. It was pretty sticky. One of the men, a Texan named Mike Cassidy, made over Butch. Mother could see what was happening. That's where he got the Cassidy name."

"Butch was high spirited. He was a good cowpuncher. He left home at 18 and went to Rock Springs, Wyo., where he worked in a butcher shop for a spell. That's how he come onto the nickname Butch. Then he got into mining at Telluride, Colo. That's where he robbed his first bank. He and another Mormon boy from Circleville, Elza Lay, went up to Telluride together. They got mixed up with notorious characters like Matt Warner, Tom McCarthy, Flat Nose George Curry and others."

Continued Career

Mrs. Betenson said that the first time Butch was jailed at Montrose, Colo., "Dad rode over on his horse to see what it was all about and tried several times to get Butch to straighten out and come home, but he never did."

"He'd come to the house at different times through the years when he was being hunted, but always alone. Butch would come but none of the others. The family never saw any of the others."

"In later years, after he was supposed to have been killed, he told the family he had the time of his life in New York City when he left the West to retire and run a ranch in South America."

"He and the Sundance Kid—Harry Longabaugh —had a big haul they took with them. The Sundance Kid brought along his lady friend, Etta Place, a schoolteacher. Butch didn't want the woman to go along, but Sundance insisted. They went to South America and instead of retiring started all over again robbing trains and banks."

Mrs. Betenson says she's not sure what happened to Longabaugh, but does know that Etta Place later returned to Denver.

"My brother did a lot of traveling the rest of his life under an assumed name when he came back to the United States in 1912. He never married. He worked as a trapper and as a cowboy. He spent some time in Alaska," she said.

Although she was active in Utah politics the last 40 years, few of Mrs. Betenson's acquaintances knew her brother was Butch Cassidy. It has just been since the movie that she has been willing to talk openly about him. Mother of five, grandmother seven times and great-grandmother of 13 boys and girls, Mrs. Betenson served as a representative to the Utah State Legislature during the 1950s.

Retracing Trail

The past nine years she's been retracing her brother's trail through the West, visiting his old hideouts, talking with oldtimers and sons and daughters of those who had contact with Cassidy. She has compiled all the family stories about her brother.

"The movie was a good film that captured his friendly manner and showed the daring train and bank holdups by Butch and his gang," said Mrs. Betenson. "But there actually was very little of his life portrayed in the film. He was one of the truly fascinating characters of the West. The film was a sort of a teaser."

QUESTIONS

1. From whom did the author of the article get his information? _____
2. What was Butch Cassidy's real name? _____
3. Where did he get his nickname "Butch"? _____
4. In what state was he born? _____
5. What two centuries did Butch Cassidy's life span? _____
6. To what character in classical literature has Butch Cassidy been compared? Why? _____
_____
7. By checking the article, find (a) one incident in the movie that was based on fact and (b) one incident where the movie departed from the truth.
   A. _____
   B. _____

For Discussion:

1. Why do you think Butch Cassidy's sister said "We never talked about my brother outside the family . . . . But within the family, seems like it's all we talked about"? Do you think the same situation exists among members of his family now? Why or why not?
2. In the last paragraph of the article, Butch Cassidy's sister makes a comment that might indicate that she did not think the film about her brother's life was true-to-life. By what standards do you think a movie based on a person's life should be judged? Does she use any words in discussing the film that might help you formulate a standard by which to judge films based on the lives of real people?

The Editorial

A newspaper article that differs considerably from news items or feature articles is the editorial. An editorial expresses an opinion on current issues or events in the news. Editorials are grouped together in a part of the paper known as the *editorial section*. They may be written by syndicated columnists—writers whose articles are sold by an agency to many newspapers—or they may be written by a writer employed by the newspaper in which the editorial is printed. The articles written by the syndicated columnists will carry a byline, while the article written by the staff writer may not. The staff writer's article will usually express the official opinion of the paper that employs him. Good newspapers are very conscientious about separating their opinions on current affairs from their reporting of the news. Regular readers of a newspaper look to the editorial pages for help in filling out their background for reading the news and in forming their own opinions. Therefore, the editorial writer and the newspaper that prints what he writes can have considerable influence upon legislators, voters, and other people who in various ways make news.

EXERCISE 10

The following editorial appeared in the Los Angeles Times shortly after 18-year-olds were given the vote in California. Read the editorial carefully and answer the questions that follow it.

Equal Rights for 18-Year-Olds

California legislators have nearly completed work on two major pieces of legislation designed to match the extension of the vote to 18-year-olds with the extension of other legal elements of adulthood.

The initial piece of legislation is almost ready for the signature of Gov. Reagan. It extends downward from 21 to 18 the age of eligibility for major legal activities, thus matching the privilege of the vote with the responsibility of full citizenship.

Senate approval is still needed on the second piece of legislation, clearing for the ballots next year a constitutional amendment lowering the legal age limit for drinking to 18.

Rights, privileges and responsibilities are not easily separated. So it is a good thing that the government of California is moving promptly, in the wake of new voting age, to take these complementary steps. It was nonsense to deny the vote to those old enough to be drafted. It would be nonsense to deprive young people of the remaining elements of adult status.

None of these steps has been taken without misgivings. Some exceptions have been provided, including an option for criminal courts to refer immature convicts up to 21 to the Youth Authority, which already is handling some prisoners to the age of 25.

A survey of secondary school students in San Mateo County, showing a marked increase in the use of alcohol and drugs by junior high school students, notably seventh graders, is alarming. But this problem will not be solved by maintaining the present 21-year minimum drinking age.

The first response of young people to winning the vote has not been the militancy and radicalism that some feared, but apathy. Apathy is not theirs alone. The extension of the other rights of adulthood can encourage the broader exercise of responsibility.

No doubt about it, young people in America already are making a contribution rivaled by few if any other societies. The quality of their contribution will be no less than the trust placed in them.

Copyright, 1972, *Los Angeles Times*. Reprinted by permission.

QUESTIONS

1. A. What particular complementary privilege for 18-year olds does the writer mention?

   B. Does the writer favor granting this privilege?

   C. Does his newspaper favor granting the privilege?

   D. Do you agree with the writer? Why or why not?

2. List three reasons the writer gives to support the position he and his paper are taking on this issue.

   A.

   B.

   C.

3. In what way does the writer anticipate opinions that are contrary to those expressed in the editorial? State an argument that he thinks will be used against his position, and present his answer to it.

Opposing argument: _____

_____

_____

Writer's answer: _____

_____

_____

The Encyclopedia

The most complete all-purpose reference source for the average person is the encyclopedia. Encyclopedias are found in the reference section of libraries and usually consist of sets of several volumes. Different sets are written to meet the various needs of different people. Some people's needs are for short, relatively simple selections, while others engaged in scholarly research may require longer, in-depth treatment of a subject. You will probably find one encyclopedia that most often meets your needs and tastes. However, your approach to reading a selection in an encyclopedia has to be as varied as the subject matter treated in its many volumes. Read the following biographical item taken from *The World Book Encyclopedia*.

> **APPLESEED, JOHNNY** (1774-1847), was the name given John Chapman, a pioneer who has become a legendary figure in American history. He was a strange mixture of plant nurseryman, herb doctor, minor military hero, and religious enthusiast. At the beginning of the 1800's, he appeared along the Ohio River and became known to his frontier neighbors as "Johnny Appleseed" because of the ardent way he distributed apple seeds and sprouts in central and northern Ohio. He accepted almost any object or amount of money in payment for his seeds and sprouts.
>
> Chapman was also religious, and he preached the teachings of Emanuel Swedenborg with force (see SWEDENBORGIANS). To the Ohio frontiersmen, he seemed like an American version of a Hebrew prophet wandering in the wilderness. He combined the services of herb doctor and botanist with his religious sayings. He also distributed herbs and medicinal plants, and served as a frontier messenger during the War of 1812.
>
> By the time of his death, Chapman had become part of the Ohio Valley legend. He defied religious and social customs. His apple trees strengthened the economy of the rich farming areas of northern Ohio and Indiana. He was born in Massachusetts. THOMAS D. CLARK
>
> From *The World Book Encyclopedia*, © 1972, Field Enterprises Educational Corporation.

The chronological facts about any man's life are easy for almost anybody to read. What you attempt to learn from these facts depends upon your reasons for using the reference material. You may refer to the same encyclopedia for information on another subject and find a difficult reading task because you are dealing with a complex subject with which you are totally unfamiliar. In most cases encyclopedia items are prepared by noted scholars.

EXERCISE 11 Read the following news item pertaining to a proposal to Congress that would bring about changes in the life of every United States citizen. The news item is directed more to the purpose of reporting news than providing background information. Therefore, this item is typical of the type of reading that sends the reader to another reference source for more information.

Can't Drag Feet, He Warns
Stans Will Urge Timetable to Put U.S. on Metric Track

By Victor Cohn
Exclusive to The Times from the Washington Post

WASHINGTON—A massive 10-year program to switch the entire nation to the metric system—meaning measuring almost everything in meters and grams instead of feet and pounds—will be urgently recommended to Congress today by Secretary of Commerce Maurice H. Stans.

Such a switch, if voted by Congress, would mean a gigantic change in every American's habits, and in every job.

Industry would have to reconvert vast amounts of measuring and manufacturing machinery. Farmers and shirt-buyers would have to learn new measurements. A housewife would have to buy a new set of measuring cups—and refer to a converter in her purse to learn that a "meter" of cloth equals 39.37 inches.

© *The Washington Post.* Reprinted with permission.

But the 100-yard football field and many other entrenched measurements, Stans will reassure Congress, will probably survive.

At the same time, the Bureau of Standards report says that the changeover may cost manufacturers between $10 billion and $40 billion over 10 years.

Yet failing to make it, the study finds, could eventually cost even more in jobs and trade in a day when the United States has become the only major nation that has not decided to switch.

Also, it argues, the United States inevitably will be forced to go more and more metric anyway, and doing it by plan would cost far less than doing it slowly and haphazardly.

Stans will argue in terms of trade, ... of relations with other countries, national security and adoption of worldwide standards in a smaller and smaller world.

Congress, the metric system's best friends concede, could take a minimum of two or three years of convincing. Some industries and businesses are expected to support a change, others—those that would have to retool most massively—to oppose it.

Specifically, Stans and the Bureau of Standards report will urge:

—A "deliberate and careful" change through a coordinated national program, with a target date 10 years ahead, "by which time the U.S. will have become predominantly though not exclusively metric."

—Establishment by Congress of a "central coordinating body," which would precede the 10-year change period with two years' study during which each affected sector would work out its own plans and timetables.

EDUCATION GOAL

—A "general rule" that changeover costs shall "lie where they fall." In other words, each business sector and its consumers would pay its costs.

—That "early priority be given to educating every American schoolchild and the public at large to think in metric terms."

—"A firm government commitment," finally, to the metric goal.

Britain, long non-metric, started a 10-year changeover six years ago. Canada announced a like decision 18 months ago, but is said to be waiting for action by the remaining holdout, the United States.

EXERCISE 12

Now read the following entry on the metric system, also taken from *The World Book Encyclopedia.* Read it through without interruption and then respond to the self-evaluation statements that follow it.

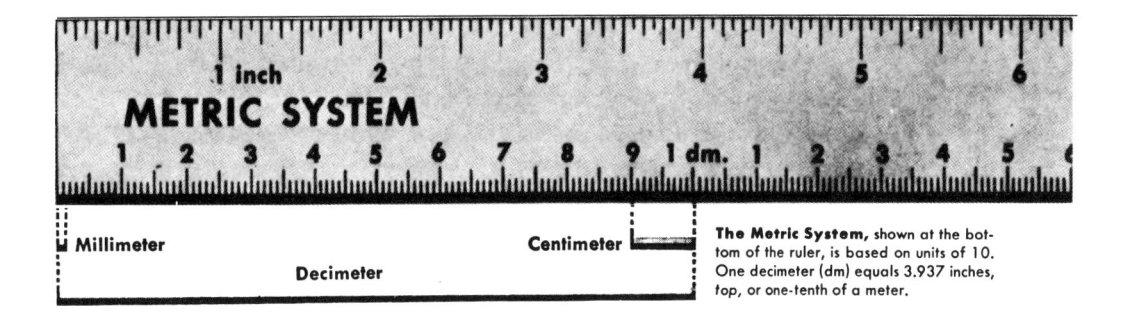

The Metric System, shown at the bottom of the ruler, is based on units of 10. One decimeter (dm) equals 3.937 inches, top, or one-tenth of a meter.

[SECTION I]

METRIC SYSTEM, *MET rick*. Scientists throughout the world measure lengths, distances, weights, and other values by a standard method, called the *metric system*. The word comes from *meter,* the principal unit of length in this system.

A commission of French scientists developed the metric system. France adopted it as the legal system of weights and measures in 1799. Its use was made compulsory in 1837. Most countries now use the metric system. After World War II, China, Egypt, and India adopted it. During the 1960's, Great Britain and most of the Commonwealth of Nations began to convert to the system. But the United States and Canada still use the English system. The metric system is generally considered easy to learn and to use.

[SECTION II]

How It Is Organized. In the metric system all units have a uniform scale of relation, based on the decimal. The principal unit is the *meter* which corresponds to the *yard* as a unit of length. The meter is 39.37 inches, or 1.093 yards. The scale of multiples and subdivisions of the meter is ten. All units of surface, volume, capacity, and weight are directly derived from the meter.

The relation between them is very simple because a definite volume of water is taken as the unit of capacity and mass. The *liter* corresponds to the *quart* as a unit of capacity. The liter also has multiples and subdivisions of ten. One liter contains one cubic *decimeter* of water and weighs one *kilogram*.

The following table shows the use of the decimal scale:

Ten millimeters = one centimeter

Ten centimeters = one decimeter

Ten decimeters = one meter

Ten meters = one decameter

Ten decameters = one hectometer

Ten hectometers = one kilometer

Ten kilometers = one myriameter

The same system applies to the other units, the *liter* and the *gram*. Ten *liters* are equal to one *decaliter,* or *dekaliter,* and ten *decigrams* are equal to one *gram*.

This uniform system of names is one of the advantages of the metric system. The various units of measure get their names by adding other prefixes to the chief units. Divisions of the chief units are tenths, hundredths, thousandths, and so on. They are formed by adding Latin prefixes. For example, *deci* means *one-tenth* (.1), *centi* means *one-hundredth* (.01), and *milli* means *one-thousandth* (.001). Higher denominations are formed by multiplying the basic unit by ten, a hundred, a thousand, and so on. Greek prefixes are added to the chief unit. For example, *myria* means 10,000; *kilo* means 1,000; *hecto* means 100, and *deca* means 10. The units to which these prefixes are added are the *meter, liter,* and *gram*.

Metric numbers are written decimally. The decimal point is placed immediately after the unit. For example, 156.735 m. reads 156 meters and 735 millimeters. Or, 156.735 g. reads 156 grams and 735 milligrams. Calculations with the metric system are easy because they are made according to

The Basis of the Metric System is the distance between the North Pole and the equator, which is about 6,200 miles. A line running from the North Pole to the equator has 10,000,000 equal parts. Each part is a meter, or 39.37 inches.

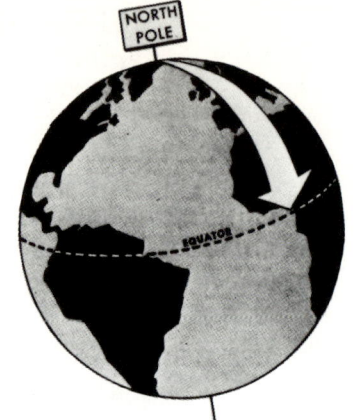

the decimal system. Any denomination may be changed to the next higher by moving the decimal point to the left. Any denomination may be reduced to the next lower by moving the decimal point to the right.

[SECTION III]

The Unit of Length. The unit of length is described in the article METER. The kilometer (1,000 meters) is used, like the English mile, to measure long distances. For example, Versailles is nineteen and one-half kilometers from Paris.

The Unit of Surface. Surface is measured with the square meter which is the area of a square whose sides each measure one

English Measurements

Length			
	Yard	=	0.9144 meter
	Foot	=	0.3048 meter
	Inch	=	0.0254 meter
	Mile	=	1.609 kilometers
Surface			
	Square yard	=	0.836 square meter
	Square foot	=	0.092 square meter
	Square inch	=	6.45 square centimeters
	Square mile	=	2.590 square kilometers
	Acre	=	0.405 hectare
Volume			
	Cubic yard	=	0.764 cubic meter
	Cubic foot	=	0.028 cubic meter
	Cubic inch	=	16.387 cubic centimeters
	Cord	=	3.624 steres
Capacity			
	U.S. liquid quart	=	0.946 liter
	Dry quart	=	1.111 liters
	U.S. gallon	=	3.785 liters
	English gallon	=	4.543 liters
	U.S. bushel	=	0.352 hectoliter
	English bushel	=	0.363 hectoliter
Weight			
	Grain	=	0.0648 gram
	Troy ounce	=	31.103 grams
	Avoirdupois ounce	=	28.35 grams
	Pound	=	0.4536 kilogram
	Short ton	=	0.907 metric ton

meter. The multiples and subdivisions go by the square of ten, which is 100. One square decameter is equal to 100 square meters. One square decimeter is one-hundredth part of a square meter. The *are* and the *hectare* are used in most land measurements. The are has 100 square meters. The hectare has 100 ares or 10,000 square meters. Large areas, such as countries, are measured by square kilometers.

The Unit of Volume. A cubic meter is the unit used to measure volume. A cubic meter is a cube of which each edge is one meter. The multiples and subdivisions go by the cube of ten, which is 1,000. One cubic decameter is equal to 1,000 cubic meters. One cubic decimeter is equal to one-thousandth part of a cubic meter. When the cubic meter is used to measure wood it is called a *stere.*

The Unit of Capacity. A *liter* is the unit of capacity. A liter contains the quantity of one cubic decimeter of distilled water at its greatest density, or, at the temperature of 39.2 degrees Fahrenheit and at sea level. The liter is used to measure liquids such as milk and wine, and also for small fruit. Grain, vegetables, and liquids in casks are usually measured with the *hectoliter.*

The Unit of Weight. A *gram* is the unit of weight. A gram is the weight of one cubic centimeter of distilled water at its greatest density, or at a temperature of 39.2° F. at sea level. One thousand cubic centimeters, which equal one cubic decimeter, have the capacity of one liter and weigh 1,000 grams, or a kilogram. The kilogram is used to compute most weights. The metric ton (1,000 kilograms) is used for heavy articles. All the units in the metric system are related. A thousand kilograms, or a metric ton, is the weight of 1,000 cubic decimeters, or a cubic meter of water with a capacity of 1,000 liters, or a kiloliter.

The American five-cent piece weighs five grams and has a diagram of two centimeters. A silver half dollar of United States money weighs twelve and one-half grams. Eighty half dollars weigh one kilogram. In fine scientific weights, the unit is the *microgram,* which is a thousandth part of a milligram, or a millionth part of a gram. The *carat,* the weight for measuring diamonds and other precious stones, also has been standardized since 1913. The new international carat weighs 200 milligrams, or one fifth of a gram. Before it was standardized, the carat weighed 205.3 milligrams.

[SECTION IV]

Use in the United States. In 1866 Congress passed a law making the metric system legal in the United States for those who wish to use it. The Bureau of Standards in Washington adopted the metric system in 1893 as the standard to be used in legally defining the yard and the pound. It is now used in the Coast and Geodetic Survey, in all government departments dealing in tariff operations, in coining money, and in weighing foreign mail. Government departments dealing in tariff operations use it, and it is the legal unit for electrical measure. Eyeglass lenses are prescribed and ground by metric tables. Radio stations use it in defining the wave lengths which are assigned to them.

Several attempts have been made to bring the metric system into general use in the United States. As far back as 1790, Thomas Jefferson, who was then Secretary of State, recommended that Congress introduce a decimal system in this country. Later, in 1821, John Quincy Adams advocated the adoption of the metric system in a report to Congress on weights and measures. With engineers and the business world using both the metric and older units of measure, there is some confusion. Probably in a few generations the metric system will be used generally. Anyone who plans a career in business, foreign trade, civil service, engineering or any branch of pure or applied science should understand the metric system.

Underline your response:
1. I already have some knowledge of and experience with the metric system. (yes—no)

2. I am very confused by this article. (yes—no)
3. I understand a little about the metric system from reading this article. (yes—no)
4. I feel I understand the metric system after reading this article. (yes—no)

For most people effective study techniques need to be applied when reading an article such as this in order to get a workable basic understanding of its contents. This is because it presents a new concept that is in conflict with something that has long been part of your daily lives. Also, because an encyclopedia entry is written for a large and varied audience, it may contain more information than some people need for an introduction to a complex subject, and it may, therefore, be confusing. For this reason, you may have to isolate the portions of the entry that give you the working information you need. The selection has been divided into sections to demonstrate a suggested study plan for you. The questions are designed to provide a way of acquiring a better understanding of the material. (Further practice in study techniques will be given in Section VI.)

EXERCISE 13

Fill in the blanks.
A. The section that gives me the most basic information about the metric system is section _____ (*give number*).
B. All units of measurement in the metric system are related on a base of _____ (*answer with a number*).
C. The basic unit of measurement is the _____ (*give term*).
D. Terms designating other units of measurement have been named by placing prefixes before the basic unit of measurement. These prefixes have been taken from the _____ (*name language*) and _____ (*name language*) languages.
E. I could probably understand this article better if I listed the prefixes in two columns, separating those of one language from another.

Prefixes Used in the Metric System

Column I
Language: _____

Column II
Language: _____

Prefix   *Meaning*   *Prefix*   *Meaning*

1. _____ _____   _____   _____
2. _____ _____   _____   _____
3. _____ _____   _____   _____
4. _____ _____   _____   _____

F. These prefixes are added to the following units of measurement.

Unit   *Used to Measure*

1. _____   _____
2. _____   _____
3. _____   _____

G. A good study technique is to tell a story to yourself as you read. Many good students actually talk aloud to themselves when they study or when they read something difficult. Filling in these blanks gives you an opportunity to talk to yourself. Where two possibilities are given in parenthesis, underline the correct response.

(1) In the metric system the principal unit of measurement is the _____ _____.

(2) To determine a distance having a Latin prefix you (divide, multiply) your basic unit of measurement, which is the _____, by the number designated by the prefix.

(3) Supply a fraction such as: 1/10, 1/100 or 1/1000.
One decimeter = _____ of a meter.
One centimeter = _____ of a meter.
One millimeter = _____ of a meter.

(4) Supply a figure:
A meter is _____ inches.
A decimeter is _____ inches.

(5) Supply a figure:
1 yard = _____ inches.
1 meter = _____ inches.

(6) Mexico uses the metric system. Mexico produces some very beautiful fabrics, many of them handwoven and with beautiful colors and combinations of colors. If you wished to buy fabric on a trip to Mexico and your pattern called for three yards of fabric, you would buy (less than, more than) three meters.

(7) *Problem:*
If you take a trip to Europe, you will find distances measured in kilometers. The prefix *kilo* means _____.

(Do your figuring here.)

(8) A kilometer = _____ meters

A mile = _____ feet

A foot = _____ inches

A mile = _____ inches

A meter = _____ inches

A kilometer = _____ meters

A kilometer = _____ inches

(9) A kilometer is a (shorter, longer) distance than a mile.

Section Five

The Power of Suggestion

This section deals with two quite different forms of suggestion. The first exercises introduce suggestion through words that say more than they appear to say. The power of the suggestions carried by these words is limited only by your ability to receive their message. The other exercises are based on reviews from newspapers and periodicals that offer suggestions for leisure-time activities. You are, of course, free to accept or reject the opinions expressed in such reviews. However, accepting, or at least reading some of the suggestions of professional reviewers about books and cultural events can be a strong factor in a personal design for a life style that recognizes education as a lifelong process.

Figurative Language

Language is almost limitless in the varieties of ways it communicates. In your everyday speech, you may be very resourceful in saying what you want to say. Without knowing it, you probably sprinkle your speech with figurative language. This means that you constantly seek out words or expressions that communicate not only in a factual, literal manner but also communicate many of the sensations and feelings that go with the facts. If you say, "The quarterback charged down the field" or "The car roared down the street" you are using figurative language. In other words, instead of settling for saying that the quarterback and the car simply went from one place to another, you are—through your choice of words—communicating some of the sound, manner, and emotions connected with the actions.

Figurative language combines what we know with what is new. It asks of readers or listeners to play a game of "let's pretend" in order that they may better understand. In the above examples the speaker pretends—and the listener goes along with him—that the quarterback is an army, in order to communicate the drive and purpose with which he went down the field; and the car becomes a ferocious animal so the readers can sense the sound and the speed of the car. English can be used figuratively in a variety of ways, but you can benefit from focusing on a few of the forms it takes. This focus should make you more aware of the depth of meaning in the language you hear and read every day and prepare you for situations in which a meaning may not be clear unless you detect that the "figurative game" is being played.

Adjectives that Borrow

A common device that packs meaning into a single word is to shift the word from its most commonly used setting, or context, to a new context. Such shifts take with them (or borrow) shades of meaning from the old context that can be added to the meaning of the word in the new context. For instance, if a person is referred to as having a *sour* personality, the word *sour* brings many associations with it from its more common use as applied to food. Actually the word *sour* is a cue to set up the "figurative game" by asking you to *compare* your reactions to a personality to your reactions to a sour food item, such as a lemon.

EXERCISE 1

The noun phrases listed contain adjectives that borrow meaning from their commonly-used contexts. Opposite each noun phrase write the association that the adjective brings with it from its more common use.

EXAMPLE:

a salty character — salty brings with it the association of flavor; food without enough salt lacks flavor and is dull and uninteresting. It could also bring the association of the sea. A salty character could be a typical sailor or fisherman.

*Noun Phrases Containing
Adjectives that Borrow*   Association

1. spicy conversation

2. warm smile

3. biting remark

4. sparkling personality

5. saucy hat

6. frosty retort

7. raw youth

8. saccharine personality

9. fluid situation

10. hard, cold facts

Word Class Shifts: The x = y Formula

The shifting of a word from one form class to another can set up the "figurative game" where the reader pretends, for the sake of determining meaning, that one thing is another thing. It is quite common to shift a word from its more common use as a noun to a verb position where the meaning takes on some of the images connected with the noun. If you say "The child wolfed his food," the verb *wolfed* means *ate*, but with the added association of some of the images of the mannerisms of a wolf when eating. This type of figurative speech can be analyzed with what can be called an x = y formula; that is, child = wolf.

EXERCISE 2   The verbs in the following sentences represent shifts from a noun form class to a verb form class. Underline the verbs and write the x = y formula in the blanks. Be prepared to discuss the association transferred from a noun to the verb.

EXAMPLE:

The radio barked out a running commentary on the positions of the frontrunners as the horses approached the finish line.

Formula (x = y)

radio = dog

1. The salesman hounded all the homeowners on the street until they bought his product. _____ = _____
2. Fog blanketed the area for several days. _____ = _____
3. The darkness swallowed up the mysterious visitor. _____ = _____
4. The student pirated his essay from the works of a professional writer. _____ = _____
5. Some political analysts feel that bad moves on the part of some businessmen abroad have torpedoed chances for peace. _____ = _____
6. Children ape their elders. _____ = _____
7. The problem of nonpayment of dues clouds the issue. _____ = _____
8. Low-hanging clouds shrouded the skyline. _____ = _____
9. The fighter, who weighed in at 227 pounds, peppered away during the first 10 rounds with left jabs. _____ = _____
10. The fullback knifed through the opposing line and gobbled up twenty yards before he was brought down. _____ = _____

EXERCISE 3   All the verbs in the following sentences are used figuratively in that the meaning comes through association rather than through literal interpretation. Write the verb in the blank opposite each sentence and be prepared to tell what association the word brings to the new context from its literal meaning.

Verb

1. The search party scoured the surrounding mountains for the missing hiker. _____
2. The sergeant barks his orders through a megaphone. _____
3. By the end of the race a score of cars will have gulped thousands of gallons of gasoline. _____
4. The students underlined their demands with demonstrations and sit-ins. _____
5. The chairman of the committee shouldered all the responsibility for the collection of funds. _____

6. The jury was closeted for eighteen hours in an attempt to reach agreement. _____
7. The candidate threaded her way through the crowd to the speaker's table. _____
8. The eager student is confident that a good report card will spell success for him in everything that he undertakes. _____
9. The speedboat hopscotched its way across the lake. _____
10. The protesters rained insults and jeers on the speakers. _____

EXERCISE 4

The following quotations come from a variety of sources ranging from informal speech to works of literature. Apply the x = y formula to each quotation. The formula may be stated, or it may be suggested by the use of the words *like* or *as* or by other words that indicate that one thing is thought of as being another. Identify and explain additional words or phrases from the quotations whose meanings might not be clear unless the reader plays the "figurative game."

EXAMPLE:

The operating budget must be trimmed—not only the fat but the muscle.

$$x = y$$
budget = whole carcass

fat (outer layer or less-needed items)

muscle (inner layer or more-needed items)

Quotation	x = y Formula	Words Formula Explains

1. Turning from the sun-blazing valley, he rode deep into the wood. Tree trunks, like people standing grey and still, took no notice as he went.
—"The Prussian Officer," D. H. Lawrence

2. The main bout in this year's political arena will be a classic match between a slugger and a puncher.
—Radio news item

3. From an inauspicious beginning has come the modern-day rodeo, bowlegged with fatigue, covered with saddle sores, but brimming with life.
—"Rodeo Cowboys Don't Take Their Hats Off to Anybody," Robert Meyers

4. If you don't want your fashion cake to fall flat, the best bet is to accept the mixture as put together by the designers. They've calculated the recipe well for perfect coordination and eye appeal. Follow it

closely, or you may end up with a casserole of left-overs.
—A NEWSPAPER FASHION ITEM

5. The Prime Minister [of Canada] memorably summed up the two countries' [U.S. and Canada's] relationship. "Living next to you is in some ways like sleeping with an elephant. No matter how friendly or even-tempered the beast,... one is affected by every twitch and grunt.
—News article, TIME, THE WEEKLY NEWSMAGAZINE

6. Even on the fringe of the town, where a man could still look off and mark where the river ran, the houses squatted freely near elbow to elbow, and farther on the buildings looked to be pushing for room, trying to keep from being pushed.
—*The Big Sky*, A. B. GUTHRIE

7. ... though once they [birch trees] are bowed so low
So low for long, they never right themselves:
You may see their trunks arching in the woods
Year afterwards, trailing their leaves on the ground
Like girls on hands and knees that throw their hair
Before them over their heads to dry in the sun.
—"Birches," ROBERT FROST*

8. He groaned to see that she was off on that topic. She went into it every few days like a train on an open track. He knew every stop, every junction, every swamp along the way, and he knew the exact point at which her conclusion would roll majestically into the station.
—"Everything That Rises Must Converge," FLANNERY O'CONNOR

* From "Birches" from *The Poetry of Robert Frost* edited by Edward Connery Lathem. Copyright 1916, © 1969 by Holt, Rinehart and Winston, Inc. Copyright 1944 by Robert Frost. Reprinted by permission of Holt, Rinehart and Winston, Inc.

Sports writers use figurative language freely. They know that figurative language produces images (pictures, sounds, and feelings in the mind) that reproduce the excitement and drama of the sports events they write about. They often use their columns to express opinions about the sports world. Since figurative language communicates feeling as well as fact, it can be a powerful device to influence the opinions of their readers.

EXERCISE 5

The following column by a well-known sports writer was published immediately after the "Indianapolis 500" in 1971. The column is an editorial; that is, it states the writer's opinions. It has been divided into sections for you. Read the first three sections in which the writer builds up to stating the changes he is recommending. Then answer the questions that follow.

Indy Ripe for Change

By Jim Murray

[SECTION I]

INDIANAPOLIS — Indianapolis the morning after the 500 is like any other ballroom after the music stops, Cinderella back at the ashes.

The garages stand silent and empty. A piece of waxpaper with mustard on it drifts down Gasoline Alley on a vagrant wind.

But there are always ghosts at Indianapolis. If you stand stock still and listen, you can hear the full deep-throated roar of the old Novis, the first high-pitched wasp whine of the first rear engines, the cannon-cracker snapping of an Offy roadster backing off as it comes off a straight and into the deadly corners.

It was 1963 when I first came to the Speedway. Over here in the middle of the middle row of garages was lovable Eddie Sachs, leprechaun in goggles, the sprite of the Speedway. It was the last time I was to see him. He had just come in from a third-turn crash, wheeling

Copyright, 1971, *Los Angeles Times*. Reprinted by permission.

his wheel as kids used to do with old tires, and waving to the crowd.

Eddie had two laps to go.

[SECTION II]

Was it over here near Garage 87 that I first saw the courtly Scotsman, Jimmy Clark, looking so pale and frail like his racer which the Indy vets predicted would not stand the pounding of this concrete and wire-rope arena, where the heat rose in searing billows? I mean, what did Clark think this was—that haybale racing of Europe where you waved to the cows? This was no lawn party for tea drinkers, these were brutish racers.

Clark, like his racing machine, was built of the steel of champions. The glint in the eye, the set of the chin behind the mild Scot farmer exterior told you that. Jimmy Clark was UNAFRAID. He may have been the best ever around this oval. With just a little luck, he could have won four in a row. A lot of important people still think he won two in a row —1965 when he did and 1966 when the pencil-pushers picked Graham Hill as the winner out of a crowd.

Last time I saw Jimmy was in a Holiday Inn restaurant in 1967 where I told him I had just bet on him in a lunch-counter pool. Jimmy laughed. "Don't," he said, "that machine of mine belongs on a carousel, not a race track."

[SECTION III]

Jimmy didn't die at Indy. He died against a tree in Germany in one of those races where you're supposed to be able to peel off in an open field and save your car and yourself. His machine at Indy that last year DID belong on a carousel. It went around for only 35 laps.

There were others you remember. Allen Crowe was in the fifth row at the start of the 1963 race and on the wall by the 47th lap. He had one week to go. Or four days. He crashed on an Ohio track and was killed.

Don Branson was on the front row that 1963. Don lost his life in Gardena three years later in a race car. Bobby Marshman was in row three in 1963. Bobby was to kill himself in a race car 20 months later. There were other grids in other years. Billy Foster was in the '65 race which Clark won, and in the '66 race

136

where his car leaped sideways on him and started a 13-car pileup at the start. Billy died at Riverside the next January.

The hearse waits for all men. But this is dangerous business. And the experience of 1971, it would seem to me would behoove the Indianapolis Motor Speedway to take a hard look at some of its procedures.

QUESTIONS:

1. What, in general, is Jim Murray writing about in these sections? _____

2. As you read, were you able to visualize the scenes and the people written about? Yes_____ No_____

3. As you finished reading what was your attitude toward the writer's ideas? Sympathetic_____ Unsympathetic_____

4. Section I contains figurative language expressions in three patterns: x is like y, x = y, and adjectives that borrow. Can you find these patterns? Copy the phrases containing them in the spaces provided.

   A. x is like y _____

   B. x = y _____

   C. Adjectives that borrow _____

5. Jim Murray makes some of his points in an indirect way; that is, some entire statements cannot be taken literally but need to be rephrased in the mind of the reader. Such statements are said to be *implied* as opposed to *stated*. When the reader rephrases in his mind the literal meaning, he is drawing an *inference*.
   A. Rephrase the statement, "But there are always ghosts at Indianapolis."

   B. Rephrase the statement, "The hearse waits for all men."

[SECTION IV]

When cars are going around this thing at 180 miles-per-hour and so finely-tuned they will stall out on you at 120, you don't put a car dealer in a stock family sedan and ask him to pace 33 of the finest engines and chauffeurs in the world at a speed twice as fast as he has ever driven before in front of a quarter of a million people. That's a job for a hardened racer at the wheel and, maybe, a hardened engine under the hood.

The business of leaving abandoned cars parked alongside the track, fully-loaded and as dangerous as mine fields, instead of towing them back to the garages is so obvious an oversight as not to need belaboring. There's barely room enough around this track for running cars without having derelicts abroad on it. It seems as simple a logic as removing logs from harbor shipping lanes.

137

6. Read Section IV and restate in brief, direct sentences what is said in each paragraph. Each paragraph contains one of the recommendations the author is making for improving conditions at Indy.

Paragraph 1 _____

_____

_____

Paragraph 2 _____

_____

_____

7. Now read the final section. Here the recommendations are repeated.

[SECTION V]

The fastest does not always win at Indy. Nor the bravest. Nor the luckiest, nor the wisest. There are times when this race is as out-of-control as a stampede for everyone in it.

The very least the drivers —and the public—are entitled to is a management which sees to it the things it CAN control are. Cars which have people in them on the tracks should have people in them who know what they are doing. Cars without people in them should not be on the track.

Like any other self-respecting freeway, there should be no parking. And pace the race cars with something and someone that has the braking power and the reflexes the rest of the field has. Lord knows the one thing Indy doesn't need is more danger.

Select one sentence from this section that restates each recommendation. Then select a sentence that generalizes about the recommendations. The ideas are restated twice, so they have actually been presented three times. To have missed them even once would have lessened the impact that Mr. Murray hoped to make on his readers.

Section V _____

_____

_____

Generalization _____

_____

Television Review

Although some television reviews are limited in their influence upon your program viewing because they often appear after the shows are run, many reviews appear before programs are seen by the public. Because of the increasing number of series, specials, and movies filmed for television, television reviews can be very helpful in planning the use of your leisure time. They can also be of interest in following the careers of your favorite stars, writers, and directors. Reviews appear on the entertainment pages of all newspapers. You will soon find reviewers who reflect your tastes or whose suggestions can build upon your present interests.

EXERCISE 6

The typical television review should supply you with information concerning the *format* (general form, arrangement) of a show as well as something of the substance and tone of the production. And of course it will contain facts about performers, directors, and viewing time. Read the following review, fill in the information called for below, and answer the questions that follow the review.

1. Stars _____
2. Supporting performers _____
3. Network and time _____
4. Name of writer of this episode _____

Van Dyke's Show Bows Tonight at 9

The New Dick Van Dyke Show arrives tonight at 9 on CBS and all the loyal viewers who watched Van Dyke for five years on his previous series shouldn't have any trouble taking up with him again in his new digs.

Carl Reiner, who was writer - director - producer of Van Dyke's first series, is creative consultant on this one (he was also writer-director of tonight's episode) and he has provided a comfortable format which (as before) allows Dick to be easygoing, personable, fun, sometimes a bit square, occasionally Mr. Bumbles.

Just how new, then, is the New Dick Van Dyke Show? Well, Dick has a new TV wife, Emmy-winner Hope Lange; a new job (this time around he hosts a TV talk show); new surroundings (Arizona, where the series is filmed); new supporting players (Marty Brill, Fannie Flagg, Nancy Dussault).

As for tonight's story, it probably leans more to vintage Van Dyke than to completely new (but if you're going to lean, that's not a bad direction). The plot is simple: Dick breaks a nonsmoking pact with his wife and associates then suffers the agony of trying to fight off the desire for just one more puff.

Actually, the choice of this particular episode for the opener is a curious one, since a preview of two additional segments indicates there is much better material in the wings. This one is a little thin when stretched over 30 minutes.

Nevertheless, the vibes seem good between Van Dyke and Miss Lange, and though Brill and Misses Flagg and Dussault don't have much to do this time out, they are experienced players and should contribute as the weeks go along.

So even though to smoke or not to smoke is not the strongest of stories, you won't find it dangerous or hazardous to your health. You'll be amused and there's promise of more laughs ahead.

And in Van Dyke's case, that's one thing that is definitely not "new." He's been making people laugh for years and probably can stay around CBS for another five years if he chooses.

—**Aleene MacMinn**

THE NEW DICK VAN DYKE SHOW

Half-hour comedy series filmed before a live audience at Carefree, Ariz. Created by Carl Reiner. Executive producer Byron Paul. Producers and story consultants Bernie Orenstein and Saul Turteltaub. Associate producer Norman S. Powell. Creative consultant Carl Reiner; premiere episode written and directed by Reiner. With Dick Van Dyke, Hope Lange, Marty Brill, Fannie Flagg, Nancy Dussault, Angela Powell. Airs 9 p.m. Saturdays on Channel 2.

Copyright, 1971, *Los Angeles Times*. Reprinted by permission.

QUESTIONS:

1. Do you know of any other productions Carl Reiner has been associated with?

_____

2. What statements in this review express a definite opinion of the reviewer and not just information about the show? _____

3. Did you notice the use of figurative language? What is meant by the following phrases?

   A. comfortable format _____

   B. better material in the wings _____

   C. vintage Van Dyke _____

   D. this segment is a little thin _____

Movie Review

EXERCISE 7

After looking up the vocabulary words, read the review and fill in the statistical information. Reread the review and answer the questions for discussion.

Vocabulary
diabolic _____

abyss _____

sleazy _____

decadence _____

Statistics
Title _____

Stars _____

Director _____

The Lively Arts

By Margaret Ronan

When Sally Bowles (Liza Minnelli) gets up on the stage at the Kit Kat Klub and invites us to "come to the cabaret!" there's no doubt that movie musicals have grown up. The smoky, sleazy Klub in *Cabaret* is a symbol of Germany in the early 1930's, teetering on the edge of the abyss of Nazism. The Berliners who gather at the Klub are interested only in pleasure and survival. They turn a deaf ear to the Storm Troopers who beat up citizens in the streets just outside.

Everything about *Cabaret* is far-reaching and big—its theme; its bitter, mocking songs; its cool, imaginative direction by Bob Fosse that invites us to think about what we are looking at and listening to. And last, but far from least, are the superb performances by Liza Minnelli as the Kit Kat Klub's star singer, and Joel Grey as its diabolic master of cere-

Reprinted by permission from Senior Scholastic. © 1972 by Scholastic Magazines, Inc. Illustration—courtesy of Allied Artists, Inc., N.Y.

monies. The numbers performed on the Klub's stage in this most mature of musicals are not just numbers. They are mocking comments on the behavior and beliefs of the crowd and the main characters themselves. In stand-out numbers like "Money" and "Why Can't They Leave Us Alone?," the M.C. needles the crowd for its prejudices and materialism. But at the same time he seems to be winking at the audience, as if to say, "Why talk sense to these fools? They're headed for disaster, anyway!"

Unlike the M.C., Sally Bowles isn't too hip to politics. She's a movie-struck American girl who dreams of being discovered by a big film director she's sure will one day wander into the Klub. Instead, she falls in love with Brian (Michael York), a young Englishman teaching languages in Berlin. Their disastrous love affair has a bittersweet parallel in the love of a would-be-fortune hunter (Fritz Wendel) for a Jewish heiress (Marisa Berenson)....

Although *Cabaret* is set in 1931 Germany, it mirrors many disturbing things about America today—public apathy, the rise of lawlessness, the pursuit of pleasure, the acceptance of decadence.

Cabaret paints an eye-opening picture in drama and song of the period that led to the rise of Nazism. One of its most effective moments is when an angelic-looking, blond young man gets up to sing "Tomorrow Belongs to Me" in a beer garden—and only as the camera slowly pulls back do we see the Nazi emblem on his arm.

Liza Minnelli and Joel Grey

From the film "Cabaret" an Allied Artists—ABC Pictures presentation

QUESTIONS

1. The reviewer has included several phrases using figurative language. Play the "figurative game" (page 131) with the writer by filling out the x = y formula and then explain the meaning of the phrase.

    A. "movie musicals have grown up"

    _____   _____
            (x = y)   (meaning of phrase)

    B. "Germany . . . (was) teetering on the abyss of Nazism"

    _____   _____
            (x = y)   (meaning of phrase)

    C. "the M.C. needles the crowd"

    _____   _____
            (x = y)   (meaning of phrase)

    D. "it (Cabaret) mirrors many disturbing things about America today"

    _____   _____
            (x = y)   (meaning of phrase)

2. List five movie musicals of the past. On the basis of what you have read in this review, discuss the reviewer's statement that "movie musicals have grown up."

    (1) _____
    (2) _____
    (3) _____
    (4) _____
    (5) _____

3. List the "disturbing things about America today" that the reviewer states are mirrored in *Cabaret*. If you have seen the movie, discuss specifically in what way these things are mirrored in the picture. Do you agree that these conditions do exist in America today?

    (1) _____
    (2) _____
    (3) _____
    (4) _____

Book Review

A book review tells what a story is about. If a book is fiction, a reviewer usually summarizes the story. He will describe what he believes the author was trying to accomplish in writing the story and also make some judgment as to the skill of the author in achieving his objective. If a book is nonfiction, a review will clearly define the scope of the treatment of the subject matter. In most cases, it will give some indication of the kind of readers who would find the book interesting. For example, many people today are interested in ecology. However, ecology is a very broad and complex subject. Therefore a review of a book on ecology would probably reveal, either directly or indirectly, whether the book is written for the layman or for the scientist. Reading book reviews can be a very interesting pastime. Regular reading of these reviews in newspapers and periodicals can keep you informed about new books that are available, even if your leisure time allows for reading only a few of them.

EXERCISE 8 Look up the words in the vocabulary list and record their meanings opposite each word before reading the review. After you have read the review, answer the questions that follow it.

Vocabulary

primeval _____

nonentity _____

paleontologist _____

orgy(ies) _____

appal(led) _____

promiscuity _____

platonic _____

fidelity _____

harem _____

offspring _____

ninny _____

A Hairy Mirror

IN THE SHADOW OF MAN by Jane van Lawick-Goodall.

"I saw a black shape hunched up on the ground. I hunched down myself ... in the thick undergrowth. Then I heard a

Reprinted by permission from *Time, The Weekly Newsmagazine;* © Time Inc. 1971.

soft hoo *to my right. I looked up and saw a large male directly overhead. All at once he uttered a long drawn-out* wraaaai... *one of the most savage sounds of the African forest... I forced myself to appear uninterested and busy, eating some roots from the ground. The end of the branch above me hit my head. With a stamping and slapping of the ground a black shape charged through the undergrowth ... I expected to be torn to pieces. I do not know how long I crouched there before I realized that everything was still and silent again, save for the* drip-drip *of the raindrops."*

With this scene of primeval terror, a young Englishwoman named Jane Goodall began an intimacy with the chimpanzees in the rain forests of Tanzania that has lasted a decade

Photograph by Baron Hugo van Lawick. © National Geographic Society.

A wild chimpanzee gets a handout of bananas from Jane Goodall.

and produced one of natural history's most impressive field studies. In this book she has greatly expanded the preliminary report on her experiences. *My Friends: The Wild Chimpanzees* (1967); the photographs speak a volume in themselves. *In the Shadow of Man* should become an instant animal classic.

Scary Scrapes. Jane was 26 and a scientific nonentity when she began her work. Born in London in modest circumstances, she worked as a secretary when she arrived in Nairobi. Struck by her feelings for animals, Africa's world-renowned paleontologist, Dr. L. S. B. Leakey, wangled a grant and packed the young lady off to chase chimps. At first she could not get within 500 yards of her subjects. Real discoveries started, however, when a bold chimp she called David Graybeard strolled into her camp one day and began chewing on a palm nut. Lured by bananas, his friends followed. Jane in turn followed the band on its jungle journeys—sometimes, despite scary scrapes with leopards, she even stayed with them all night—and gathered impressive evidence that the chimpanzee has a far more complex life-style than anybody had supposed.

Like men, she quickly discovered, chimpanzees are technological animals. They chew leaves to make sponges, which they use to sop water out of hollow branches. They also strip grass stems to make long probes, which they use to fish tasty termites out of their mounds. Jane also found out that chimps, long considered vegetarians, also eat meat. Like primitive humans, they form hunting parties and carry out fairly intricate plans to capture young bush pigs, monkeys, baboons—and even, she reports, human babies.

Prodigies of Imagination. Compared with the behavior of any species except man, the chimp's social life is richly sophisticated. They have a wide range of intelligible expressions: fear, rage, hunger, shock, confusion, boredom, irritation, amusement, worry, pleading, mischief, tenderness, embarrassment—even a look of comic alarm

Photo by Baron Hugo van Lawick. © National Geographic Society.

Flint, at 11 months, seeks out his tall friend. Like a child taking his first steps, Flint wanders on short exploratory trips away from mother's sheltering arms. But Flo stays nearby, keeping an eye on her offspring.

that reminded Jane of refined English girls watching horror movies. The chimps also smile, hold hands, dance when it rains, play simple games and stage hugging-and-back-slapping orgies when they discover a new fruit tree.

Status is important to both sexes, but among the males it seems to matter as much as food, perhaps more than sex. The struggle to achieve it calls forth prodigies of creative imagination. Mike, a low-ranking male of unremarkable physique, seized supreme power in his group by a stroke of genius. He grabbed a couple of empty kerosene cans from the author's camp and then charged at the other males, bellowing ferociously and banging the cans together as he came. Appalled by the din, his rivals fled. Swaggering absurdly, Mike challenged Goliath, the dominant male, and in a drama of display and roaring counterdisplay he broke the older male's nerve. After that, whenever the two met, they rushed up to each other like a couple of rival jocks and worked off their anxiety by hugging, slapping, grooming—and kissing each other on the neck. "Never, however," the author reassures us, "have we seen anything that could be regarded as homosexuality in chimpanzees."

On the whole, in fact, sex was the least serious problem in a chimpanzee's relations. Total promiscuity was the rule, but now and then a male developed a platonic passion for a special female and followed her everywhere, whether or not she was in heat. Sometimes his feeling was returned, and in that case something like a chimpanzee marriage was made. At times sexual fidelity was a part of the contract. At the other extreme, one of the dominant males would sometimes try to assemble a harem. At the first opportunity, the females usually flew the coop.

A Model Mother. Most females were more interested in children than they were in males. Jane found that chimp mothers who made their babies get out on their own at an early age wound up with clinging, frightened children. Steady, loving and even indulgent mothers, in contrast, generally had happy, independent offspring. Flo, a perfectly hideous old chimp who for reasons be-

Photo by Baron Hugo van Lawick. © National Geographic Society.

A five-year-old chimpanzee in Tanzania's Gombe Stream Reserve uses a tool she made herself by stripping down a blade of grass. With the improvised instrument, "Fifi" pokes into a termite mound to fish for insects.

yond human imagination made all the males go ape at mating season, was a model mother when the study began. She played with her babies continually, picked them up at the first whimper, followed every slap with a squeeze and cleverly distracted her child when she saw misbehavior in the making: but as she grew older she became grandmotherly and spoiled one little chimp rotten. As he approached maturity, he was still a screaming ninny.

.... A woman as well as a scientist, Jane loves her subjects and makes the reader love them too—not as clever pets but as serious and struggling individuals. All the more painful, then, to be told that throughout Africa chimpanzees are being shot for the pot by natives and pursued by professional hunters who knock off the mothers and ship the babies to zoos and laboratories. To one who has read this book, the fact that people kill chimpanzees seems only slightly less sickening than the fact that people kill people.

Brad Darrach

QUESTIONS

1. The book is _____
   A. fiction
   B. nonfiction
2. The book is about _____
   _____
3. _____ is the author.

4. The author was a _____
   A. layperson
   B. trained scientist

5. The book appears to have appeal _____
   A. only to the trained scientist
   B. only to the layperson
   C. to both the layperson and the trained scientist

6. The review contains _____
   A. an excerpt from the book
   B. no excerpt from the book

7. List facts or information from the book that you found interesting.
   A. _____
   B. _____
   C. _____
   D. _____
   E. _____

GRIN AND BEAR IT   BY LICHTY

"As soon as your child gets over the shock that it's not battery operated, I'm sure he'll really enjoy a book!"

Courtesy Publishers-Hall Syndicate

Section Six

Power Through Integration

You hear a great deal about integration these days. It is a good word used in connection with sound purposes and high ideals. If you consult a dictionary, you will find the verb *integrate* defined as *to make or form into a whole, to bring all parts together, to unify, to unite with something else, to bring into common membership in a society or organization.* You are no doubt familiar with the last definition as applied to attempts to integrate all ethnic groups into full membership in American society. Integration is a good goal for many enterprises that involve several parts working together in harmony. As you approach the final section of this text, you should be aware that no single skill will produce reading power. Reading power involves the integration of many skills that interact with each other.

Many factors that are not in themselves reading skills contribute to your reading performance. Some of these add to your skill and others detract from it. Knowledge acquired without formal instruction (outside of school) becomes part of your input. Such knowledge differs from one individual to another. Therefore, one student's performance will be different from another student's even though each has had the same schooling. And an individual's performance will differ from one task to another according to what he knows about the subject or how highly motivated he is.

Critical Reading

Emotional reaction to what you read can add or detract from your reading performance. One of the most valuable effects that formal training, or education, should have is to provide you with proper direction for your emotional reactions. If emotional response to what you read helps you to visualize more clearly what a writer is describing and to feel more deeply what he feels, your emotions are well directed. Of course you will realize that there may be many points of view on a subject. If you react emotionally to what you read in such a way that it is impossible for you to determine what a writer is saying or to follow his logic, then your emotions are not well-directed and will detract from your reading performance.

When you read with good comprehension of the content and the ability to evaluate what you read in the light of many points of view, you have become a critical reader. Articles on the same subject may seem to be—or actually may be—contradictory. Apparent contradictions need to be analyzed carefully. They can be the result of looking upon a subject from a general rather than a specific point of view. They can have to do with a writer's purpose. An author who writes to entertain his readers has a different purpose from one who is writing a deeply analytical report. A television reporter repeats news releases that give highlights of the news. A newspaper account of the same subject—in which the writer has the time to explore background material and report reactions to an event—may leave a reader with a different impression than he might have received from hearing the television report. The reports may seem to contradict each other, but actually it may be the reporters' purposes that differ. Some people seem to enjoy criticizing the quality of the media (a term used to refer to all forms of mass communication). These people would undoubtedly benefit more from trying to improve their own abilities to read critically.

On the following pages are three articles on the same subject. Read them carefully and answer the questions as directed. You will be asked to record opinions at various points. Observe yourself in the opinion-forming process. Note the sources of the articles (periodicals in which they first appeared) and try to determine the purposes of the writers.

EXERCISE 1

Read Selection I from beginning to end. Read for information and enjoyment. You will get neither information nor enjoyment unless you absorb the principal facts and visualize clearly much of the action described. *Before reading the article,* fill in the meanings of the vocabulary words listed below as you think they would be used in the context of the subject (rodeos).

VOCABULARY

1. stock _____

2. resin _____

3. cinch _____

4. spurs _____

5. chaps _____

6. steer _____

7. bareback riding _____

8. chute _____

9. human _____

10. humane _____

[SELECTION 1]
Rodeo Cowboys Don't Take Their Hats off to Anybody

By Robert Meyers

Rodeo cowboys. Some compete for pleasure, some for profit. Year-round competitions give away over $4 million in prize money. To professional cowboys, mustang, pinto and colt are horses not cars.

Rodeo seems as old as the hills. The paradox is that its earliest form first appeared a little more than a century ago. That epic moment undoubtedly came about when two cowpokes found themselves face to face with a bronc that didn't want to be "rode." They challenged each other—and the rodeo was born.

The word "rodeo" means "roundup," and on the roundups cattle were herded together and driven to market. The drives along such legendary trails as the Chisholm and the Western in the 1860s and

Reprinted by permission of Ann Elmo Agency, Inc., 52 Vanderbilt Ave., New York, N.Y. 10017. Copyright © 1971 by *Westways*.

1870s were long and lonely; cowboys spent months on the plains with no companionship other than the dozen or so men they worked with. Naturally, when a herd from the Bar J met with a herd from the Lazy Y, the pent-up energy exploded in a frenzy of competition. Cowboys challenged each other in contests of individual skill and daring—reminiscent of ancient Minoan bull-jumping, medieval jousting and Anglo-Saxon boasting contests.

There were always wild horses that had never been broken, cow ponies that had soured, or calves that needed branding—and every cowboy in the bunch was willing to try his hand. These were competitions based on actual work experience, and, in the case of the unbroken horses, the object was not just to stay on for an eight- or ten-second ride (as is the case today), but to tame the bucking bronc. There might be some bets placed (every outfit thought it had the top bronc buster in the territory), but when a man earned less than a dollar a day, the betting wasn't exactly what you find in Vegas casinos. The roughhousing over with, the cooks would put out the grub that the men at once both loathed and respected: hot beef stew, steaming baked beans, cornmeal biscuits, molasses pie, if they were lucky, and coffee. Bed was a woolen cover roll on the ground, a saddle for a headrest, a blanket of stars overhead.

With cattle drives made obsolete in an age of railroads and flatbed trucks, rodeo has evolved into a world of its own, a year-round, nationwide competition with over four million dollars in prize money, 2,500 active professional contestants and a live, paying audience of over ten million people. Where once a cowboy made his living punching cattle, today that cowboy—a rodeo cowboy—can make a handsome income solely by competing in the more than 530 rodeos held each year in all parts of the country. One of rodeo's current superstars, for example, Larry Mahan, at the tender age of twenty-seven earned more than $60,000 in prize money alone during 1970. (That was before endorsements for everything from boots to saddles.)

Other top hands in each of the six recognized events (bareback, saddle bronc and bull riding; calf roping, team roping, and steer wrestling) can make over $25,000 a year, and it's possible to finish as low as fifteenth place in the annual standings and still clear over $10,000. Professional rodeo, a sport that didn't even exist in any organized way a hundred years ago, and didn't really get started until after World War II, now holds a secure place on the American sports scene.

A major factor in rodeo's growth has been the organization by the cowboys themselves into a professional guild-type setup, and the development and improvement of the rodeo production companies. Cowboys get their "pro cards" after they win $1,000 during a season, and are then covered by a generous insurance policy for their thirty-five-dollars-a-year dues. With the exception of the RCA secretary-treasurer (currently Dave Stout, a well-liked rodeo hand), the officials headquartered in the RCA's Denver facilities are unsalaried—businessmen, ranchers, farmers, breeders and plain rodeo fans who do it out of devotion to the sport.

The largest rodeo production company in the world is the Golden State Rodeo Company, with main offices in Marysville, California.

The largest part of the rodeo job falls to the stock contractors, who are hired for a fee to stage a rodeo.

"We can go into an arena in the morning, have our equipment up by noon, rehearse the acts by five, put on a performance by eight and be out of there by midnight," says the current head of the Flying U division of Golden State. "And we do everything ourselves, from publicity to films to even bringing in the dirt, if necessary. We develop our own acts, raise our own livestock, put on the kinds of shows in the six western states that you can't find anywhere else."

In order to do all this, Golden State Rodeo keeps 250 bucking horses, 150 bulls, 50 saddle horses, 600 steers, 200 calves and 50 Texas Longhorns on five ranches scattered throughout the state. To move their stock and equipment (including chutes, pens and barriers), Golden State uses four specially built, $45,000, sixty-foot-long, double-decker diesel trucks, which can haul twenty-six horses on the bottom and twelve bulls on top. Golden State is constantly experimenting with their half-time acts, and recently added a group of trick riders known as "The Blackouts," who race around the arena illuminated only by ultra-violet lights. Rosser says coming innovations might include colored sawdust on the floor (for indoor shows), and hydraulically operated chute gates that would open in the middle, rather than be hinged on one side.

The cynical city slicker might feel that the mating of high finance and show biz has bred the life out of rodeo, but that's not the case at all. There's nothing phony about the block-busting action that goes on in the ring, or the smaller, finer details—like tooling on a saddle, the glint of sun off a silver spur, the ripple of muscle in a cow pony's shoulder.

Unlike baseball and football, which plays to audiences of thousands of people, most of whom are sitting a good distance back from the action, rodeo usually plays to a small audience of about one thousand people.

Indoors or out, afternoon or evening, summer or winter, all rodeos begin with a Grand Parade. This is rodeo's traditional opening event, and at Golden State shows it's done with enough precision to make the Rockettes turn in their tap shoes with envy. Led by a mounted color guard of cowgirls dressed in sexy, spangled outfits, the day's contestants come galloping in and make a huge figure eight around the arena. Drawing their horses to a sharp halt, they face the grandstand as the loudspeaker blares the national anthem, after which they whoop and yell as the announcer introduces the ring officials and other honored guests. Then they're off, and the rodeo begins.

The first people in the arena are the judges, two stripe-vested officials who are themselves active contestants (though of course they don't compete at the rodeos they judge). In bareback, saddle bronc, and bull riding, each judge marks the rider up to twenty-five points for his ride, and also scores the animal up to twenty-five for its performance. Therefore, no cowboy wants a lazy animal, because that would only hurt his chances of winning. In calf and team roping, and steer wrestling, events that are waged mainly against the clock, the judges function only to make sure that the rules aren't broken. (It would be pretty obvious if a roper missed catching his calf.)

Bareback riding is usually the first of the roughstock events. The cowboy mounts his horse in the chutes, sitting on a double-thick pad. His handhold is fitted on a cinch rigging which encircles the animal. The man wears gloves, and chaps, usually coated with a sticky resin to prevent slippage. But if the man isn't on securely in the first place, he's in trouble. The rules say the rider must keep his spurs over the horse's shoulders until the first jump is completed, that he can use only one hand to hold on with and that he can't touch either the horse or the rigging with the other, and that to qualify he's got to stay on for the full eight seconds. Other than that, he's on his own. Bareback riding is strictly a rodeo event, matching nothing in a cowboy's working life. It's been a standard event for only twenty years, but is one of the most popular.

Rodeo stock is used only in the arena. The horse that bucks furiously for the eight seconds is probably "worked" no more than ten minutes *a year*. The rest of the time he's put out to pasture. The spurs a cowboy uses are dulled so they wouldn't cut butter; anything else might not only injure the animal, but could catch in the animal's flesh and flip the cowboy off. (All rodeo contractors abide by their state's veterinary rules, and there's always a county animal regulation official on hand to see that they do.)

The quintessential rodeo event, saddle bronc riding, is a direct descendant of the days when, if a man needed a horse, he had to tame one to get it. It is similar to bareback riding, except that the cowboy mounts a regulation RCA saddle and hangs on to a manila rope running from the bridle. Ideally, the rider falls into the horse's bucking "rhythm," moving in perfect if ferocious harmony with it. A good ride is a joy to behold. Each judge, scoring both horse and rider from one to twenty-five points, calls his score up to the announcer's booth. On a scale of 100, a score in the high seventies will usually take it.

Steer wrestling or bulldogging, is a product of the rodeo arena, its beginning generally laid to a black cowboy, Bill Pickett, who traveled with the Miller Brothers rodeo in the early 1900s. In this event, the cowboy has to glide from his galloping horse onto the neck of a running steer (often weighing upwards of 500 pounds), and throw him to the ground in the shortest possible time. The steer is given a ten-foot jump out of the chute at the far end of the arena before the cowboy and his hazer take off after him. It's the hazer's job to race on horseback along the steer's right flank and make sure he doesn't veer off course. At the same time the cowboy is sliding off his horse and onto the steer, he's getting his hand under the steer's chin. Digging his boots hard into the ground, he twists the animal's neck until it falls to the ground, all four legs extended. Unlike bronc and bull riders, who are often lean and wiry, some extra weight helps here, and bulldoggers can be pretty hefty fellows. A good time in this event is twelve seconds.

In calf and team roping (which derives directly from ranch work), a mounted cowboy takes off after a 150-pound calf that has been given a ten-foot head start; the cowboy has a rope in one hand and a pigging string between his teeth. When he's just behind the calf he throws the loop, pulls his horse back in a jarring, hind-legs-in-the-dust stop, jumps off and races to the calf. The horse's action has literally thrown the calf off its feet, and the roper should reach him before he gets his balance back. Throwing the calf down on its side and straddling him, the roper whips the pigging string out of his mouth and ties any three of the calf's legs, throwing his hands up when he's through. Then he walks back and mounts his horse, who all the while has been playing a major part by backing up to keep the rope taut. Roper's horses are among the most skilled and highly trained in rodeo, and a good one will bring upwards of $1500. The cowboy, now mounted, moves toward the calf, letting the rope go slack. If the calf stays tied for six seconds, the roper has qualified. A good time for this event, from start to finish (when the roper throws his hands up) is ten seconds.

In team roping, two cowboys go after the calf, one roping the calf's head, the other his two hind feet. When the calf is hung up between the header and heeler, the official drops his flag. Team roping, when done by the best, draws gasps of amazement from the crowd.

Bull riding, traditionally the last event of the afternoon, is acknowledged the most dangerous of all rodeo contests. Not only is it sheer hell for a cowpoke weighing no more than 200 pounds to stay *on* the bull, who weighs more than 1500 pounds, but he's got to worry about getting gored or trampled once he's off. Bull riding was introduced to the arena in the 1920s, and immediately became the roughest, toughest, rankest competition going.

The cowboy's problems start in the chute. He's got to be careful that, once he's mounted, the bull doesn't swerve to the side and crush his leg against barriers. The cowboy, wearing gloves and chaps rubbed with resin, sits directly on the bull's back. He holds on to a cinch girth that's got a cowbell on it—and the only thing holding the cinch on is the cowboy, who's holding the free end. When he lets go of the rope, it'll fall free. The object in this event, of course, is to stay on—and show as much poise as possible while doing it.

The cowboy isn't required to spur the animal, as he is in bareback and saddle bronc riding, but he gets extra points if he does. Outside of his own ability, the one other thing the rider depends on are the two clowns—here more properly known as bull fighters. If the cowboy is thrown off, the bull is going to take off after him. It's here that the clowns will rush in, waving rags and parasols in the bull's face, offering themselves as targets. The bull turns to look at the clown—and the cowboy gets away free. Riding a bull—be it Brahma, short horned, or white face—can be the longest eight seconds in a cowboy's life.

Cowboys, all of them, are a breed apart. The ranching West and the rodeo arena have become bastions for some of the most colorful language left to the tongue: you don't rope a calf, you tie some veal or you hitch up his axles; your horse doesn't stop short, he digs his tail in. Western clothes worn by cowboys remain unique

James Fain
Saddle bronc

QUESTIONS

and distinctive—and envied around the world: a high-crowned hat, metal-snapped shirt, stovepipe jeans hanging well below the heel of pointy-toed, fancy-stitched, calf-high boots (among the most comfortable footwear a man can own), the cowboy's pants, held up by a fancy leather belt with his name carved on it, and the biggest buckle you ever saw, awarded to him for his last big rodeo win.

Cowboys are also guardians of western humor, that peculiarly American form of boasting and jest, sometimes dry, sometimes rollicking, which pops up around the chutes more often than a scared calf. Ask a cowboy about the bronc he rode last week and he'll tell you it stayed in the air a full ten seconds, and the poor thing nearly died for oxygen; ask another about that bull he rode in Yuma and he'll say the damn thing was so tall he needed a ladder to mount it. Pretty soon talk like this grows so big it starts bouncing off the Rockies, and you see that the legend of Paul Bunyan and his ox Babe was only the first and tallest of all tall tales, told by men whose descendants are still laughing.

Something else about cowboys: they don't take their hats off. In the shade, in a car, in a restaurant, in a store, the hat—not the dude's ten-gallon variety, but the kind that looks like it could hold a good three quarts—stays firmly on. He might tip it forward when he meets someone, and tip it back so he can see the girls better, but the hat never comes off. And the reason for this isn't clear at once, since businessmen, soldiers and protesting construction workers all take their hats off at some point or another. Perhaps it's a custom from the days of the frontier, when a man never knew when he'd have to leave the saloon in a hurry; perhaps it's a reflection of the inordinately high hat-casualty rate in days when people tended to sit down rather suddenly and crush a new Stetson beneath them; perhaps it's a reminder that there were very few hat racks in the Old West.

Perhaps, perhaps.

But maybe it's because they honestly feel—and who can really blame them?—that cowboys don't have to take their hats off to anyone.

A. *Impressions*
1. My general impression of rodeos as exciting, wholesome entertainment is _____
    A. favorable
    B. unfavorable
    C. not sure

2. My general impression of the life of a rodeo cowboy is that it is exciting, financially rewarding, and on the whole a good career for those qualified and interested. _____
    A. yes
    B. no
    C. not sure

3. My general impression of the treatment given to the animals in rodeos is _____
    A. favorable
    B. unfavorable
    C. not sure

B. *Opinions*
1. In the field of entertainment rodeos appear to be a very profitable business for most of those involved. _____
    A. agree
    B. disagree
    C. not sure

2. If I were a good rider, liked competition, and wanted to make money, I think that being a rodeo cowboy would make a good career. _____
   A. agree
   B. disagree
   C. not sure

3. Rodeos have all the essential elements of a good spectator sport. _____
   A. agree
   B. disagree
   C. not sure

4. Rodeo cowboys appear to be interesting people both as individuals and as a group. _____
   A. agree
   B. disagree
   C. not sure

5. Rodeos provide good working conditions and good pay for the participating cowboys. _____
   A. agree
   B. disagree
   C. not sure

6. Rodeos seem to provide humane treatment for the animals. _____
   A. agree
   B. disagree
   C. not sure

EXERCISE 2 Read Selections II and III carefully. After Selection III the questions you answered after Selection I have been reprinted. Answer them again on the basis of what you have read in all three articles. You will probably find it interesting to discuss your responses with others in your class.

[SECTION II]
Lively debate

Rodeos: Sport or 'Spectacles of Brutality'?

By Charles Hillinger
Times Staff Writer

The newspaper ads begin with large bold letters that ask:

"Is This The Way The West Was Won?"

Copyright, 1971, *Los Angeles Times*. Reprinted by permission.

A photograph accompanying the ad shows two men jabbing a horse with electric prods as a cowboy aboard the rearing animal charges from a rodeo chute.

"Look closely at the picture," urges the ad by the Humane Society of the United States. "It shows how to turn a quiet, domesticated horse into a frightened savage animal.

"Around the horse's loins is a leather belt known as a bucking strap being pulled so tight that the horse goes 'wild' to be rid of the pain.

"To make the horse leap from the chute, he is being goaded near his tail with the electric prods."

The Humane Society has launched a nationwide campaign charging rodeos with being "spectacles of brutality in which each year hundreds of animals are maimed, crippled and killed."

'IN NAME OF SPORT'

"And all this is done in the name of sport, under the guise of entertainment."

"Hogwash!" declares Dave Stout, secretary-treasurer of the 3,000-member Rodeo Cowboys

Assn., at his Denver headquarters.

"Of course animals are occasionally hurt, just as they are in thoroughbred horse racing, steeplechasing, polo, in circuses or in fact wherever animals are used.

"But RCA rules aim specifically at lessening the danger of injury. We make every effort to make sure animals are not mistreated. We don't like to see the animals hurt any more than members of humane societies do."

Each year 25 million Americans fill stadiums and arenas across the country to see the traditional cowboy extravaganza. Last year, of the roughly 3,000 rodeos staged in the United States, 547 were RCA sanctioned. The RCA gate totaled more than $25 million.

Many more were put on by 4-H Clubs, Future Farmers of America, high schools, colleges, other rodeo associations and groups.

The Humane Society, headquartered in Washington, D.C., recently petitioned the Federal Trade Commission to ban telecasting of rodeos and to compel the rodeo industry "to cease false and deceptive advertising."

In a letter to the FTC, the society's general counsel asked for public hearings and demanded the rodeo industry "tell it like it is."

"Horses in bucking events," he charged, "are neither wild nor unbroken. The horse is in a state of fear, frenzy and torment, propelled from the chute with kicks and electric prods, forced to thrash and buck by means of the bucking strap."

An RCA representative maintains that the RCA has never identified its bucking horses as wild horses.

"They are miscreants of the equine world, horses that have soured under the saddle or harness," he said. "They buck because they want to, not because they are forced to."

"The flank strap is a leather strap 2 inches wide and covered with sheepskin." It's an irritant, like a tightened belt and makes a horse kick high with his hind legs.

"But it causes no pain. When a bucking horse grunts or snorts it's from exertion, not pain. Bucking is an integral part of a horse's being."

In a brochure published by RCA to refute the Humane Society claims, the editor of the Western Horseman writes:

"If he doesn't buck enough, the horse is sold to canners and he ends up inside somebody's lap dog.

"If he bucks well, a rodeo producer save his life and buys him for his bucking string. That horse works less in the next few years than anybody's riding horse."

Also quoted in the RCA brochure is a veterinarian, who reports:

"Bucking and flank straps are not painful devices. They serve to increase the bucking animal's action and to cause him to kick higher. If pulled too tight the animal can't buck. In fact he will be unable to stand.

"I believe rodeos must be supervised to minimize injuries and prevent instances of cruelty. Rodeo contestants and personnel who are guilty of cruelty to animals ought to be penalized."

As for electric prods, a common device used by ranchers to move their stock, the RCA representative countered: "In RCA rodeos electric prods are not used to propel bucking horses or calves out of chutes. They are used, however, to position animals in the chute if the need arises.

"The photo used in the humane society ads was not taken at an RCA-sanctioned rodeo.

"It should be remembered, too, the prod gives off an electric shock equivalent to one a person receives when he scuffles his feet on a carpet and touches a door knob."

The American Humane Assn. and its 400 affiliates throughout the nation maintains charts and statistics on injuries and deaths to rodeo animals.

"We do not approve or condone rodeos," a spokesman for the AHA stated.

"But as long as these performances continue to be attended by millions of people, we will continue to work on a practical level making every possible effort to eliminate and reduce animal injury and suffering."

Injury Rates

He said the AHA found 5% of the rodeo animals were injured sufficiently to require medical attention in nonsupervised rodeos.

"The AHA currently is able to supervise about 10% of the rodeos, that is have humane officers in attendance," he noted.

"Injuries at these events have dropped from 5% to about three-fourths of 1%."

It was the AHA, headquartered in Denver, that compiled the 19 rules under which the Rodeo Cowboys Assn. has operated the last 10 years.

One of the rules, for example, requires that calves used in rodeo events weigh a minimum of 250 pounds.

One of the nation's most outspoken rodeo foes is Elizabeth Sakach, a vivacious 38-year-old redhead.

Mrs. Sakach, long-time member of the Internal Revenue Service's investigative staff, has been a trumpet player with a band for 20 years.

DIFFERENT VIEW

The band always plays at the annual local rodeo.

"I always looked forward to the rodeo," said Mrs. Sakach, "I enjoyed the color, the excitement.

"But being in the band we got a different view than most spectators. The band sits right above the chutes. I didn't like some of the things I saw.

"The last straw happened in 1965. Two horses broke their legs."

Since that day Mrs. Sakach has spent most of her free time campaigning against alleged cruelty in rodeo arenas.

"The 19 rules the RCA adopted are fine," says Mrs. Sakach, "except it's impossible to enforce them.

"Legislation isn't needed," insists Mrs. Sakach. "If anticruelty laws in every state were enforced most abuses would be outlawed."

[SELECTION III]
Most Still Broke

Today's Rodeo: Top Cowboys Are Airborne

By David Lamb
Times Staff Writer

LEHI, Utah—The prize money was only $6,500—not much considering the miles traveled and the risks taken—but a slice of it would be enough to get Jay Ventress to the next rodeo town.

Ventress, who is 25 and rides Brahman bulls for a living, pulled into Lehi in his dusty Chevrolet after a

Copyright, 1971, *Los Angeles Times*. Reprinted by permission.

sleepless night. Fifty bucks, he figured, would meet expenses and get him back on the road.

Larry Mahan, who is 27 and has earned $292,000 riding bulls and broncs since 1963, arrived in his twin-engine Cessna after a 700-mile flight from a rodeo in Canada. He makes commercials for Wheaties but he, too, was tired and hungry.

He had left Ponoka at dawn, stopped in Livingston, Mont., to drop off two cowboys who would share their winnings with him in exchange for the ride, cleared customs in Cutbank, Mont., picked up a saddle in Blackfoot, Ida., and made it to Lehi one hour before the saddle bronc event.

THREE RODEOS PLANNED

Tomorrow he would compete in Cody, Wyo., in the afternoon, Rupert, Ida., in the evening, then leave for St. Paul, Ore., where a rodeo started the next day. He would cover 1,700 miles in three days. Not an unusual journey for a rodeo cowboy these days.

For Lehi, a Mormon town of 5,000 located beneath the Wasatch Mountains just north of Provo, this rodeo was the big event of the year, the only thing, said Mayor Morris Clark, "we really have to offer the public."

For the 172 cowboys who entered, it was just another stop and another skipped meal on the circuit, one of 11 rodeos some would enter in the single weekend, a brief layover on Mahan's 200,000-mile annual trek.

159

They straggled into Lehi from yesterday's rodeo in Reno, lugging duffle bags and saddles, hauling horses behind their campers and pickups, talking about the places they had been and the stock they had ridden.

Superstitions are as much a part of their lives as broken bones. Don't eat peanuts in the arena. Don't put your hat on a bed. And for some, don't change the clothes you wore during a winning ride. (One cowboy set an unofficial record this year by riding 19 straight broncs without changing.)

There are 3,446 cowboys on the circuit and all but 221 made less than $5,000 last year. Most are broke by the time they get to the national finals in Oklahoma City and only the top money winners get to the finals.

Last year, 288 of them were hospitalized with injuries, but they get no closer to admitting the presence of fear than hinting, as did bareback rider Marty Backstrom, "Sure, you got your motor runnin' a bit when the chute opens."

Backstrom recently had been "crippled" for a month after taking "a little draggin' up in South Dakota." It would take, however, more than a couple of bum legs to get him back to his carpenter's job in Wickenburg, Ariz., for $7.50 an hour.

"You don't get rich rodeoing," said Ventress, a black cowboy from Burbank, "but what you get, you get on your own. No one subsidizes you. You pay your own entry fees. (Up to $100 an event in big rodeos.) You make all the plays. No one else."

But for Larry Clayman, 29, rodeoing was the only profession that ever entered his mind. He is a third-generation rodeo clown, one of a handful making $20,000 a year. He is a man with a dual disposition:

—Serious and intent as he sits in his 24-foot house trailer with his wife and beer-drinking chimpanzee, Toto, talking about how he must psyche out each bull and know his reactions to every situation.

—Silly and funny and recklessly daring as he prances in the arena, taunting the bulls, turning them in circles to give cowboys a better ride, distracting them from fallen riders and shouting, "Ride 'em, Jay. Ride 'em. Attaboy, Jay. Stay with him, boy, stay with him."

Clayman runs two miles a day so he will be as fresh for the first bull of the night as for the last. Still, his recent injuries include two broken feet, a broken right leg, eight teeth knocked out, four cracked ribs, his right arm and shoulder dislocated, his right eye displaced from its socket, part of one finger severed and his jugular vein gored, requiring a transfusion.

... Old-time rodeo hands talk about a new breed on the circuit. They are younger and smarter and they fly airplanes and invest their money. Many move into the professional ranks not from ranches as in the past, but from the 87 colleges which offer rodeo scholarships and field rodeo teams.

"It's just not good business management to operate any other way," says one of the new breed, C. W. Adams, 29, a graduate of Cal Poly San Luis Obispo, who won $13,000 riding bulls in his top year, 1967.

"I don't drink, but I have nothing against it. There's no way, though, that I can hang around a bar all night, then fly my plane across two states the next day to compete in a rodeo."

Like other cowboys, Adams scoffs at recent charges by the Humane Society that rodeos are cruel. (For the cowboys, maybe, but not the animals, they laugh.)

There was a breeze off the mountains and rain clouds in the night when Lehi's rodeo began with the "world's most famous miniature parade" on Main St. Only a few hundred spectators turned out, but that was to be expected. Most of Lehi was in the parade.

At the nearby 5,000-seat arena, the rodeo chairman . . . was eyeing the early arrivals. Three capacity performances would bring in about $17,000. . . . Golden State would get just over half, $1,500 already had gone for advertising and $3,150 for purse money. The profits, per- perhaps $1,500, would buy new uniforms for the high school band and get its rodeo team to other contests in Utah.

Of the 172 contestants, only about 25 would share in the prize money. The rest would leave empty handed. Among them: Jay Ventress, who would still manage to get to Rupert; C. W. Adams, who would tumble off Blue Smoke before the eight second limit (no time, no dough); and Larry Allen who would leave in an ambulance.

The arena is filled by the time Larry Mahan climbs into chute No. 5 with Yellow Jacket.

The kids perched on the railing are staring intently, their expressions perhaps a bit distant. They come from the surrounding ranches and they understand the violent world of rodeo.

One day, it will be their turn.

James Fain
Bull riding

Fill in the full names of the organizations referred to in Selection II.

1. RCA _____
2. FTC _____
3. AHA _____

QUESTIONS

A. *Impressions*
1. My general impression of rodeos as exciting, wholesome entertainment is _____
   A. favorable
   B. unfavorable
   C. not sure

2. My general impression of the life of a rodeo cowboy is that it is exciting, financially rewarding, and on the whole a good career for those qualified and interested. _____
   A. yes
   B. no
   C. not sure

3. My general impression of the treatment given to the animals in rodeos is _____
   A. favorable
   B. unfavorable
   C. not sure

B. *Opinions*

1. In the field of entertainment rodeos appear to be a very profitable business for most of those involved. _____
   A. agree
   B. disagree
   C. not sure

2. If I were a good rider, liked competition, and wanted to make money, I think that being a rodeo cowboy would make a good career. _____
   A. agree
   B. disagree
   C. not sure

3. Rodeos have all the essential elements of a good spectator sport. _____
   A. agree
   B. disagree
   C. not sure

4. Rodeo cowboys appear to be interesting people both as individuals and as a group. _____
   A. agree
   B. disagree
   C. not sure

5. Rodeos provide good working conditions and good pay for the participating cowboys. _____
   A. agree
   B. disagree
   C. not sure

6. Rodeos seem to provide humane treatment for the animals. _____
   A. agree
   B. disagree
   C. not sure

EXERCISE 3

On the basis of the judgments you made and opinions expressed in Exercises 1 and 2 what statement could you make about the effects of *a writer's point of view* on a reader's opinions?

_____
_____
_____
_____

What do you think would be a good policy for a reader to follow before he forms strong opinions on a subject?

_____
_____
_____
_____

Study Skills

The reading task that is probably the most difficult is one that students are most concerned with—the reading of textbooks. There are many reasons why textbook reading is difficult. Different subject fields and different textbooks require different approaches. Some subject fields often work with specialized vocabularies. And to complicate matters—each student differs from every other student in what he brings with him to the learning task from previous study or experiences. But probably the principle reason why textbook reading (studying) is so difficult is that it is not just reading; it is reading *plus* many other things, all of which can be loosely classified as study skills. These study skills must be *integrated* into your reading performance.

Here are some of the things you probably will have to do in textbook reading.

1. *Project* (predict) what you expect to find in a particular section of a book or chapter. You should do this before you read and as you read. Leafing through a chapter and looking at the bold type can help you to project. However, you are still not relieved of the task of constantly relating what you *have* read to what you expect to find and integrating all the information into a larger whole. It takes more than a simple survey of the book to do this. Students who place too much faith in any mechanical step and ignore the necessity of sustained involvement will waste time.

   Much of the task of projecting what to expect from a text involves adjusting to an author's style of writing. An author's style becomes apparent only as you read. Some authors may give several examples of important points, enabling you to learn as you read. Other authors present new principles one after the other in such rapid succession that a totally new manner of reading must be structured. Many authors change their style as they move from one phase of their subject matter to another. In some textbooks, the various chapters are actually written by different authors.

2. *Ask yourself questions as you read.* Structuring questions, answering them, and discarding some questions and some answers is a task involving very rapid decision-making and some adjustments. Projecting is not reading; you must build what you read into a framework that is meaningful to you. Some of the questions you might find yourself asking are:

   A. Do I understand what the author has said in the paragraph I have just read?
   B. Is there anything in this paragraph or section that I should stop to learn?
   C. Is there anything I can do now that will make a second reading more effective? (That something could be taking some notes either in a notebook or in the margins of your book.)
   D. How does what I have just read relate to what I am expecting to find from this chapter or section. Do I need to alter my previous expectations for this section or chapter?

3. *Shift gears.* This involves recognizing material that can be read at different rates of speed and developing the skill to read effectively at different rates.

4. *Settle the conflict* between what you may find interesting about the book and what you must do to meet the instructor's requirements. Reading for study can be different from reading for pleasure. There can be pleasure, however, in the rewards gained from effective study.

5. *Make judgments.* Careless work wastes time, but some judgment is necessary as to how much time should be spent on the whole task or any part of it. Sometimes it is very wise to take the time to reread a paragraph. Sometimes the meaning of that paragraph will reveal itself as you continue reading or in a second reading of the entire chapter. Charts and graphs can be helpful, but reading them is a skill in itself. Time spent on them has to be an individual judgment determined by your needs and the time available to you.

6. *Learn.* Because reading a text often involves having a working knowledge of what has come before—particularly definitions of terms—you often need to do some actual learning as you read. Comprehending what you read and learning what you read are two separate and quite different tasks.

> Study Reading Is Reading *Plus*
> Projecting
> Asking Questions
> Shifting Gears
> Settling Conflicts
> Making Judgments and Decisions
> Learning

The next selection is a chapter from a psychology text. The chapter has been divided into five sections. Ordinarily, you would have to make such divisions yourself. The tasks you are asked to do in each section are typical of tasks a good student might structure for himself. Read each section and answer the questions that follow it. Before you start the first section you may want to glance through the entire selection, taking note of the bold-type headings. Surveying a chapter in this way can give you an idea of where you are going and help you to see relationships between segments of a chapter. Some students read through an entire chapter at a rapid rate before they break the content into sections and engage in study-learning tasks.

Many of the aids in textbooks are directed toward providing reference sources rather than structuring initial study of the text. Thus, in a good textbook you may find a glossary (alphabetized lists of special vocabulary words and their definitions), and an index (alphabetized list of topics covered in the text with page numbers for references). At the end of each chapter you may find study questions and a bibliography (sources from which author got his information) as well as other aids for review or further study.

At the end of this chapter there is a list of "terms to remember." However, if you are to study effectively, you must recognize specialized terminology *as you come to it.* You should note the meanings of these terms, and in many instances learn them or write them down. Otherwise, your comprehension of the subject matter will suffer because the author will probably make use of the terminology throughout the chapter and the book. Special vocabulary is often introduced and defined at the beginning of a chapter.

EXERCISE 4

It is often advisable to learn meanings of terms as you study. Learning usually requires reading a meaning over several times and even reciting the meaning to yourself. Read Section I. In the blanks below write the words that you identify as special terminology as you come to them. Record their meanings. Be sure to record the meaning given to you by the author, and not just what you think the words mean.

	Special Vocabulary	*Definitions*
EXAMPLE:	ovum	egg cell
1.	_____	_____
2.	_____	_____
3.	_____	_____
4.	_____	_____
5.	_____	_____
6.	_____	_____
7.	_____	_____
8.	_____	_____

General Vocabulary

1. Nature–nurture _____
2. latent _____

Heredity and Environment

[SECTION I]

Billy has been warned repeatedly concerning his misconduct in school. The teacher has now decided to ask Billy's mother to come in and talk over the situation with her in an effort to arrive at an understanding of—and with—Billy. The mother admits that Billy's behavior is not what she would like it to be. Then she confides to

Abridged from "Heredity or Environment?" from *Psychology,* 5th Ed. by T. L. Engle and Louis Snellgrove. Copyright © 1969 by Harcourt Brace Jovanovich, Inc. and reprinted with their permission.

the teacher, "Poor boy, he comes by it naturally; everyone on his father's side of the family is like that." If it is Billy's father who comes to school, the observation will probably be, "Poor boy, he comes by it naturally; everyone on his mother's side of the family is like that." Both parents are accounting for Billy's present behavior by his heredity—although there is disagreement concerning which side of his ancestry is responsible for his good traits and which for his bad traits.

Or the parents may say, "Oh, yes! We know Billy is bad. But all the other children in the neighborhood are bad, and Billy learns his naughtiness from them." That is, they account for Billy's present behavior in terms of his environment rather than in terms of his heredity.

HEREDITY OR ENVIRONMENT?

The question is often asked, "Which is the more important factor in the development of the individual, his heredity or his environment?" Is he to be understood more in terms of what he has received biologically from his ancestors, or more in terms of the external forces, conditions, and influences that surround him and affect his activities? Although you may hear the problem expressed in terms of nature and nurture instead of heredity and environment, the meaning is the same. Psychologists have been very much interested in this question and have done a great deal of work in trying to answer it. Let us look at some of the evidence.

What are Mendel's laws of heredity? Often it is said of a child, "He is the very picture of his father (or mother)." This remark implies that in some way he has inherited outstanding physical features from one side of his family or the other. How does this inheritance take place?

Mendel spoke of the separate features of parents as *unit characters*. He said that unit characters are passed on to children independently and as wholes, sometimes becoming apparent in the first generation, sometimes not appearing until later generations. Characteristics that appear in all individuals of the first generation of descendants are said to be *dominant* characteristics. Those which are latent and do not appear in the first generation of descendants, although they may appear in subsequent generations, are said to be *recessive* characteristics. A few dominant and recessive characteristics in man are as follows:

Dominant	Recessive
Brown eyes	Blue eyes
Curly hair	Straight hair
Dark hair	Light hair
Dark skin	Light skin

Mendel's law may be seen operating in domestic animals. For example, if a rose-comb black bantam is crossed with a rose-comb white bantam, all the offspring of the first generation will be black. (For this kind of chicken, black is dominant and white is recessive.) Now if these black offspring are crossed, part of their offspring will be black and part will be white, the ratio of black to white being approximately three to one. That is, the hereditary units ultimately reappear without change, even though there is an apparent absence of these characteristics in the generation of the first cross. It should be added that sometimes a characteristic is neither dominant nor recessive. For example, there is a species of poultry in which the mating of a black with a splashed-white fowl produces blue offspring. In human beings we find blue-eyed children born to parents both of whom have brown eyes. We know, therefore, that somewhere in the ancestry of the blue-eyed child there were blue eyes and that this characteristic has been passed down from one generation to another as a recessive characteristic. Remember that as far as physical appearance is concerned, it is impossible to distinguish between persons who have "pure" brown eyes and persons who have brown eyes but carry recessive determiners for blue eyes. The laws of heredity are complicated; for further information on them, turn to a text in biology.

How are characteristics passed on from one generation to another? In reproduction the female contributes an egg cell (ovum), and the male contributes a sperm cell, or spermatozoon (spûr′mə·tə·zō′on). Although the egg cell is very, very small (smaller than a period on this page), it is still many times larger than the sperm cell. When a sperm cell enters an egg cell, fertilization occurs.

What are chromosomes and genes? Most cells of the body contain rod-shaped "colored bodies" called *chromosomes* (krō′-mə·sōms). There is evidence that 46 chromosomes exist in each cell. These chromosomes are in pairs. Prior to fertilization, the number of chromosomes in the egg and sperm cells segregate so that one of each pair finds itself in different daughter cells; the net effect of this is that each sperm and egg contains 23 chromosomes. When the sperm fertilizes the egg, the fertilized egg cell contains 46 chromosomes, or 23 pairs. By a process of cell division, more and more cells are formed. Each new cell in the human species normally contains 46 chromosomes. In other species, the number of chromosomes in each cell is different from the number in the human species; for example, the crayfish has 100 pairs; the moth, 31 pairs; the salamander, 14 pairs; the mosquito, 6 pairs. Recent investigations have revealed that approximately 95 percent of all mongoloids have 47 chromosomes instead of the usual 46. Thus, a study of chromosomes as they relate to mongolism suggests that possession of an extra chromosome may even be responsible for this type of mental retardation. Chromosomes often provide an explanation of some physical irregularity present at birth.

It was thought for a while that heredity could be understood in terms of combinations of the chromosomes. It is now known that heredity is far too complicated to be explained in such simple terms. Scientists now speak of tiny parts within each chromosome called *genes* (jēns). The term "genetics," which stands for the branch of biology dealing with the scientific investigation of the mechanisms of heredity, comes from the word "genes." In the human species there are probably at least a thousand genes in each of the 46 chromosomes. An individual's genetic make-up for any characteristic is called a genotype (jen′ə-tīp). A *genotype* refers either to the sum of all the biological characteristics that an individual is capable of transmitting to his or her offspring, or to a single such characteristic. Thus, if one parent contributes a gene for blue eyes and the other parent contributes a gene for brown eyes, the fertilized egg contains brown-blue as a genotype for eye color. The actual, observable characteristic which an individual manifests is called a *phenotype* (fē′nə-tīp). Thus, although an individual's genotype for eye color is brown-blue, his actual eye color or phenotype will be brown. If the pair of genes an individual receives from his parents differ, the one which always wins out (and therefore becomes the phenotype) is said to be dominant, the one which does not exhibit itself is said to be recessive.

Do we inherit characteristics from our parents or from remote ancestors? It is customary to say that parents reproduce themselves in their children, but in terms of biological heredity, it is not correct. When a man and a wife have children, they do not reproduce themselves. They merely pass on to their children some of those characteristics which they received from their parents, and so on back through all the generations of life. Therefore, it is not strictly correct to speak of a child as inheriting tallness, musical ability, or any other specific trait from his parents. The genes within the chromosomes within the reproductive cells are not believed to be changed by the individual carrying them. Instead, parents transmit to their children, unchanged, genes which they have inherited from their own parents.

A characteristic acquired by parents themselves and not possessed by preceding generations is not transmitted by heredity. A man and his wife may have spent years in the serious study of music, yet their child will not know one note from another—unless he is taught, just as other children are taught whose parents were not musicians. One biologist cut off the tails of mice for twenty generations, yet each new litter of mice appeared with full-length tails. For generations Chinese women bound their feet; but each baby—girl or boy—was born with normal feet.

Whenever we say that a child inherits such-and-such characteristics from his father, we mean from the ancestors on his father's side. If a father and child, or a mother and child, look alike, it is because they have a common ancestry rather than because the parent in some way reproduces his appearance in the child. We can say that a child inherits characteristics from his parents only if we mean that the parents were the immediate carriers of the characteristics of their ancestors.

Does the mother influence the unborn child? There is a very common superstition that the thoughts of a pregnant woman affect the unborn baby she is carrying in her body. It is said that if the mother reads good literature, the child will of necessity have literary ability; that if the mother reads crime stories and sees crime movies, the child is likely to become a criminal. It is said that if the mother looks intently at strawberries, the child will be born with a red spot, which—by a stretch of the imagination—may appear to be a picture of a strawberry. All these ideas are groundless. Scientists know that there is absolutely no connection between the nervous system of the mother and the nervous system of the fetus developing in her body.

This statement does not mean that the mother has no influence on the developing baby. Although the blood of the mother does not flow through the veins of the child, some things do pass from the mother to the child. Some disease germs, such as those of diphtheria, typhoid, and syphilis, may succeed in passing from the body of the mother to the body of the child. It is believed by some biologists that if the mother worries a great deal or has a severe emotional shock, the chemicals formed in her body as a result of this worry or shock may be carried to and affect her unborn child. Of course, the health of the mother affects the health of the developing child; if the mother damages her health, by excessive use of alcohol, for example, the child is affected. Poisons in the mother's system or narcotics like opium or morphine in excessive doses may also cause damage to the child.

Such influences as these are of environment and not of heredity. They may affect the child long before his birth, but his heredity was complete at conception. After conception, for nine months the child lives in the limited environment of the mother's body.

Birth itself is only an incident in life; it is not the beginning of life. Conditions at the time of birth may, however, have a great influence on the infant's later life. The infant may be damaged in the birth process. Research at a medical school gives some indication that very rapid births or births in which the infant is deprived of oxygen for a time (anoxia) may result in damage which causes the child's IQ to be lower than that of a child born under more normal conditions. Since, however, the medical school also found that some children of well above normal intellectual ability were born under these adverse conditions, it concluded that parents need not be overanxious in cases of unusual birth conditions.

If you are especially interested in biology, you will wish to study more about reproduction and the laws of heredity. For our purposes it is not necessary to go into a further discussion of the biology of heredity. Instead, we shall turn to some of the studies of heredity that are particularly important for the science of psychology.

EXERCISE 5 Read Section II through without interruption. After you have read it, answer the questions that follow it.

[SECTION II]
STUDIES EMPHASIZING THE IMPORTANCE OF HEREDITY

One way to study the effects of heredity is to trace a family tree. It is sometimes assumed that whatever similarity there is among members of a family is largely due to common heredity. Many studies of family histories have been made. We shall

Answers to problems on page 170 (geonotypes precede phenotypes): Grandparents—Mr. M and Mrs. F, dark-dark, dark; Mrs. M and Mr. F, light-light, light. Parents—Mr. M and Mrs. M, dark-light, dark. Children—Joan, dark-dark, dark; John and Ruth, dark-light, dark; Bill, light-light, light.

investigate to what degree the results of these studies are scientific.

What do animal experiments show? First, let us look at an experiment with subhuman animals. One psychologist took 142 rats at random and set them the task of learning to run through a maze in order to secure food. He found that the rats differed greatly in ability, just as human beings differ in ability. Some rats entered as few as seven or eight blind alleys. Others, with no greater opportunity to make errors, made as many as 214 entrances into blind alleys. Thus, it seemed that some rats were more intelligent than others.

The psychologist segregated the bright rats and let them mate and then permitted the mediocre and dull rats to mate. This selective breeding went on for eight generations. Descendants of the original bright rats always bred with other descendants of the original bright rats; dull and mediocre rats always bred with other descendants of the original dull and mediocre rats. By the end of the eight generations, there was practically no overlapping of the two lines of descendants so far as ability to learn a maze was concerned. That is, the

168

descendants of the original bright rats were very bright; the descendants of the dull and mediocre rats were very dull. The dullest of the bright group was about as bright as the brightest of the dull group.

Selective breeding was continued through the eighteenth generation but resulted in no greater differences than those found in the eighth generation. Then the bright and the dull rats were mated. The offspring, when tested in the maze, showed a distribution much like that with which the experiment began. That is, there were some dull rats and some bright rats, but most of the rats were in between the extremes.

This experiment is very impressive, but the data must be interpreted with caution. Further experimentation with the two strains of rats revealed that the bright rats were much more active than the dull rats, thus achieving higher scores. Possibly it was this capacity for activity which was transmitted from one generation to the next rather than a general intellectual ability. When the two strains of rats were tested on a variety of other learning tasks not so dependent upon mere activity, the bright rats were not necessarily bright nor were the dull rats necessarily dull. In a more recent experiment, however, a maze was used in which scores were not so directly related to activity, and breeding was more carefully controlled. Nevertheless, in a few generations there was a distinct separation of the scores made by the bright strain as compared with the scores made by the dull strain. From these and other animal experiments, it seems clear that learning capacities are inherited to some extent.

Although such experiments cannot be carried out with human beings, it is possible to work backward and study interesting family trees.

What do studies of human families show? There was a time when psychologists and sociologists placed a great deal of confidence in studies which have been made of family trees. These studies were often quoted as "proof" of the great importance of heredity. In them, the descendants of selected families were traced through a number of generations. It was found that when one or both parents were considered mentally retarded, they tended to produce a larger percentage of mentally retarded children than would be expected in the general population. Conversely, tracings of the family trees of unusually intelligent couples have resulted in descendants who became top public officials, college professors, lawyers, physicians, and clergymen.

Are studies of family trees scientific proof of the importance of heredity? At first glance, tracings of family trees seem to indicate that heredity plays almost an all-important part in the development of any individual. Certainly, heredity is important, but there are at least three reason why such studies are no longer considered of great scientific value.

1. The men making these studies were not always as scientific as they should have been in collecting their data. In many cases they depended upon hearsay rather than upon carefully collected facts.

2. There was a tendency to omit cases that did not prove the point. For example, all undesirable members of a family with some history of mental retardation were noted with care, but not so much attention was paid to the normal or superior members of the family.

3. Probably the most serious criticism of these studies is that no account was taken of environment. That is, the children of unusually bright or unusually dull parents grew up in that particular environment. Would the results have been the same if, in some way, exceptionally intelligent children could have been raised in the homes of mentally retarded families?

Because of the many uncontrolled variables in the tracing of family trees, these studies are not regarded as scientific evidence today.

Are there practical applications for controlling heredity? In a province in northern Italy, there existed for many years an excessive number of mentally retarded persons of a certain kind. Then, beginning in 1890, these mentally retarded persons were prevented from marrying. Within twenty years this form of mental retardation had almost disappeared from the province. Although this study was not made with the scientific care used in the study of rats... it does show the great importance of heredity.

Eugenics (yōō·jen′iks) is the science dealing with methods for improving the hereditary qualities of a species, especially of the human species. One method some eugenicists advocate is the method described above—that of preventing defective people from reproducing. Some states in the United States now have laws providing for the sterilization of certain defective people, so that they cannot reproduce. Others interested in eugenics try to educate the public to the value of choosing marriage partners with good hereditary background.

Eugenics is a controversial subject—one in which legal, social, and religious as well as scientific attitudes enter. You should be reminded, however,... that some married couples of normal or superior intelligence may produce a mentally retarded child, since many defective characteristics are recessive. Eugenics could not control these cases.

Also, as mentioned in our discussion of family trees, we cannot be sure to what extent defective characteristics are hereditary unless we are able to control environmental factors.

Much research in the area of human heredity still needs to be done. Perhaps some of you will be geneticists and will contribute to this research.

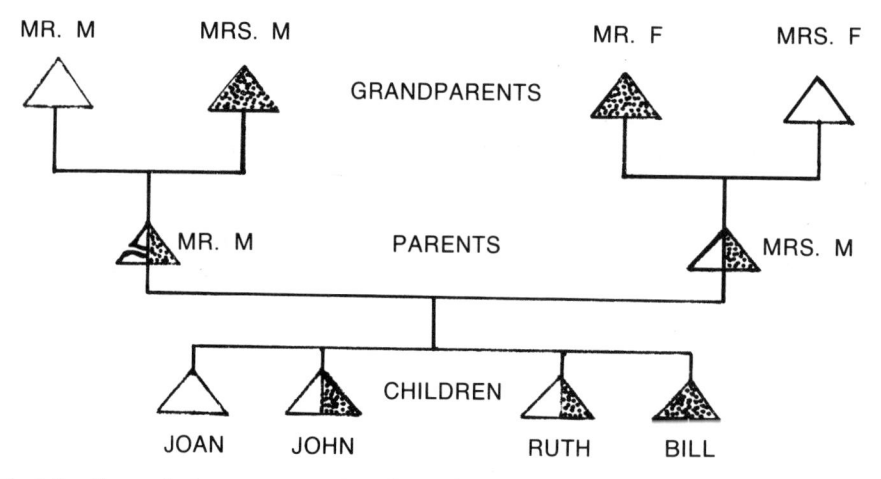

Assume that the figure below represents a hypothetical family's genetic make-up for hair color. Assume, too, that black represents the dominant gene, dark hair, and that gray represents the recessive gene, light hair. What, then, is the genotype for hair color for each member of the family? What is the phenotype for each? (Answers on page 168.)

QUESTIONS

1. What is the subject of this section? _____

2. What scientific term appears in this section that should be added to your list of special vocabulary words? _____

3. How could the answers to questions 1 and 2 be determined for review purposes without reading the section? _____

4. Explain and give examples of *selective breeding*.

5. Explain and give examples of a *variable*.

6. Look at the chart in this section. What does the chart illustrate? (Write your answer in your own words.)

7. The terms *genotype* and *phenotype* are used in the directions for reading the chart. Where can you find the meanings of these terms if you do not know them?

8. If you had the entire text, where might you find the meanings of any other scientific terms used in the directions to the chart?

9. Work out the problems in the chart. Check your answers on page 168.

10. Was this chart easy to use?   Yes _____   No _____
    What is the value of the chart in this section?

EXERCISE 6

Read Section III at a reasonable rate without stopping. After you have finished, answer the questions that follow it.

[SECTION III]
STUDIES EMPHASIZING THE IMPORTANCE OF ENVIRONMENT

It is impossible to go around taking children out of their homes and putting them in other homes in order to see what effect another environment will have on them. But sometimes children are raised in homes other than those of their biological parents. Psychologists have made careful studies of some of these cases. ... the IQ tends to remain constant, but changes in environment can have some influence on IQ.

Can a change in home conditions cause a change in IQ? In one case a study was made of twenty-six children in an orphanage. This particular orphanage was conducted with little thought for the welfare of the children. There was overcrowding, those in charge were not trained for the work, play and study equipment was lack-

171

ing or very poor, the children received very little individual attention. Upon entering the orphanage, the children all had IQ's of 80 or above, the average IQ being 90. After these children had lived in the undesirable environment for less than two years, their average IQ dropped 16 points, that is, to 74. An IQ of 74 is not so far above what is generally considered mental retardation. Yet none of the children gave indications of mental retardation before living in the poor environment of the orphanage.

How do various community environments affect children? Children living in five "hollows" in a mountainous section of the US were studied because their home and community environments differed radically.

One hollow consisted of a few scattered families living in an area so isolated that it did not even have a road to the outside world. There was neither a school nor a church, and none of the citizens could read or write.

A second hollow was connected with the outside world by a rocky mountain trail. Occasionally, the townspeople held meetings in a combined church and schoolhouse, and a few of the men could read and write.

A third hollow could be reached by automobile, although the road was a very poor one. There were a combined church and school and a general store which contained the post office. The people of this community did most of their buying from mail-order catalogues, and they sold some agricultural products.

A fourth hollow could be reached by a fair road connecting with a state highway. There was daily mail service. About 75 percent of the people could read, and they kept in touch with events by means of newspapers. There was an organized school in session seven months out of the year.

The fifth community was on a hard-surfaced road. There was a modern school, and church services were held regularly. The people kept in touch with events by means of newspapers, magazines, radios, and automobile travel. This community was a rather typical small American town.

When the children in these five communities were given intelligence tests, it was found that there was a direct relationship between scores and the conditions under which the children lived. The more isolated the hollow, the lower the intelligence-test scores.

There was no reason to believe that the poor performance of the children in the isolated hollows could be blamed on "poor heredity." The children in the remote hollows were all from the same general ancestral background as the children living in the fifth community. Limitations of the environment—lack of schools, books, social life, and so forth—seemed the most plausible explanation.

How do different socioeconomic levels affect test scores? In one testing survey which involved several hundred students, all students in a school system were tested at the twelfth, ninth, sixth, and third grades. The students at each grade level were composed of individuals representing two different backgrounds and socioeconomic levels. Group A represented those from a higher socioeconomic level than Group B. When the scores of twelfth-grade students were compared, Group A achieved at the twelfth-grade level and Group B scored at the sixth-grade level, a difference of six years. The difference between scores of the two groups at the ninth-grade level was three years; at the sixth-grade level, only one and a half years; and at the third-grade level only nine months. In other words, at every three-grade decrease, the difference between the groups was divided in half. If this progression had continued to the first-grade level, where tests were not given to the students, theoretically there would have been no appreciable difference between the groups.

The question is, "If the two groups showed no appreciable difference at the first grade but did at the twelfth grade, what caused the difference?" Did the difference in background cause the difference in scores, or was it that Group B had a lower potential as determined by heredity? These questions, like many others, cannot be adequately answered at the present time. Perhaps in the future, as we gather more data, we shall be better able to provide more scientific conclusions.

What further study of environment is needed? Most studies showing the importance of environment have been concerned primarily with measurement of intelligence. At present, psychologists feel that they know how to measure intelligence much better than they know how to measure personality, social habits, and attitudes. For that reason, most of the studies of the influence of environment have been limited to intelligence. Although it is valuable to know about changes in IQ as measured by tests, one must always remember that saying an IQ increases is not necessarily the same as saying that there has been an improvement in the way the individual adjusts to his environment. Furthermore, there are many other aspects of personality that should be studied. Some experiments with small children have indicated that shyness and lack of self-confidence can be overcome by means of environment. In the experiments, the children were given opportunities to do things and to do them well. More studies will be made in the future on many phases of the effects of environment.

QUESTIONS

1. Environment appears to have an effect upon intelligence. _____ (true–false)
2. There appears to be a positive relationship between a community's contact with the outside world and the intelligence of its citizens. _____ (true–false)
3. Research on the effects of heredity and environment on a child's total development is quite conclusive. _____ (true–false)
4. What is meant by a *socioeconomic* group? _____
   _____
5. The assumed progress of Group A described in the testing survey of two socioeconomic groups on page 172 has been plotted on the graph below. In red pencil chart the progress of Group B from the information in the account of the results of the study.

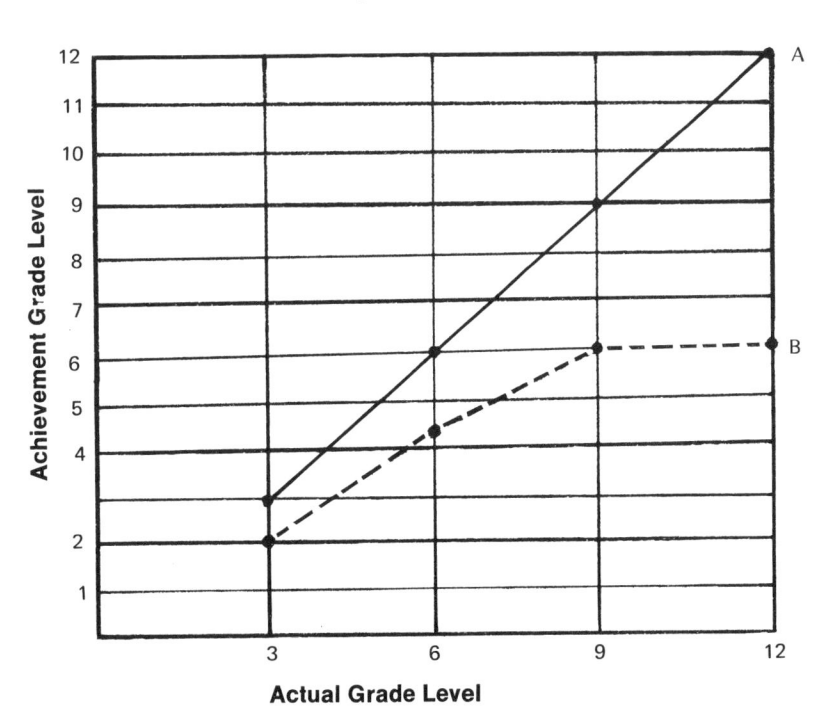

EXERCISE 7A   As you read Section IV write the italicized terms that are introduced, with their definitions, in the blanks below.

　　　　Term　　　　　　　Definition
1. _____   _____
2. _____   _____
3. _____   _____

Special terminology is usually defined only once in a textbook. Occasionally, it is necessary to consult the glossary, a dictionary, or possibly a reference listed in the index to refresh your memory on a term you have forgotten. In Section IV the way the term *coefficient of correlation* is used indicates that the student is expected to understand it. The glossary entry and a reference from a previous chapter are printed below.

EXAMPLE:

Glossary entry:

coefficient of correlation—A number to express the degree of relationship between paired measures. Usually designated by the letter *r*.

Reference:
(from a chapter entitled "Personality" and a section headed "Correlation") "Statistics, used in all sciences, is the mathematical procedure for gathering, organizing, analyzing, and interpreting data. In studying scientific measures of personality—and in much other work with psychology—you will find reference to a statistical device known as *correlation*. Psychologists often use correlation to tell how much relationship there is between two scores. . . . A single number, called a *coefficient of correlation* can be used to express whatever relationship may exist. . . . A result could produce a coefficient correlation of 1.00 (note that this is not one hundred), indicating a perfect positive relationship. . . . The size of the coefficient indicates the degree of relationship." (Relationships that are not perfect would progress from .001 to .999.)

[SECTION IV]
STUDIES OF TWINS

You have seen that some studies show the tremendous importance of heredity, while others show the tremendous importance of environment. It would be ideal for purposes of research if we could permit a group of babies to grow up under one environment, then, by some magic, change them back to babies again and let them grow up under a very different environment. In this way we could determine the effects of different environments when the hereditary basis was the same. Quite obviously, such an experiment is impossible. Fortunately, however, studies of twins go a long way toward giving us the answers desired.

In the United States twins occur about once in every ninety births. Some twins dress alike and act very much alike. They may be so similar in appearance that their friends cannot tell them apart. Other twins look no more alike than any two brothers, two sisters, or brother and sister.

What is the difference between fraternal and identical twins? There are two kinds of twins, fraternal and identical. *Fraternal twins* are children of the same parents who simply happen to be conceived and born at approximately the same time. In terms of heredity they are no more alike than other children of the same parents. Two ova (eggs) were fertilized by two sperms, and two individuals developed from the start. There may be two boys or two girls, or there may be a boy and a girl. Sometimes fraternal twins decide that they wish to appear very much alike. A typical case is that of two high school girls, who are fraternal twins. There is some resemblance between them, as there often is between two sisters, but their faces and figures differ. However, they do not like to admit this. They dress absolutely alike (one has to have her dresses slightly tight, and the other slightly loose), they go to the same places, they study the same subjects in school.

If a psychologist makes a study of fraternal twins, he cannot tell with any certainty how much of their individual development is due to heredity and how much is due to environment. Their environments are often similar, and in some cases every effort is made to have their environments as nearly alike as possible. There is not a good opportunity for a scientific measure of the relative influences of environment and heredity.

From a scientific point of view, psychologists are much more interested in identical twins than in fraternal twins. *Identical twins* result from a single ovum, which is fertilized by a single sperm. Seemingly, one new life is started. Then, for some reason not yet known, this cell divides and two individuals develop instead of one. Since both of the individuals come from a single fertilized cell, it is believed that they have the same heredity. They are always of the same sex. There is great similarity in such characteristics as eye color, skin color, hair form, length and shape of fingers, height, weight, body shape, and facial details. These are the twins that look so very much alike. Since identical twins have the same heredity, whatever differences may appear in them must be due to the influence of environment.

How much alike are twins reared together? A number of scientific studies have been made of twins and of siblings other than twins. (*Siblings* [sib′ lingz] are children of the same parents, whether twins or not, and regardless of sex.) In general it has been found that identical twins are much more alike than fraternal twins and that in many cases fraternal twins are more alike than siblings who are not twins.

In IQ, pairs of identical twins tend to differ, on the average, about 5 points. Pairs of fraternal twins differ about 9 points, while other siblings differ about 11 points. Unrelated pairs of individuals selected at random tend to differ about 15 points. The difference in IQ's for identical twins (5 points) is no greater than is often found for two tests given to one individual. Furthermore, one study of 150 pairs of identical and fraternal twins showed that identical twins were much more alike in each of the primary mental abilities . . . than were fraternal twins. Thus, it seems that identical twins, having the same heredity, are much more alike than the other pairs of children who have different heredities.

Secondly, fraternal twins are more alike than siblings who are not twins. This difference cannot be accounted for in terms of heredity, for there is no reason to believe that fraternal twins have common heredity to a greater extent than any two children of the same parents. However, fraternal twins probably have a more common environment than other siblings. Identical twins are likely to have a still more common environment.

Most pairs of twins, both identical and fraternal, are reared in the same homes, go to the same schools, attend the same social events, and so on. They are of the same age and so have a more common environment than siblings who are not twins.

At first thought it might seem that siblings other than twins reared in the same home would have just as similar an environment as twins reared in the same home, but this is not the case. Suppose there are two boys in a family, one twelve years of age, the other nine. The one twelve years of age has had three years of the home environment which his younger brother has not had. Furthermore, the twelve-year-old boy has a younger brother in his environment. The nine-year-old has an older brother in his environment. If the two children are of different sexes, one has a younger brother or sister and the other has an older brother or sister. These circumstances all make differences in what seem otherwise to be very similar environments.

How much alike are twins reared in different envi-

ronments? In most cases identical twins live in very similar environments. Once in a while, however, it does happen that identical twins are separated early in life and grow up in quite different environments.

Scientists succeeded in finding nineteen pairs of identical twins who had been separated early in life and who were at least twelve years of age when studied. Thus, there had been a considerable length of time in which environment had had a chance to play its part in their development. Now there was an opportunity to study the effects of different environments with individuals having the same heredity. In several cases the twins grew up in total ignorance of each other's existence. The average difference between the IQ's of these nineteen pairs of twins was 8.2, as against about 5 for identical twins living together.

This difference of 8.2 points in IQ can perhaps be accounted for in terms of a few of the nineteen pairs. In these few cases there had been marked differences in educational opportunity. Except for the few cases of very unequal educational opportunities, the rest of the pairs of identical twins differed only 5.5 points on the average. This is almost the same difference that has been noted for identical twins reared in the same homes. Furthermore, the difference of 8.2 points for all pairs of identical twins reared apart is less than that usually found between siblings living in the same home environments (11 points). Certainly it is less than the 15 points found on the average for unrelated individuals living in different home environments. This study seems to suggest that heredity is a very important factor in the development of the individual, regardless of the influences of the environment.

Some of the data presented in this section are summarized in the ... table on page 177. Obviously no figure can be put in the middle space of the top row, because identical twins cannot live in the same family otherwise than as twins. In the top horizontal row of the table, note that the factor of heredity seems to be strong, regardless of differences in environment. The bottom horizontal row indicates that greater similarity in environment tends to make fraternal twins more alike than siblings other than twins raised in the same home. Nontwin siblings, remember, differ no more in heredity than do fraternal twins. The greatest difference is found where both heredity and environment are different—that is, among unrelated individuals living in different families.

How much correlation is there in height and weight for twins? Further light is thrown on the influence of heredity and environment by studying various physical measurements of twins reared together and twins reared apart. The coefficient of correlation for height of identical twins reared together has been found to be +.981; for identical twins reared apart, +.969. Fraternal twins reared together show a correlation for height of +.934. Height is determined primarily by heredity. Note that identical twins, even when living apart, are more alike in height than fraternal twins living together.

Weight is determined in part by heredity and in part by the kind and amount of food eaten. The coefficient of correlation for weight of identical twins reared together has been found to be +.973; for identical twins reared apart, +.886. For fraternal twins reared together, the correlation was found to be +.900.

How much correlation is there in intelligence and school achievement for twins? A British scientist made very extensive studies concerned with the inheritance of mental ability. He succeeded in finding over thirty cases of identical twins brought up in different environments. Part of his data is summarized in a table (page 177, bottom) so that you can compare identical twins reared together and apart. The table also gives coefficients of correlation for nontwin siblings reared together and apart. Finally, data are given for unrelated children who have been reared together. You will note that for intelligence as measured by intelligence tests, the correlation for identical twins, even when reared apart, is very high. It is almost as high as for successive testings of the same individuals. For school achievement, the

Point Differences in IQ for Various Combinations of Hereditary and Environmental Influences (a Summary of Scientific Studies)

	Living Together As Twins	Living Merely in the Same Family	Living in Different Families
Identical heredity	5 (Identical twins)	(Could be no such condition)	8.2 (5.5 for most cases)
Nonidentical heredity	9 (Fraternal twins)	11 (Siblings) Nontwin	15 (Unrelated)

Correlation Between Measures of Intelligence and School Achievement for Twins and Nontwins

	Identical Twins Together	Identical Twins Apart	Fraternal Twins Together	Nontwin Siblings Together	Nontwin Siblings Apart	Unrelated Children Together
Intelligence	+.925	+.876	+.551	+.538	+.517	+.269
School achievement	+.898	+.681	+.831	+.814	+.526	+.535

correlation is much lower for identical twins reared separately than for those reared together. In fact, this correlation is lower than for fraternal twins and nontwin siblings reared together.

What can be learned from case studies of twins raised in separate homes? The study of twins is interesting, not only in terms of average figures and general conclusions but also in terms of specific cases. One example is the case studies of identical twin boys who were born in an isolated village and whose mother died at the time they were born. The paternal grandparents adopted one, known in psychological writings as R. The maternal grandparents adopted the other, known as J. The grandparents who took J were industrious and gave him many advantages. He was graduated from high school and became an engineer. He was fond of reading good literature.

The grandparents who took R were rather shiftless. The grandfather tried blacksmithing, working on the railroad, and coal mining, but he did not stick to any kind of work. R attended school for eight grades but was not interested in schoolwork. Something of his environment can be seen from the fact that in the community in which he lived school was in session for only five months of the year. After leaving school, R did some work of various kinds, but he seemed to avoid all work as much as possible. At the age of twenty-seven, J's IQ was found to be 96 and R's 77 (Stanford-Binet).

What conclusions have been reached from studies of twins? As a result of their studies of twins, some psychologists have reached certain tentative conclusions: that physical characteristics are least likely to be affected by environment; that intelligence, as measured by the IQ, is more likely to be affected; that education and achievement are still more likely to be affected; that personality is most likely to be affected.

EXERCISE 7B

Section IV presented a great deal of data that may be difficult to understand. What aids does the author give you in summarizing the contents of this section?

(1) _____

(2) _____

After referring to these aids, check the appropriate answers to these questions.

1. Studies of twins reveal that differences in environment will have the greatest effect upon _____
   A. personality
   B. intelligence as measured by IQ
   C. physical characteristics
   D. achievement

2. Differences in IQ level for two children brought up in different environments will be the greatest for _____
   A. siblings
   B. fraternal twins
   C. unrelated children
   D. identical twins

3. The correlation between intelligence and school achievement will be the highest for _____
   A. fraternal twins living together
   B. identical twins living together
   C. siblings living together

[SECTION V]
MOTIVATION

Psychologists who study motivation can tell us a great deal about the influences of heredity and of environment on an individual. Motivation refers to the regulation of behavior that satisfies needs and leads toward goals. By studying motivation, psychologists can understand something of the conditions which predispose individuals to one kind of behavior rather than toward another. How an individual behaves is determined in part by biological drives and in part by social considerations.

All men, as well as lower animals, have certain biological drives which are to be understood in terms of inherited structures. Biological drives which serve to motivate man are the drives for nourishment, water, oxygen, elimination, and reproduction. Man is also motivated to keep his body at a comfortable temperature and to provide sleep and other rest for his body. The biological drives help man and lower animals to maintain their bodies in a state of equilibrium.

How an individual satisfies these drives depends on his learning from his social environment. For example, let us consider an individual who is motivated by hunger. He may work for the money with which to buy food, or he may steal to eat; he may eat his food according to accepted rules of table etiquette, or he may stuff it into his mouth; he may insist that his meat be well cooked, or he may prefer to eat it raw.

Man is also motivated by psychological and social drives. For example, he has the need for the security found in group living (gregariousness). Man forms social groups varying from the family to international organizations. The infant's group living is limited to the mother and other individuals in the family circle. These individuals satisfy the infant's early biological needs, but soon he learns to value companionship even when it is not necessary for the satisfaction of his biological needs. It is not necessary to think of our desire for group living as inborn or inherited, but rather we should think of it as learned behavior, and as growing out of a period of dependence through which we all pass.

Throughout your present study of psychology, you will find many references to motivation. If you do supplementary reading in more advanced textbooks, you may find a different organization of material. Perhaps there will be several chapters devoted to a unit on motivation instead of a discussion of the topic throughout the book. In your supplementary reading you may find certain differences in the definitions given for such terms as motivation and drives. Psychologists have not yet fully agreed on the definitions for these terms. Nevertheless, you will find much interesting evidence from experiments and from many field studies concerning the general problem of motivation.

MATURATION

... [The] process of physical growth and development of an organism over a period of time is called *maturation*.

Maturation is not the same as learning, since changes due to maturation are determined by heredity. For example, a newborn baby cannot learn to walk, no matter how much instruction he is given. Only when his body structure has developed sufficiently as a result of maturation can he be taught to walk.

Different species of animals have different rates of maturation as a result of heredity. An eight-week-old puppy can run about, eat from a dish, and do most of the things he will do as a grown dog. An eight-week-old baby, on the other hand, is still quite helpless and could not survive if he were not cared for. Dogs mature more rapidly than do human beings—but, of course, their capacity for development is far more limited.

An experiment with a simple organism. How do organisms such as salamanders "learn" to swim? In one experiment, a large group of salamander eggs was divided into two groups. One group served as a control for the experiment. The eggs of this group were placed in ordinary water and permitted to develop as they normally do in nature. The other group of eggs served as the experimental group. These eggs were placed in a drug solution which did not interfere with the normal processes of growth but which did paralyze the animals so that they could not move. The control group developed the usual swimming ability. After these salamanders had been swimming for five days, the ones that had been in the drug solution were removed and placed in ordinary water. Within thirty minutes they were able to swim about with as much ease as the members of the control group that had had five days' practice. Apparently the development of a salamander's ability to swim depends upon maturation rather than upon practice or learning.

Why did it take these experimental salamanders about thirty minutes to develop swimming? Why didn't they swim as soon as they were placed in ordinary water? What effect did the drug have? To answer these questions, the experimenters placed in the drug solution other animals which had been raised in ordinary water and had developed normal swimming. Of course, they now became motionless. After twenty-four hours in the drug solution, they were put back in ordinary water. It took them up to thirty minutes to regain swimming ability.

What is imprinting? Have you ever seen baby chicks following their mother around the barnyard? Perhaps you assumed that such following was "natural," without realizing that there was involved a very interesting relationship between maturation and learning. Psychologists use the word *imprinting* to refer to a special kind of very rapid learning that takes place in some animals—notably birds—at an early stage of their development. A specific reward or reinforcement is not involved. Imprinting does involve presenting to the animal a large moving object. Also, imprinting may take place only at the time maturation makes it possible. Such learning is relatively insusceptible to forgetting or extinction.

As early as 1873, it was noted that incubator-hatched chicks tended to follow the first moving object to which they were exposed. Much more recently, another scientist reported that goslings followed the first large moving object they saw—in this case, the scientist, and would have nothing to do with their mother when she appeared later on. In one experiment, the scientist imprinted a group of goslings upon himself and imprinted another group of goslings upon their mother. All of the goslings were placed together under a box while the mother goose and the scientist stood nearby. When the mother started to walk away, so did the scientist but in a different direction. The box was lifted. The goslings imprinted upon their mother followed her, and the goslings imprinted upon the scientist followed him.

Imprinting varies with the age of the animal and the conditions of the imprinting. For example, with ducklings the tendency to follow is strongest when imprinting occurs thirteen to sixteen hours after hatching. Merely allowing the bird to see a large moving object does not necessarily produce imprinting. The young bird must spend effort to stay near its object. In one experiment, ducklings were imprinted on a large wooden decoy duck which was moved mechanically around a circular track. Those required to walk only a few feet showed less strength of imprinting than those required to walk one hundred feet.

Wouldn't it make an interesting experiment for a fair or other exhibit to imprint baby chicks on a mother duck and to imprint ducklings on a hen? Such a demonstration might be quite disturbing to people who had thought it was "natural" for baby chicks to follow a hen and for ducklings to follow a duck.

What does maturation have to do with human learning? In order to answer this question, we must turn to some experimental studies. In one experiment

"They think I'm their mother."

identical twin babies were used. At the age of forty-six weeks, one of the twin girls was given an opportunity to climb a set of stairs. She did not climb any of them. She was then given training in climbing stairs, and after four weeks of such training she was able to climb the stairs without assistance. The other twin was not given any experience with stairs until she was fifty-three weeks of age. In her first test at this age she climbed the stairs unaided in 45 seconds. After two weeks of training, this twin, who had had no training until she was fifty-three weeks of age, was actually climbing stairs better than her twin, who had had five weeks of training. Remember that these were identical twins and therefore had the same heredity.

Another study of twins has a bearing on our question. Twin boys, Johnny and Jimmy, were placed under very different environmental conditions at the age of twenty days and were used as experimental subjects until they were about two years of age. It was thought that these boys were identical twins, but later it was found that they were fraternal twins. Nevertheless, the study does contribute to our understanding of the importance of maturation and of environment. Johnny was given training in such acts as diving, swimming, roller skating, and use of language. By the age of eight months he swam 7 feet; at eighteen months he swam 50 feet. At fifteen months he would dive headfirst from a springboard 5 feet above the water. Before most children can walk, Johnny was learning to roller skate, and before he was two years of age, he was quite a proficient skater. Johnny was trained largely on the sink-or-swim basis. That is, he was made to face hardships in the hope that he would be bold and self-reliant.

Jimmy had no such special training and could not perform the acts Johnny could perform. Furthermore, Jimmy would not even attempt these acts. That Jimmy was more timid than Johnny may well be explained by the difference in their training.

It is significant to note that the training given Johnny did not make him permanently superior to Jimmy in such behavior as crawling and creeping, sitting up, reaching and grasping objects. Maturation in itself seemed to produce these activities. Training did make Johnny superior to Jimmy in the less essential skills such as swimming, diving, and skating. We must not, however, overlook the fact that later, when he was given an opportunity to learn these activities, Jimmy usually acquired them more easily than had Johnny at an earlier age, owing to the fact that he was more mature when he undertook the learning.

We shall consider just one more illustration of the effects of maturation. Traditionally, Hopi Indian babies are attached to cradle boards for most of their first nine months of life and so have very little opportunity to exercise the muscles to be used in later walking. Some Hopi Indians, however, allow their babies to move about freely, unconfined by cradle boards. In one study it was found that both Hopi babies raised in the traditional way and Hopi babies who moved about "learned" to walk at almost exactly the same age (about fifteen months).

Can maturation be depended upon to guarantee learning? The importance of maturation is receiving more and more attention in modern education. For example, at what age should a child be taught to read? There is no simple answer. The answer depends in part upon the degree of maturation of the child. Some children are ready to read at an earlier age than other children because of their more rapid biological growth rate. Children do not, however, suddenly mature into being able to read without training. How soon a child learns to read depends in part upon how much he is read to before he is able to read himself. The child growing up in a home where there is a good deal of reading and other broadening experiences will wish to learn to read at an earlier age than a child growing up in a home where reading is neglected and where life is very monotonous. Learning to read is influenced partly by the processes of maturation and partly by environmental influences. The child may be forced to learn to read at an early age, but he can learn more efficiently if he has achieved a sufficient degree of maturation before instruction in reading is given.

In general, we can say that human learning is too complex to be accounted for solely in terms of maturation, but learning does take place most efficiently when the environmental stimulation is keyed to the degree of maturation of the individual.

The discussion of maturation has led us a little nearer to an understanding of the effects of heredity and environment on individuals. Before attempting to reach any general conclusions about the comparative importance of heredity and environment, we might consider some studies of extremely unusual cases.

UNUSUAL STUDIES

You have seen that children raised in foster homes serve well as subjects for studies in the effects of environment. There have been documented cases of some individuals who were reared as foster children of animals and of others who, in some way, managed to survive alone in the forest. After these individuals were discovered, attempts were made to teach them to speak, read, and perform the usual social customs of civilized life. Few of the attempts were successful, however. These persons continued to function and perform as animals in many ways; they were human only in shape. The essential question involved is whether the lack of early training, guidance, and association with other humans resulted in behavior resembling that of a mentally retarded individual or whether the individuals were retarded before being reared by animals or before roaming the forests alone. Wild animals cannot be thoroughly trained unless they are captured soon after birth. The early years are very important in child training. These "wild" children may have been so impressed with their early training that later attempts to train them in the ways of human society were not very successful.

Owing to the lack of adequate data, no one knows whether to account for the behavior of these "wild" children in terms of heredity or environment. It is obviously out of the question to abandon children of known heredity in forests in order to learn what will happen to them—or to place one child of a pair of identical twins in a human home and abandon the other to the home of a wolf or other animal.

What about the other side of the story? What about placing a nonhuman in a human environment?

What would happen to an ape raised with a child? Many persons keep animal pets in close contact with human environment. Even so, the animals are treated as animals rather than as human beings. They are taught tricks and seem to learn a great deal about human customs, but fundamentally they are treated like nonhuman animals. What would be the result if a nonhuman animal were placed in a human home and treated just as a human child is treated? Such an experiment has been performed.

A professor of psychology and his wife undertook to rear a baby female chimpanzee with their own baby boy. When the experiment began, the baby chimpanzee, named Gua, was seven and one-half months of age; the baby boy, Donald, was ten months old. The two lived together as playmates and as the "children" of the psychologist and his wife for nine months.

Gua learned to walk like a human being instead of like a chimpanzee. She learned bladder control and to use the toilet—well but not perfectly. She kissed and hugged. Gua understood 95 words by the end of the nine-month experiment (Donald could understand 107). She did not learn to speak (although in a similar experiment made more recently a chimpanzee named Viki was taught to say four words). On the other hand, she was able to eat with a spoon and drink from a glass at an earlier age than Donald. Since chimpanzees mature more rapidly than do human beings, Gua could learn certain bits of behavior before Donald, although in time Donald caught up and surpassed her.

Gua never behaved altogether like a human being. In those acts in which anatomical structure was important for performance, her behavior remained apelike. Yet some of her behavior was very much like a human being's. That is, both heredity and environment were involved in her development.

In all studies of human children living with nonhuman animals and of nonhuman animals living with human beings, both heredity and environment play a part.

PRACTICAL CONCLUSIONS

Is it possible to tell whether heredity is more important than environment, or vice versa? Now look back at the question at the beginning of this chapter: "Which is the more important factor in the development of the individual, his heredity or his environment?" To help answer this question, compare an individual with a rectangle. Which is the more important factor in a rectangle, its base or its altitude? Obviously we cannot have a rectangle without both base and altitude. Neither can we have an individual without both heredity and environment. Did you ever see an individual without any environment? Did you ever see an individual who did not have ancestors? We might represent an individual by a four-sided figure, with heredity as the base and environment as the altitude, as in the figure below.

Although we cannot have a rectangle without both a base and an altitude, the base and the altitude can vary in length. A rectangle may have a narrow base and a high altitude, or a wide base and a low altitude, as shown in the figure on page 183.

An individual may have an inferior heredity and a superior environment, or an individual may have a superior heredity and an inferior environment. Suppose there are two individuals with approximately equally good heredity. One is placed in a rich cultural environment, the other in a poor cultural environment.

The resulting total individuals will be quite different. Or suppose two individuals with considerably different heredities are placed in approximately the same environments. The individuals will be quite different, owing to the factor of heredity.

Psychologists do not know enough about either heredity or environment to speak in terms of specific measureable units. Hence, it is not possible to say that one individual's environment is three times as good as another's or that one individual's heredity is twice as good as another's. Neither can it be said that as a result of both heredity and environment, one total individual is, for example, three times as capable as another. Individuals cannot be appraised by a geometrical formula. The analogy to rectangles suggests, however, the related contributions of heredity and environment to the development of the individual.

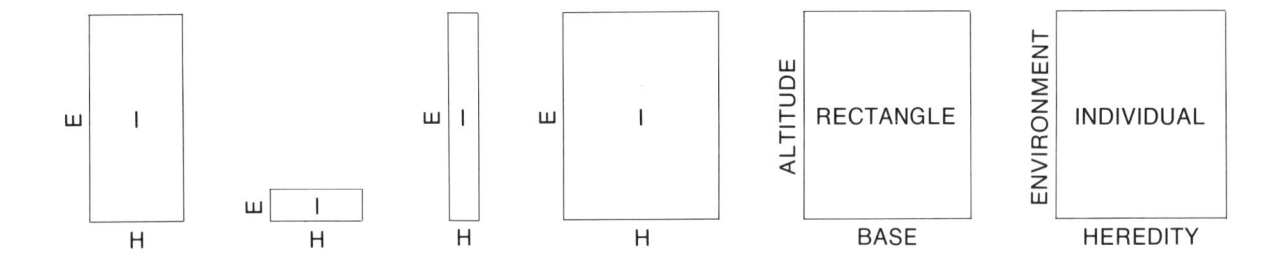

How important are eugenics and euthenics? The farmer who tries to improve his crops must take account of both heredity and environment. If, for example, he is trying to raise premium corn, he will first carefully select the best seeds available and then plant them in rich soil. He may have to improve the soil environment by fertilizing it, and he will have to plow the soil. By combining good seed (heredity) and good soil (environment), he can expect to secure premium corn. In raising premium cattle, the farmer must mate good stock and then give the resulting cattle every advantage in food and shelter.

Human beings are often not as careful in their own mating as the farmer is in cattle mating or in the selection of seeds for plantings. Eugenics . . . aims at the improvement of the human race by calling attention to the importance of heredity.

In trying to improve the human race, we should give careful consideration to the factor of environment. Unfortunately, . . . society is often not as careful of human environment as the farmer is of the environment that he provides for his premium stock. Yet by means of education, religion and ethics, social work, and medicine, the human species can be improved. The branch of applied science that aims at the improvement of man by regulating his environment is called *euthenics* (yōō·then´iks).

Go back to the case of Billy, who misbehaved in school (page 165). Was that misbehavior owing to heredity or environment? Perhaps Billy inherited a small body; he is shorter and weighs less than the other boys his age. Perhaps where Billy lives, the larger boys make fun of him and make him feel inferior. Billy does not wish to be the subject of jokes about his size, does not wish to feel inferior. He believes that by misbehaving in school, he will cause the other children to think that he is tough. If Billy's heredity had been different, he might not have had the small body and would not have been the subject of jokes about his size. If Billy's heredity had been the same but he had lived in a community where other children did not make fun of him, his misbehavior would not have developed. In effect, his present behavior is to be understood in terms of both his heredity and his environment. Heredity and environment always interact.

Terms to Add to Your Vocabulary

chromosomes	genes	phenotype
deoxyribonucleic acid (DNA)	genetics	recessive characteristics
dominant characteristics	genotype	ribonucleic acid (RNA)
environment	heredity	siblings
eugenics	identical twins	unit characters
euthenics	imprinting	
fraternal twins	maturation	

Suggestions for Further Reading

Coleman, James, *Personality Dynamics and Effective Behavior*, Scott, Foresman. Part I, "The Human System," discusses the mechanics of heredity and the role of heredity in development, as well as the roles of physical and sociocultural environments in development.

Hilgard, Ernest R., and Richard C. Atkinson, *Introduction to Psychology*, 4th ed., Harcourt, Brace & World. Chapter 6, "Human Motivation"; Chapter 17, "Behavior Genetics."

Itard, Jean-Marc-Gaspard (English translation by George and Muriel Humphrey), *The Wild Boy of Aveyron*, Appleton-Century-Crofts. A paperback edition of this famous account of an inarticulate, and probably mentally retarded, child found roaming in a French forest in 1799.

Kalish, Richard A., *The Psychology of Human Behavior*, Wadsworth. Chapter 5, "An Introduction to Human Personality and Development," especially pages 96–104.

McKeachie, Wilbert J., and Charlotte L. Doyle, *Psychology*, Addison-Wesley. Chapter 4, "Heredity and Maturation."

Mead, Margaret, *New Lives for Old*, New American Library (Mentor Books). The effects of environmental influences on a primitive people.

Montagu, Ashley, *Human Heredity*, rev. ed., New American Library.

Morgan, Clifford T., and Richard A. King, *Introduction to Psychology*, 3rd ed., McGraw-Hill. Chapter 2, "Maturation and Development."

Munn, Norman L., *Psychology*, 5th ed., Houghton Mifflin. Chapter 4, "How Individual Differences Originate."

Ruch, Floyd L., *Psychology and Life*, 7th ed., Scott, Foresman. Chapter 3, "The Development of Behavior," pages 74–82, "The Mechanism of Heredity," and "Inherited Structures."

Sanford, Fillmore H., *Psychology: A Scientific Study of Man*, 2nd ed., Wadsworth. Chapter 3, "The Developing Organism."

Singh, J. A. L., and Robert M. Zingg, *Wolf-Children and Feral Man*, Shoe String Press. This book includes material by Reverend Singh, the missionary who cared for the "wolf-children" of India, as well as accounts of other individuals who have lived wild or isolated lives.

Whittaker, James O., et al., *Introduction to Psychology*, W. B. Saunders. Chapter 3, "The Development of Behavior."

The Essay Question

Essay questions in examinations often involve answering several questions and incorporating the answers to each of them into a well-organized unit, or essay. The terminology in essay questions is precise and the questions usually request specific content—such as definitions, examples, discussions (pros and cons of a subject), evaluations, or conclusions. You should always read the question carefully and plan your answer before you write. You may want to jot down some notes beside the question or on scratch paper. You should usually answer each part of the question in the order in which it appears in the question. Write in simple, direct language. Allow time to read your answer and make minor corrections or changes.

EXERCISE 8

Answer the following questions based on the material in Section V. Some words, phrases, and connecting sentences are provided for you to help you to structure your answers.

1. What is imprinting? Give an example.

Imprinting is _____

Imprinting has been observed in _____

2. What is maturation? Is maturation related to learning? Give examples of studies with nonhuman and human subjects.
Maturation is _____

The relationship of maturation to learning can be observed in the average home; for example, _____

An experiment with salamanders was very interesting. _____

Studies have been made with sets of twins and with Hopi babies. _____

These studies show that maturation _____ learning.

However, in general we can say _____

Many students do not know how to review a text in preparation for an examination. A second reading of the material covered by the examination is advisable if the quantity is not too great. If you have kept up with the regular assignments, your familiarity with the material should allow you to do a second reading that is different from the first reading. Skim over every page of the text, take note of all bold type, and tell yourself what is included under each heading. If you cannot remember, reread that section. Recite aloud definitions of all important terms. Formulate in your mind possible test questions based on definitions and theories. As you skim the text, take special note of sections devoted to examples and general discussion and reread them. Often this rereading can be done at a fairly rapid rate because much of the material is familiar to you. Check whether you can remember a reasonable number of examples and discussion points. Be sure to read all sections that summarize or state conclusions.

EXERCISE 9 Review "Heredity and Environment" in its entirety as you would for an examination. Answer the following essay questions.

1. Define *genotype* and *phenotype*. Explain each by tracing a specific characteristic within one family.

   _____
   _____
   _____
   _____

2. Define *eugenics*. Would it be possible for eugenics to eradicate mental retardation? Explain.

   _____
   _____
   _____
   _____

3. Define *heredity* and *environment*. What are the important factors involved in each? Discuss studies designed to show the effects of heredity and environment upon human development. What practical conclusions can be made from these studies?

Talking About Short Stories

Discussion of a short story or any work of fiction often begins in an organized manner by talking about the *characters, setting,* and *plot.* The *characters* are, of course, the people in the story. Usually, there are only one or two principal characters in a short story. *Setting* refers to the time and place of the story. Setting is important because people's actions and attitudes are affected by when and where they live, or where they find themselves at the time of the story. *Plot* refers to what actually happens in the story. We can understand a story only if we are sure of what happens and have the sequence of these events clearly in mind. On the following pages is a complete short story by a well-known contemporary writer. Read it through at one sitting. Then do the exercises that follow the story and discuss your answers with other students in your class.

A Diamond Guitar

Truman Capote

The nearest town to the prison farm is twenty miles away. Many forests of pine trees stand between the farm and the town, and it is in these forests that the convicts work; they tap for turpentine. The prison itself is in a forest. You will find it there at the end of a red rutted road, barbed wire sprawling like a vine over its walls. Inside, there live one hundred and nine white men, ninety-seven Negroes and one Chinese. There are two sleep houses—great green wooden buildings with tarpaper roofs. The white men occupy one, the Negroes and the Chinese the other. In each sleep house there is one large pot-bellied stove, but the winters are cold here, and at night with the pines waving frostily and a freezing light falling from the moon the men, stretched on their iron cots, lie awake with the fire colors of the stove playing in their eyes.

The men whose cots are nearest the stove are the important men—those who are looked up to or feared. Mr. Schaeffer is one of these. Mr. Schaeffer—for that is what he is called, a mark of special respect—is a lanky, pulled-out man. He has reddish, silvering hair, and his face is attenuated, religious; there is no flesh to him; you can see the workings of his bones, and his eyes are a poor, dull color. He can read and he can write, he can add a column of figures. When another man receives a letter, he brings it to Mr. Schaeffer. Most of these letters are sad and complaining; very often Mr. Schaeffer improvises more cheerful messages and does not read what is written on the page. In the sleep house there are two other men who can read. Even so, one of them brings his letters to Mr. Schaeffer, who obliges by never reading the truth. Mr. Schaeffer himself does not receive mail, not even at Christmas; he seems to have no friends beyond the prison, and actually he has none there—that is, no particular friend. This was not always true.

Copyright 1950 by Truman Capote. Reprinted from *Breakfast at Tiffany's,* by Truman Capote, by permission of Random House, Inc.

One winter Sunday some winters ago Mr. Schaeffer was sitting on the steps of the sleep house carving a doll. He is quite talented at this. His dolls are carved in separate sections, then put together with bits of spring wire; the arms and legs move, the head rolls. When he has finished a dozen or so of these dolls, the Captain of the farm takes them into town, and there they are sold in a general store. In this way Mr. Schaeffer earns money for candy and tobacco.

That Sunday, as he sat cutting out the fingers for a little hand, a truck pulled into the prison yard. A young boy, handcuffed to the Captain of the farm, climbed out of the truck and stood blinking at the ghostly winter sun. Mr. Schaeffer only glanced at him. He was then a man of fifty, and seventeen of those years he'd lived at the farm. The arrival of a new prisoner could not arouse him. Sunday is a free day at the farm, and other men who were moping around the yard crowded down to the truck. Afterward, Pick Axe and Goober stopped by to speak with Mr. Schaeffer.

Pick Axe said, "He's a foreigner, the new one is. From Cuba. But with yellow hair."

"A knifer, Cap'n says," said Goober, who was a knifer himself. "Cut up a sailor in Mobile."

"Two sailors," said Pick Axe. "But just a café fight. He didn't hurt them boys none."

"To cut off a man's ear? You call that not hurtin' him? They give him two years, Cap'n says."

Pick Axe said, "He's got a guitar with jewels all over it."

It was getting too dark to work. Mr. Schaeffer fitted the pieces of his doll together and, holding its little hands, set it on his knee. He rolled a cigarette; the pines were blue in the sundown light, and the smoke from his cigarette lingered in the cold, darkening air. He could see the Captain coming across the yard. The new prisoner, a blond young boy, lagged a pace behind. He was carrying a guitar studded with glass diamonds that cast a starry twinkle, and his new uniform was too big for him; it looked like a Halloween suit.

"Somebody for you, Schaeffer," said the Captain, pausing on the steps of the sleep house. The Captain was not a hard man; occasionally he invited Mr. Schaeffer into his office, and they would talk together about things they had read in the newspaper. "Tico Feo," he said as though it were the name of a bird or a song, "this is Mr. Schaeffer. Do like him, and you'll do right."

Mr. Schaeffer glanced up at the boy and smiled. He smiled at him longer than he meant to, for the boy had eyes like strips of sky—blue as the winter evening—and his hair was as gold as the Captain's teeth. He had a fun-loving face, nimble, clever; and, looking at him, Mr. Schaeffer thought of holidays and good times.

"Is like my baby sister," said Tico Feo, touching Mr. Schaeffer's doll. His voice with its Cuban accent was soft and sweet as a banana. "She sit on my knee also."

Mr. Schaeffer was suddenly shy. Bowing to the Captain, he walked off into the shadows of the yard. He stood there whispering the names of the evening stars as they opened in flower above him. The stars were his pleasure, but tonight they did not comfort him; they did not make him remember that what happens to us on earth is lost in the endless shine of eternity. Gazing at them—the stars—he thought of the jeweled guitar and its worldly glitter.

It could be said of Mr. Schaeffer that in his life he'd done only one really bad thing: he'd killed a man. The circumstances of that deed are unimportant, except to say that the man deserved to die and that for it Mr. Schaeffer was sentenced to ninety-nine years and a day. For a long while—for many years, in fact—he had not thought of how it was before he came to the farm. His memory of those times was like a house where no one lives and where the furniture has rotted away. But tonight it was as if lamps had been lighted through all the gloomy dead rooms. It had begun to happen when he saw Tico Feo coming through the dusk with his splendid guitar. Until that moment he had not been lonesome. Now, recognizing his loneliness, he felt alive. He had not wanted to be alive. To be alive was to remember brown rivers where the fish run, and sunlight on a lady's hair.

Mr. Schaeffer hung his head. The glare of the stars had made his eyes water.

The sleep house usually is a glum place, stale with the smell of men and stark in the light of two unshaded electric bulbs. But with the advent of Tico Feo it was as though a tropic occurrence had happened in the cold room, for when Mr. Schaeffer returned from his observance of the stars he came upon a savage and garish scene. Sitting cross-legged on a cot, Tico Feo was picking at his guitar with long swaying fingers and singing a song that sounded as jolly as jingling coins. Though the song was in Spanish, some of the men tried to sing it with him, and Pick Axe and Goober were dancing together. Charlie and Wink were dancing too, but separately. It was nice to hear the men laughing, and when Tico Feo finally put aside his guitar, Mr. Schaeffer was among those who congratulated him.

"You deserve such a fine guitar," he said.

"Is diamond guitar," said Tico Feo, drawing his hand over its vaudeville dazzle. "Once I have a one with rubies. But that one is stole. In Havana my sister work in a, how you say, where make guitar; is how I have this one."

Mr. Schaeffer asked him if he had many sisters, and Tico Feo, grinning, held up four fingers. Then, his blue eyes narrowing greedily, he said, "Please, Mister, you give me doll for my two little sister?"

The next evening Mr. Schaeffer brought him the dolls. After that he was Tico Feo's best friend and they were always together. At all times they considered each other.

Tico Feo was eighteen years old and for two years had worked on a freighter in the Caribbean. As a child he'd gone to school with nuns, and he wore a gold crucifix around his neck. He had a rosary too. The rosary he kept wrapped in a green silk scarf that also held three other treasures: a bottle of Evening in Paris cologne, a pocket mirror and a Rand McNally map of the world. These and the guitar were his only possessions, and he would not allow anyone to touch them. Perhaps he prized his map the most. At night, before the lights were turned off, he would shake out his map and show Mr. Schaeffer the places he'd been—Galveston, Miami, New Orleans, Mobile, Cuba, Haiti, Jamaica, Puerto Rico, the Virgin Islands—and the places he wanted to go to. He wanted to go almost everywhere, especially Madrid, especially the North Pole. This both charmed and frightened Mr. Schaeffer. It hurt him to think of Tico Feo on the seas and in far places. He sometimes looked defensively at his friend and thought, "You are just a lazy dreamer."

It is true that Tico Feo was a lazy fellow. After that first evening he had to be urged even to play his guitar. At daybreak when the guard came to rouse the men, which he did by banging a hammer on the stove, Tico Feo would whimper like a child. Sometimes he pretended to be ill, moaned and rubbed his stomach; but he never got away with this, for the Captain would send him out to work with the rest of the men. He and Mr. Schaeffer were put together on a highway gang. It was hard work, digging at frozen clay and carrying croker sacks filled with broken stone. The guard had always to be shouting at Tico Feo, for he spent most of the time trying to lean on things.

Each noon, when the dinner buckets were passed around, the two friends sat together. There were some good things in Mr. Schaeffer's bucket, as he could afford apples and candy bars from the town. He liked giving these things to his friend, for his friend enjoyed them so much, and he thought, "You are growing; it will be a long time until you are a grown man."

Not all the men liked Tico Feo. Because they were jealous, or for more subtle reasons, some of them told ugly stories about him. Tico Feo himself seemed unaware of this. When the men gathered around him, and he played his guitar and sang his songs, you could see that he felt he was loved. Most of the men did feel a love for him; they waited for and depended upon the hour between supper and lights out. "Tico, play your box," they would say. They did not notice that afterward there was a deeper sadness than there had ever been. Sleep jumped beyond them like a jack rabbit, and their eyes lingered ponderingly on the firelight that creaked behind the grating of the stove. Mr. Schaeffer was the only one who understood their troubled feeling, for he felt it too. It was that his friend had revived the brown rivers where the fish run, and ladies with sunlight in their hair.

Soon Tico Feo was allowed the honor of having a bed near the stove and next to Mr. Schaeffer. Mr. Schaeffer had always known that his friend was a terrible liar. He did not listen for the truth in Tico Feo's tales of adventure, of conquests and encounters with famous people. Rather, he took pleasure in them as plain stories, such as you would read in a magazine, and it warmed him to hear his friend's tropic voice whispering in the dark.

Except that they did not combine their bodies or think

to do so, though such things were not unknown at the farm, they were as lovers. Of the seasons, spring is the most shattering: stalks thrusting through the earth's winter-stiffened crust, young leaves cracking out on old left-to-die branches, the falling-asleep wind cruising through all the newborn green. And with Mr. Schaeffer it was the same, a breaking up, a flexing of muscles that had hardened.

It was late January. The friends were sitting on the steps of the sleep house, each with a cigarette in his hand. A moon thin and yellow as a piece of lemon rind curved above them, and under its light, threads of ground frost glistened like silver snail trails. For many days Tico Feo had been drawn into himself—silent as a robber waiting in the shadows. It was no good to say to him, "Tico, play your box." He would only look at you with smooth, under-ether eyes.

"Tell a story," said Mr. Schaeffer, who felt nervous and helpless when he could not reach his friend. "Tell about when you went to the race track in Miami."

"I not ever go to no race track," said Tico Feo, thereby admitting to his wildest lie, one involving hundreds of dollars and a meeting with Bing Crosby. He did not seem to care. He produced a comb and pulled it sulkily through his hair. A few days before this comb had been the cause of a fierce quarrel. One of the men, Wink, claimed that Tico Feo had stolen the comb from him, to which the accused replied by spitting in his face. They had wrestled around until Mr. Schaeffer and another man got them separated. "Is my comb. You tell him!" Tico Feo had demanded of Mr. Schaeffer. But Mr. Schaeffer with quiet firmness had said no, it was not his friend's comb—an answer that seemed to defeat all concerned. "Aw," said Wink, "if he want it so much, Christ's sake, let the sonofabitch keep it." And later, in a puzzled, uncertain voice, Tico Feo had said, "I thought you was my friend." "I am," Mr. Schaeffer had thought, though he said nothing.

"I not go to no race track, and what I said about the widow woman, that is not true also." He puffed up his cigarette to a furious glow and looked at Mr. Schaeffer with a speculating expression. "Say, you have money, Mister?"

"Maybe twenty dollars," said Mr. Schaeffer hesitantly, afraid of where this was leading.

"Not so good, twenty dollar," Tico said, but without disappointment. "No important, we work our way. In Mobile I have my friend Frederico. He will put us on a boat. There will not be trouble," and it was as though he were saying that the weather had turned colder.

There was a squeezing in Mr. Schaeffer's heart; he could not speak.

"Nobody here can run to catch Tico. He run the fastest."

"Shotguns run faster," said Mr. Schaeffer in a voice hardly alive. "I'm too old," he said, with the knowledge of age churning like nausea inside him.

Tico Feo was not listening. "Then, the world. The

world, *el mundo,* my friend." Standing up, he quivered like a young horse; everything seemed to draw close to him—the moon, the callings of screech owls. His breath came quickly and turned to smoke in the air. "Should we go to Madrid? Maybe someone teach me to bullfight. You think so, Mister?"

Mr. Schaeffer was not listening either. "I'm too old," he said. "I'm too damned old."

For the next several weeks Tico Feo kept after him— the world, *el mundo,* my friend; and he wanted to hide. He would shut himself in the toilet and hold his head. Nevertheless, he was excited, tantalized. What if it could come true, the race with Tico across the forests and to the sea? And he imagined himself on a boat, he who had never seen the sea, whose whole life had been landrooted. During this time one of the convicts died, and in the yard you could hear the coffin being made. As each nail thudded into place, Mr. Schaeffer thought, "This is for me, it is mine."

Tico Feo himself was never in better spirits; he sauntered about with a dancer's snappy, gigolo grace, and had a joke for everyone. In the sleep house after supper his fingers popped at the guitar like firecrackers. He taught the men to cry *olé*, and some of them sailed their caps through the air.

When work on the road was finished, Mr. Schaeffer and Tico Feo were moved back into the forests. On Valentine's Day they ate their lunch under a pine tree. Mr. Schaeffer had ordered a dozen oranges from the town and he peeled them slowly, the skins unraveling in a spiral; the jucier slices he gave to his friend, who was proud of how far he could spit the seeds—a good ten feet.

It was a cold beautiful day, scraps of sunlight blew about them like butterflies, and Mr. Schaeffer, who liked working with the trees, felt dim and happy. Then Tico Feo said, "That one, he no could catch a fly in his mouth." He meant Armstrong, a hog-jowled man sitting with a shotgun propped between his legs. He was the youngest of the guards and new at the farm.

"I don't know," said Mr. Schaeffer. He'd watched Armstrong and noticed that, like many people who are both heavy and vain, the new guard moved with a skimming lightness. "He might could fool you."

"I fool him, maybe," said Tico Feo, and spit an orange seed in Armstrong's direction. The guard scowled at him, then blew a whistle. It was the signal for work to begin.

Sometime during the afternoon the two friends came together again; that is, they were nailing turpentine buckets onto trees that stood next to each other. At a distance below them a shallow bouncing creek branched through the woods. "In water no smell," said Tico Feo meticulously, as though remembering something he'd heard. "We run in the water; until dark we climb a tree. Yes, Mister?"

Mr. Schaeffer went on hammering, but his hand was shaking, and the hammer came down on his thumb. He looked around dazedly at his friend. His face showed no reflection of pain, and he did not put the thumb in his mouth, the way a man ordinarily might.

Tico Feo's blue eyes seemed to swell like bubbles, and when in a voice quieter than the wind sounds in the pinetops he said, "Tomorrow," these eyes were all that Mr. Schaeffer could see.

"Tomorrow, Mister?"

"Tomorrow," said Mr. Schaeffer.

The first colors of morning fell upon the walls of the sleep house, and Mr. Schaeffer, who had rested a little, knew that Tico Feo was awake too. With the weary eyes of a crocodile he observed the movements of his friend in the next cot. Tico Feo was unknotting the scarf that contained his treasures. First he took the pocket mirror. Its jellyfish light trembled on his face. For a while he admired himself with serious delight, and combed and slicked his hair as though he were preparing to step out to a party. Then he hung the rosary about his neck. The cologne he never opened, nor the map. The last thing he did was to tune his guitar. While the other men were dressing, he sat on the edge of his cot and tuned the guitar. It was strange, for he must have known he would never play it again.

Bird shrills followed the men through the smoky morning woods. They walked single file, fifteen men to a group, and a guard bringing up the rear of each line. Mr. Schaeffer was sweating as though it were a hot day, and he could not keep in marching step with his friend, who walked ahead, snapping his fingers and whistling at the birds.

A signal had been set. Tico Feo was to call, "Time out," and pretend to go behind a tree. But Mr. Schaeffer did not know when it would happen.

The guard named Armstrong blew a whistle, and his men dropped from the line and separated to their various stations. Mr. Schaeffer, though going about his work as best he could, took care always to be in a position where he could keep an eye on both Tico Feo and the guard. Armstrong sat on a stump, a chew of tobacco lopsiding his face, and his gun pointing into the sun. He had the tricky eyes of a cardsharp; you could not really tell where he was looking.

Once another man gave the signal. Although Mr. Schaeffer had known at once that it was not the voice of his friend, panic had pulled at his throat like a rope. As the morning wore on there was such a drumming in his ears he was afraid he would not hear the signal when it came.

The sun climbed to the center of the sky. "He is just a lazy dreamer. It will never happen," thought Mr. Schaeffer, daring a moment to believe this. But "First we eat," said Tico Feo with a practical air as they set their dinner pails on the bank above the creek. They ate in silence, almost as though each bore the other a grudge, but at the end of it Mr. Schaeffer felt his friend's hand close over his own and hold it with a tender pressure.

"Mr. Armstrong, time out . . ."

Near the creek Mr. Schaeffer had seen a sweet gum

tree, and he was thinking it would soon be spring and the sweet gum ready to chew. A razory stone ripped open the palm of his hand as he slid off the slippery embankment into the water. He straightened up and began to run; his legs were long, he kept almost abreast of Tico Feo, and icy geysers sprayed around them. Back and forth through the woods the shouts of men boomed hollowly like voices in a cavern, and there were three shots, all highflying, as though the guard were shooting at a cloud of geese.

Mr. Schaeffer did not see the log that lay across the creek. He thought he was still running, and his legs thrashed about him; it was as though he were a turtle stranded on its back.

While he struggled there, it seemed to him that the face of his friend, suspended above him, was part of the white winter sky—it was so distant, judging. It hung there but an instant, like a hummingbird, yet in that time he'd seen that Tico Feo had not wanted him to make it, had never thought he would, and he remembered once thinking that it would be a long time before his friend was a grown man. When they found him, he was still lying in the ankle-deep water as though it were a summer afternoon and he were idly floating on the stream.

Since then three winters have gone by, and each has been said to be the coldest, the longest. Two recent months of rain washed deeper ruts in the clay road leading to the farm, and it is harder than ever to get there, harder to leave. A pair of searchlights has been added to the walls, and they burn there through the night like the eyes of a giant owl. Otherwise, there have not been many changes. Mr. Schaeffer, for instance, looks much the same, except that there is a thicker frost of white in his hair, and as the result of a broken ankle he walks with a limp. It was the Captain himself who said that Mr. Schaeffer had broken his ankle attempting to capture Tico Feo. There was even a picture of Mr. Schaeffer in the newspaper, and under it this caption: "Tried to Prevent Escape." At the time he was deeply mortified, not because he knew the other men were laughing, but because he thought of Tico Feo seeing it. But he cut it out of the paper anyway, and keeps it in an envelope along with several clippings pertaining to his friend: a spinster woman told the authorities he'd entered her home and kissed her, twice he was reported seen in the Mobile vicinity, finally it was believed that he had left the country.

No one has ever disputed Mr. Schaeffer's claim to the guitar. Several months ago a new prisoner was moved into the sleep house. He was said to be a fine player, and Mr. Schaeffer was persuaded to lend him the guitar. But all the man's tunes came out sour, for it was as though Tico Feo, tuning his guitar that last morning, had put a curse upon it. Now it lies under Mr. Schaeffer's cot, where its glass diamonds are turning yellow; in the night his hand sometimes searches it out, and his fingers drift across the strings: then, the world.

Discussion of characters first centers around what we *know* about them—what they look like, what we know about their past, what their personalities seem to be, how they react to other people, and how other people react to them. Later discussion may have more to do with why they did what they did in the story or what their reactions or apparent feelings have revealed to us about people or life in general.

CHARACTERS

EXERCISE 10 Complete the following statements about the two principal characters in the story. In some instances you are asked to supply a word to complete the verb; in other instances you are asked to supply both the verb and the word to complete it.

Mr. Schaeffer

1. *(Give age.)* He / was _____.
2. *(Tell something about his status at the farm.)* He / was _____.
3. *(Tell something about his physical appearance.)* He / was _____.
4. *(Give an important fact about his past.)* He / _____.
5. *(Tell how he spent much of his time at the farm.)* He / _____.

Tico Feo

1. *(Tell something about his physical appearance.)* He / was _____.
2. *(Make a statement about his past.)* He / _____.
3. *(Make a statement about things he owned.)* He / _____.
4. *(Make a statement about his character or personality.)* He / _____.

SETTING

EXERCISE 11 Fill in the blanks in the sentences below to produce a statement about *where* and *when* the story took place. Note that sometimes we have to draw inferences to make such a statement.

The story takes place on a _____ _____ located in a _____. The action occurs in the (*time of year*) _____. The author, Truman Capote, was brought up in the (*look this up if necessary*) _____ part of the United States and possibly may have been writing about a place he had seen in his youth. Although the author does not give a date for the story, it might be concluded that the story took place in the (*1st, 2nd*) _____ half of the twentieth century.

I concluded this because of the following details mentioned in the story.
_____
_____

PLOT

EXERCISE 12

Following is an outline of the plot of the story. After each step in the plot state in the space provided whether this step was *stated* (actually told to you in the story) or *implied* (communicated to you by something else the author said that lead you to make a conclusion). On p. 190 the author states, "Mr. Schaeffer hung his head. The glare of the stars had made his eyes water." The author has implied in the previous paragraph that meeting Tico Feo had reminded Mr. Schaeffer of his own youth. The statement about his eyes watering leads us to conclude that Mr. Schaeffer cried. The fact that he hung his head when he found this happening leads us to conclude that Mr. Schaeffer was surprised or ashamed at this display of emotion on his part.

Outline of Plot of the Story	*Stated or Implied*	*Page and Line*
I. Tico Feo arrives at prison farm.	_____	_____
II. Mr. Schaeffer and Tico Feo become friends.	_____	_____
III. Tico Feo suggests that they escape.	_____	_____
IV. They agree that escape will be made when a particular guard is on duty.	_____	_____
V. They agree to escape by water.	_____	_____
VI. Escape is made.	_____	_____
VII. Mr. Schaeffer falls.	_____	_____
VIII. The Captain covers up for Mr. Schaeffer.	_____	_____
IX. Life at the prison farm goes back to normal.	_____	_____

IMAGERY

Writers use adjectives skillfully and sometimes in unusual ways to help us see things vividly. Adjectives can point out details that we might overlook in daily situations. Sometimes an adjective does more than merely describe a character. Well-chosen adjectives can produce feelings as well as mental pictures. A good writer, through his skill with words, can extend a reader's experiences.

EXERCISE 13

Following are some noun phrases taken from the story. These phrases are made up of nouns preceded by adjectives. In the blanks to the right of these phrases indicate whether the adjectives (1) merely describe or (2) produce a feeling. A writer can arouse the emotions of a reader by using an adjective that might ordinarily be used to describe something else. This is, in effect, an implied comparison. An implied comparison can make adjectives doubly effective. For instance, if a town is described as sleepy, you associate with the town all the feelings of a sleepy person—drowsiness, dullness, or the boredom connected with little activity. If you don't know the meanings of some adjectives, use the dictionary. Under *Comments* explain your answer.

Examples:

Noun Phrase	Effect of Adjective	Comments
1. *sundown* light	1 *(describes)*	The light is low at sundown. You can see, but things do not sparkle or shine.
2. *pulled-out* man (Mr. Schaeffer)	1 & 2 *(describes and produces a feeling)*	"Pulled-out" tells you he's thin, but it also suggests that he is worn out from the life he's led and makes you feel sorry for him.

Noun Phrase	Effect of Adjective	Comments
1. *attenuated* face	_____	
2. *ghostly* winter sun	_____	
3. *worldly* glitter (of the guitar)	_____	
4. *stale* place (the sleep house)	_____	
5. *garish* scene	_____	
6. *vaudeville* dazzle (of the guitar)	_____	

7. *shattering* season _____
   (spring)

8. *jelly fish* light _____
   (of pocket mirror)

9. *tropic* voice _____
   (Tico Feo's)

10. *smoky* morning light _____

EXERCISE 14

Besides using unusual and vivid adjectives the author of "A Diamond Guitar" makes many direct comparisons to stimulate his readers to *see* and *feel* as they read. Direct comparisons use the words *like* or *as*. He either states that something is like something else ("Tico's Cuban accent was [as] soft and sweet as a banana") or he states that something acted like something else ("Sleep jumped [beyond them] like a jack rabbit [would jump]").

Find five direct comparisons in the story and write enough of the sentence in which they are found to make it clear which two things are being compared. Indicate the page and line of story for each choice.

Comparison   *Page and Line*

1. _____   _____

2. _____   _____

3. _____   _____

4. _____   _____

5. _____   _____

THE TITLE

Authors have many options when they choose a title for a book or a story. Many of these options (or choices) would make satisfactory titles. We never know why an author decides on the title he does, how much he intends to say through the title, or even if he takes the title very seriously. Probably the only thing we *can* say about the title is that the author sees some relationship between the title and the story or between the title and something he is trying to say to us by means of the story. When we conclude that an author is trying to communicate an idea to us as well as tell us a story, we say that the story has a *theme*.

EXERCISE 15

Rate the following titles for this story as *good, fair,* or *poor,* and state in the spaces provided what the relationship of each title is to the story or to any theme you see in the story.

Title	Rating	Relationship
EXAMPLE: A Diamond Guitar	Good	The glitter of the guitar was like the excitement that Tico Feo brought to the prison.
1. Tico Feo		
2. Wooden Dolls		
3. The Twinkling Stars		
4. El Mundo		

QUESTIONS FOR DISCUSSION

1. The author includes in the story a statement that could be considered a definition of friendship. Find this statement and write it on the line below. On

what page and line in the story did you find this definition? What do you think of this definition? Can you define friendship another way?

Statement *Page and Line*

_____ _____

_____ _____

2. What did the author mean when he said of Mr. Schaeffer, "Now recognizing his loneliness, he felt alive. He had not wanted to be alive"? What, in the author's words, was "being alive" to Mr. Schaeffer? Why did he not want to be alive? What is "being alive" to you?

_____

_____

3. Why did the author continue the story beyond the failure of the escape? Why would he make this statement in the next-to-last paragraph: "Since then three winters have gone by, and each has been said to be the coldest, the longest"? Why would the readers be interested in whether the winters had been cold since this incident?

_____

_____

4. Why did the author say that the guitar did not sound the same when played later? Why did the diamonds on the guitar turn yellow?

_____

_____

_____

© United Features Syndicate, Inc. Reprinted with permission.

Appendix A

Answers to Selected Exercises

Section One—Power through Growth and Accuracy

WORD RECOGNITION TECHNIQUES

Success with the exercises in this section will come mainly from training yourself to "see" the patterns and then pronouncing *all words aloud*. Answers to some of the exercises are provided to help you check your written work.

EXERCISE 1A PAGE 4
Ten *a*'s
Ten *e*'s
Twelve *i*'s
Nine *o*'s
Six *u*'s

EXERCISE 1B PAGE 5
Four *a*'s
Six *e*'s
Nine *i*'s
Four *o*'s
Five *u*'s

EXERCISE 5 PAGE 12   Six words of one syllable; all others two syllables.

EXERCISE 7B PAGE 15
1. mopped; mopping
2. moped; moping
3. gapped; gapping
4. gaped; gaping
5. lopped; lopping
6. loped; loping
7. stripped; stripping
8. striped; striping
9. planned; planning
10. planed; planing

EXERCISE 7C PAGE 15
1. thriving
2. planning
3. glutted
4. waning
5. bogged
6. chafing

7. chugged
8. phasing
9. chastised
10. gripping
11. jutted
12. griping
13. chafed
14. conniving
15. fogged
16. taped
17. sniping
18. matting
19. tapping
20. spanned

EXERCISE 10B PAGE 19

1. e, i, u
2. e, i, u; fern, hurt, skirt (*and many others*)

EXERCISE 11A PAGE 20

CVC	CVCe	CVVC-1	CVVC-2	CVrC
17 words	17 words	14 words	15 words	15 words

EXERCISE 11B PAGE 21

CVC	CVCe	CVVC-1	CVVC-2	CVrC
14 words	8 words	5 words	5 words	8 words

EXERCISE 12 PAGE 21 (*Some possible answers*)

	ee	oo	ue	eu or ew	ui
1.	see	cool	sue	neutral	suit
2.	green	cook	flue	mew	nuisance
3.	seem	moon	hue	grew	fluid
4.	bleed	soon	cruel	slew	ruin
5.	spleen	took	fuel	hew	sluice

EXERCISE 13 PAGE 22

1. con fis cate (3)
2. tur gid (2)
3. stam pede (2)
4. im bibe (2)
5. spec trum (2)
6. ur ban (2)
7. ur bane (2)
8. con clave (2)
9. thrush (1)
10. blas pheme (2)
11. sor did (2)
12. churl ish (2)
13. ar cane (2)
14. con trac tion (3)
15. mun dane (2)
16. con fec tion (3)
17. noc turn al (3)
18. in can des(c) ent (4)
19. scoun drel (2)
20. surr o gate (3)

EXERCISE 14 PAGE 24 Drill inserts: wine, tote, muse, Pete, flake

1. no mad
2. ma tron
3. wi ly
4. va grant
5. ty rant
6. bi son
7. co bra
8. si phon
9. scu ba

10. do cent	17. mo dal	24. Ti ber
11. sa cred	18. cre tin	25. mo gul
12. po tent	19. na tal	26. fra cas
13. le thal	20. e gret	27. bla tant
14. cro ton	21. ma trix	28. qua si
15. pu trid	22. lu nar	29. fla grant
16. Mi das	23. so lar	30. po grom

EXERCISES 17A, 18A, AND 19A PAGES 27 AND 28

These are listening exercises. Speakers may accent different syllables, as in some instances more than one pronunciation is acceptable. The important thing for you is to develop ability to *hear* what the speaker is doing. In Exercise 17A, numbers 7 and 11 and numbers 8 and 20 represent a shift from one form class to another with a shift of the accent.

EXERCISE 24 PAGE 33

Primary and secondary accents are given in words of four or more syllables. Discuss with your classmates other words in which you hear more than one syllable accented. A letter in parenthesis indicates a spot where you may hear yourself attaching letters to a different syllable than you were instructed to do in earlier exercises.

1. su′et
2. sci′on
3. *try* in si′di ous
   and in sid′i ous
4. sump′tu ous
5. mau′so le′um
6. nau′se ate
7. sub stant′i ate′
8. gra tu′i ty′
9. *try* pe′di a′trics
   and pe′di at′rics
10. par′si mo′ni ous
11. con temp′tu ous
12. vi′a (b)le
13. i o′ta
14. ob se′qui ous
15. bi′op sy
16. pro mis cu′i ty
17. stri′a ted
18. *try* cho′re o′gra phy
    and cho′re og′ra phy
19. *try* di aph′an ous
    or di aph an ous
20. co erce′

EXERCISE 26 PAGE 35

1. caus′tic (2)
2. prog no′sis (3)
3. ob′fus cate (3)
4. prog nos′ti cate (4)
5. syn′drome (2)
6. shibb′o leth (3)
7. es pouse′ (2)
8. ga ze′bo (3)
9. flac′(c)id (2)
10. bor dell′o (3)
11. pla ce′bo (3)
12. con cen′sus (3)
13. con′fis cate (3)
14. skir′mish (2)
15. shrift (1)
16. strin′gent (2)
17. pre pos′ter ous (4)
18. mor′pheme (2)
19. in′grate (2)
20. gar′goyle (2)

EXERCISE 27 PAGE 36

1. om buds man (3)
2. mall e a bil i ty (6)
3. ex tem po ra ne ous (6)
4. imm in ent (3)

5. *try* e man ate   (3)
   and em an ate
6. mis an thrope   (3)
7. *try* re ne gade   (3)
   and ren e gade
8. foi (b)le   (2)
9. dys pep tic   (3)
10. imm o late   (3)
11. e clec tic   (3)
12. blas phem ous   (3)
13. pro mis cu ous
14. fall a cious   (3)
15. ob so les (c)ence   (4)
16. ob so lete   (3)
17. pon tif i cate   (4)
18. acc o lade   (3)
19. lo qua cious   (3)
20. *try* co in cide   (3)
    and co in cide   (3)
21. te na cious   (3)
22. em phy se ma   (4)
23. ter ma gant   (3)
24. phan tas ma go ri a   (6)
25. suc (c)inct   (2)

Improving Comprehension

Paragraph Analysis

The ability to reason *about* what the author is stressing is the most important skill in analyzing paragraphs. Evaluating points that must be discarded as well as points that must be included will develop your skill in arriving at reasonable conclusions.

DEMONSTRATION EXERCISE PAGE 38 (PARAGRAPH I)
1. C / C
2. E / A

DEMONSTRATION EXERCISE PAGE 39 (PARAGRAPH II)
3. Vacation trailer families / A or C.

DEMONSTRATION EXERCISE PAGE 39 (PARAGRAPH III)
4. Motor home families / A.

DEMONSTRATION EXERCISE PAGE 40 (PARAGRAPH IV)
5. Pickup camper users / B.

DEMONSTRATION EXERCISE PAGE 40 (PARAGRAPH V)
6. The converted van family / C.

DEMONSTRATION EXERCISE PAGE 41 (PARAGRAPH VI)
7. Camper trailer families / A.

EXERCISE 28 PAGE 42
1. A
2. B

EXERCISE 30 PAGE 44
1. The guitar can provide all the basics needed for an excellent start in instrumental music.
2. The popularity of the guitar is going a long way toward changing the old-fashioned notion that the guitar is for show and not for acquiring the basics of music.

EXERCISE 31 PAGE 44   C

EXERCISE 32B PAGES 46–47

(*Some possible answers*)

Attitudes Within the Military	Historical Sources for Fashion Details
1. Emphasis on tradition—U.S. adopted British uniform with little consideration for individuality or function	1. Blue and white color scheme
2. Resistance to change—few changes since uniform adopted	2. Square collar
3. Emphasis on tradition may be changing with U.S. society	3. Black tie
	4. Bell bottomed trousers
	5. Trousers with two front closings
	6. Trousers with button front closings
	7. Sailor hat

EXERCISE 33 PAGE 47

(*Possible completions—it will be interesting for you to note the many good approaches there can be to this type of problem.*)
1. / may live in the depths of Loch Ness, a lake in northern Scotland.
2. / have been fascinated since the thirteenth century by reports of a strange monster living in a lake in Scotland.

Section Two—Power from Signals

AFFIXES

EXERCISE 1B PAGE 51
1. un
2. non
3. dis
4. in
5. ir
6. im
7. il

EXERCISE 1C PAGE 52   1. disperse   2. disadvantages

205

3. disability
4. disarray
5. disbud
6. disavow
7. disband
8. discard
9. dismay
10. discord

EXERCISE 1D PAGE 54

1. pretrial
2. preconvention
   postconvention
3. intrastate
   interstate
4. pseudoscientific
5. malpractice
6. subzero
7. malfunction
8. prewar
   postwar
9. pro-union
   anti-union

EXERCISE 2A PAGE 56

1. reference IA
2. allowance IA
3. performance IIA
4. creation IA
5. hypnotist IIa
6. maintenance Ia
7. employment IA
8. annoyance IIA
9. employee IIA
10. exclusion IA
11. correspondence IIA
12. inventions Ia
13. contortionists Ia
14. employment IA
15. guidance IIA
16. dependents IIA
17. preference IIA
18. acceptance IIA
19. creativity IA
20. organization Ia
21. offender IIA
22. adoption IIA
23. prosperity IIA
24. interruptions IA
25. dependence IA

EXERCISE 2B PAGE 58

ence
ance
tion
ist
ment

ee
sion
ent
ity
er

EXERCISE 2C PAGE 58

1. (Example)
2. the allowance, my parents, my expenses
3. the performance, the acrobatic team
4. the creation, a work, an artist's gift
5. a hypnotist
6. a consideration, a complicated piece
7. his continuous employment, many benefits
8. an annoyance
9. one worker, the building, an employee, the company, ten years
10. any ethnic group, a public building, this country
11. many famous people, a large correspondence

12. each year
13. (none)
14. a large industry, many fringe benefits
15. an informed and sympathetic counselor
16. three dependents
17. his preference
18. (none)
19. her creativity, the beautiful things
20. his talent, his success
21. a chronic offender, the eyes, her supervisors
22. (none)
23. a great country
24. the progress, the filming
25. his dependence, his notes, his insecurity, the subject matter

EXERCISE 3A
PAGES 59-60

1. terrorized (or terrified) the boy
2. motivated her
3. memorize his instructions
4. threatened
5. falsified the incident
6. penalized
7. captivated her audience
8. intensified
9. beautify the parkway
10. originated
11. lengthen
12. pressurized
13. horrified people
14. lengthen his stay at the lake
15. tightened his grip on the wheel

EXERCISE 3B
PAGES 60-61

1. necessitated the use of
2. categorize the books
3. to fluoridate the city water
4. colonize the new territory
5. intensified
6. strengthen the team's passing attack
7. broaden the approach
8. formalize the initiation procedure
9. clarified the problem
10. were now mechanized

EXERCISE 3D PAGE 63

able	ory
ible	ary
ive	ent

        ing   ous
        ful   tious

EXERCISE 4 PAGE 64

I. Today, for the first time, the American public is realizing that the inflatable boat offers a cheap low-maintenance way to get in on the boating boom.
(or possibly)
Inflatables have truly come of age.
(This sentence is more catchy and less informative than the first. It is typical of final sentences, often called "clincher" sentences.)
  A. Today running whitewater rivers is one of the fastest growing sports in the country.
  B. Until recently people were not aware of the features of inflatable boats.
  C. There are two types of materials used in making inflatables.
1. Inflatable boats are   unsinkable
                          collapsible
                          maneuverable
                          cheap
2. first
   last
Title:
Suggested Title: A Healthy Exercise Program
                   Exercise and Physical Fitness
   I. C
  II. B
III. *(Suggested)* The number 130 / is a good yardstick by which to judge a sport.
     or
    A healthy sport / is one that is played with vigor.

PUNCTUATION

EXERCISE 7 PAGE 70

1. A. Muhammad Ali was so uninterested in his twelve round bout with bulky Buster Mathis that he trained seriously only for nine days. (comma pairs, parentheses)
  B. Ali divested himself of a bit of doggerel, but his heart was clearly not in it. (parentheses)
  C. Buster was out to prove that "I'm no dog." (comma pairs)
  D. Mathis suggested a pachyderm on *pointe*. (comma pairs)
  E. In the final two rounds Ali decked Mathis four times. (dash)
  F. Ali picked up $300,000 for the light workout. (parentheses, comma pairs)
  G. Trouble is, Ali and Frazier so outclass the other contenders that in tuning up for their second "fight of the century" they seem to be reviving the old bum of the month club. (parentheses)
2. A. "I'll do to Buster what the Indians did to Custer."
    "the linger on"
    "new punch"
    "Yes, I deliberately held up."
    "I don't believe in killing a man just to satisfy a crowd."
  B. "I'm no dog."

C. "fight of the century"
3. It is a French word meaning a ballet position where the dancer dances on the toes.

Use of Context Clues to Increase Vocabulary

Definitions

EXERCISE 11
PAGES 77–78
1. greatcoat—heavy overcoat
2. press—a large cabinet with shelves and drawers
3. cabinet—closet, a small private room
4. minim—smallest fluid measure, about a drop
5. draught—British for *draft,* a portion measured out for drinking
6. bull's eye—a simple lens of short focal distance or a lantern with such a lens
7. ulster—long, loose overcoat
   cravat—a necktie or scarf
8. boa—a long, fluffy scarf of fur or feathers
9. hansom—light two-wheeled carriage with driver's seat
10. beige—*cloth* made of natural undyed wool (reference to color blue excludes meaning of color)

EXERCISE 14 PAGE 82 population explosion, ecologists, extinct, increased, obvious, web, balance, environmental, deterioration, redirect, population biology, continue, unstable, simplify, exterminated, escalation, escalation, increases, insecticides, instant, simplified

Section Three—Power through Seeing Relationships

Sentences

EXERCISE 1 PAGE 84
1. after (qualifier)
2. although *or* but (contraster)
3. when (qualifier); and (extender)
4. but (contraster) *or* although (contraster)
5. and (extender)

EXERCISE 2 PAGE 85
1. when
2. and
3. but
4. and
5. but
6. and
7. which
8. but *or* although
9. and
10. but

EXERCISE 3   (*Numbers refer to lines*)
PAGES 86–87

1. but	22. and	37. although	54. because
3. when	24. after	38. however	57. thus
6. but	26. but	42. and	63. yet
8. although	26. in fact	44. which	64. in fact
12. but	28. when	46. however	65. which
14. moreover	29. who	47. because	67. so
16. if	29. who	51. and	
21. but	33. when	52. therefore	

EXERCISE 4 PAGE 88

A. emphasizer
B. extender
C. qualifier
D. contraster
E. summarizer

PARAGRAPHS

The purpose of the exercises in this section is to continue the development of the ability to *reason* about the various ideas within a single paragraph. The ability to see relationships and discuss the basis for relationships is more important at this point than placing ideas in arbitrary slots.

EXERCISE 5 PAGE 91   Primary idea: A great drawing card for the guitar is the social aspect of this versatile instrument.
Secondary ideas: (1) Teens and subteens find that guitar playing is an easy route to enhancing and increasing friendships; (2) and more important, they learn to profit from other people's accomplishments and get experience in overcoming shyness.

EXERCISE 6 PAGE 93   Primary idea: (1) concentration; (2) vital; (3) professional driver; (4) layman
Secondary ideas: A *and* D

EXERCISE 7A PAGE 94   Primary idea: 3

EXERCISE 7B PAGE 95   Primary idea: 3
Secondary ideas: 2 *and* 5
Introduction to new step: This raises certain speculations
New step: 1 *and* 4

EXERCISE 8 PAGE 96 Primary idea: 1
Secondary idea: 2
Supported by: 3 *and* 4
Secondary idea: 5
Supported by: 6 *and* 7
Secondary idea: 8

EXERCISE 10 PAGE 100
1. F
2. C

Suggested secondary ideas: (1) Kids couldn't wait to grow up to drive a motorcycle or a car so they wanted mini-bikes immediately. (2) American kids have more of a passion for wheels than for baseball or football. (3) The Y.M.C.A. has had good success working with "incorrigible" youngsters by offering mini-bike riding in supervised events as rewards.

EXERCISE 11A PAGE 101

Acts	Interpretation
1. leans back in chair, crosses arms and legs	is listening
2. shifts position: leans forward and uncrosses arms and legs or raises one forefinger	disagrees
3. leans back, crosses arms and legs or leans back, arms and legs uncrossed	is ready to listen again

EXERCISE 11B PAGE 102 ... the reactions of the listener to the ideas of the speaker can be analyzed by observing the listener's physical moves

EXERCISE 12A PAGE 102
1. A, C, D
2. B, E, F

EXERCISE 12B PAGE 103 A(S), B(G), C(G), D(S), E(G), F(S)

EXERCISE 13 PAGE 103

Causes	Effects
1. We stare at scenery	We give nonhuman status
2. We stare at people	We give nonhuman status

3. We manage our eyes	We classify as human or nonhuman
	or
	We make or break a person
4. We stare at art	We give nonhuman status
5. We stare at animals	We give nonhuman status
6. We do not stare at people	We give human status

Section Four—Power Through Reference

THE DICTIONARY

The purpose of this section is to help you to gain familiarity with the dictionary entry by focusing on one portion of the entry at a time. In learning to use the pronunciation aids, it is very important—as it was in the word recognition section—that you pronounce all the words aloud.

EXERCISE 7B PAGE 113
1. v.tr, 3
2. n., 7
3. n., 3
4. n., 5b
5. n., 10
6. v. intr., 3
7. n., 4
8. n., 4

THE NEWSPAPER

EXERCISE 9 PAGE 115
1. Butch Cassidy's sister, Mrs. Lula Parker Betensen
2. Robert LeRoy Parker
3. He worked in a butcher shop.
4. Utah
5. Nineteenth and twentieth
6. Robin Hood
7. A. His visit to New York City; his migration to South America; inclusion of the school teacher in the story
   B. The circumstances of his death

EXERCISE 10 PAGE 118
1. A. Lowering the legal age for drinking to 18
2. A. It is nonsense to deprive young people of the remaining elements of adult status.
   B. Extension of rights of adulthood can encourage broader exercise of responsibility.
   C. Contributions of young people will be no less than the trust placed in them.
3. The writer anticipates three opposing arguments:
   A. If rights are extended, young people will in turn be denied special legal privileges traditionally given them.
      Answer: Option provided to refer immature convicts up to age 21 to Youth Authority.
   B. Granting the right to drink at 18 will add to the problem of the use of

alcohol and drugs among the very young.
Answer: Keeping the drinking age at 21 will not help this problem. The writer implies that the two are unrelated.
C. Granting more rights of adulthood will increase militancy and radicalism.
Answer: See answer to 2B.

EXERCISE 13 PAGE 126
A. II
B. ten
C. meter
D. Latin, Greek
E.

	Column I Latin		Column II Greek	
1. deci	ten	deca	ten
2. centi	one-hundredth	herto	one hundred
3. milli	one-thousandth	kilo	one thousand
4. —	—	myria	ten thousand

F. 1. meter - length
2. liter - capacity
3. gram - weight
G. 1. meter
2. divide
3. 1/10, 1/100, 1/1000
4. 39.37; 39.37; 3.93
5. 36; 39.37
6. less than
7. 1000
8. 5,280; 12; 63,360; 39.37; 1,000; 39,370
9. shorter

Section Five—The Power of Suggestion

EXERCISE 2 PAGE 133
1. salesman = hound
2. fog = blanket
3. darkness = large animal
4. student = pirate
5. bad moves = torpedoes
6. children = apes
7. problem = cloud
8. clouds = shroud
9. fighter = pepper shaker
10. fullback = knife
fullback = animal that eats without pausing between mouthfuls

EXERCISE 3 PAGES 133–134
1. scoured
2. barks
3. gulped
4. underlined
5. shouldered
6. closeted
7. threaded
8. spelled
9. hopscotched
10. rained

213

EXERCISE 4 PAGE 134

	x = y	Words Formula Explains
1.	Tree trunks = people	standing grey and still, took no notice
2.	election = boxing match	bout, arena, slugger, puncher
3.	rodeo = person	bowlegged with fatigue, covered with saddle-sores, brimming with life
4.	costume = cake or some other prepared dish	mixture, recipe, casserole, left-overs
5.	U.S. = elephant	beast, twitch, grunt
6.	houses = people	squatted, elbow to elbow, pushing for room, trying to keep from being pushed
7.	birch trees = young girls on hands and knees	that throw their hair before them over their heads to dry in the sun
8.	her conversation on a particular topic = a train on an open track	stop, junction, swamp, roll majestically into the station

EXERCISE 5 PAGE 135

1. The writer is talking about race car drivers he has known who have been killed racing.
4. A. Indianapolis is like a ballroom after the music stops.
   Indianapolis is like Cinderella back at the ashes.
   Jimmy Clark was pale and frail like his racer.
   B. Eddie Sachs = leprechaun in goggles
   Eddie Sachs = the sprite of the speedway
   C. *deep throated* roar, *wasp* whine, *cannon-cracker* snapping
5. A. The presence of race driver, now dead, is always felt at Indianapolis.
   B. Everyone has to die sometime.
6. Paragraph 1: Only highly trained drivers should be allowed to be pace drivers at Indy.
   Paragraph 2: Abandoned cars should be removed from the track.

Section V
1. And pace the race cars with someone who knows what they are doing.
2. Like any other self-respecting freeway, there should be no parking.
or
Cars without people in them should not be on the track.
Generalization: The very least the drivers—and the public—are entitled to is a management which sees to it that the things it can control are controlled.
or
Lord knows the one thing Indy doesn't need is more danger.

EXERCISE 7 PAGE 140

1. A. movie musicals = people
      Movie musicals are no longer childish with subject matter based on fantasy but are concerned with real life.
   B. Germany = a person
      Germany was rocking back and forth between stable ground and Nazism
   C. M.C. = needle
      The M.C. pricks the minds of the audience with *sharp* remarks.

    D. *Cabaret* = mirror
　　　It gives us a picture of ourselves.
2. Some successful musicals of the past years have been: Oklahoma, The Sound of Music, My Fair Lady, Camelot, Fiddler on the Roof.

Section Six—Power Through Integration

EXERCISE 5
PAGES 168–171

1. Studies emphasizing the importance of heredity
2. Eugenics
3. By checking bold type and italics
4 and 5. These questions involve definitions that are more difficult to find than those in Exercise 4. The terms are mentioned in the text and you must deduce (figure out) their meanings by information given in the text. *Selective breeding* is mentioned on page 169, Col. 1. Your definition will have to be expressed in your own words. *Variable* is used on page 169, Col. 3. The situations described in the three preceding paragraphs are instances of variables. The dictionary, along with these examples, can aid you in working out a reasonable definition. You will be held responsible for this type of definition in study-reading just as much as those for which a precise definition is given in the text.
6. Understanding of the terms *genotype* and *phenotype*.
7. Section I
8. In the glossary
10. It illustrates a general principle by showing you how the principle works in a real-life situation.

EXERCISE 6
PAGES 171–173

1. true
2. true
3. false
4. A group of people having social and economic conditions in common

EXERCISE 7A
PAGES 174–177

1. *fraternal twins*—children of the same parents, conceived and born at approximately the same time.
2. *identical twins*—children from a single ovum, fertilized by a single sperm.
3. *siblings*—children of the same parents.

EXERCISE 7B
PAGES 177–184

(1) a chart
(2) a summary
1. A
2. C
3. B

215

EXERCISE 11 PAGE 195 prison farm, forest, winter, Southern, first, possible observations: pot bellied stove, mention of Bing Crosby as an active star, mention of Evening in Paris perfume which was popular in the thirties.

EXERCISE 12 PAGE 196
    I. stated   page 188, ll. 45–47
    II. stated   page 189, l. 140
    III. implied   page 191, ll. 251–253
    IV. stated   page 192, l. 298
    V. stated   page 192, l. 315
    VI. stated   page 194, ll. 379–380
    VII. implied   page 194, ll. 386–389
    VIII. implied   page 194, ll. 409–411
    IX. implied   page 194, ll. 406–407

Appendix B

Insert for Instructor

Section I   Spelling   CVC Pattern

Following are the words to be dictated for spelling on page 17. This drill can be helpful for the student in developing auditory discrimination. It can provide the instructor with a diagnostic tool that can point up confusion between specific vowels such as *i* and *e*, or *o* and *u*, or difficulty with recognition of particular consonant teams.

I.
- winch
- stomp
- stump
- rasp
- hush
- clod
- stint
- glint
- hasp
- wench

II.
- glum
- filch
- wilt
- cleft
- smut
- trek
- wend
- broth
- bland
- prod

III.
- rift
- pelt
- wisp
- josh
- lilt
- welt
- sprint
- grid
- gild
- sulk
- cult
- conch
- posh
- grist

IV.
- engulf
- consent
- reflex
- unclench
- uncanny
- abject
- contempt
- disrupt
- refract
- admonish

Appendix to Section One

Word Recognition Generalizations

SPELLING PATTERNS (NUMBERS 1, 4, 5, 6, and 8)

GENERALIZATION 1

CVC Pattern

The most common pattern in the English language is consonant-vowel-consonant. This pattern is found in hundreds of one-syllable words and is a part of hundreds more multi-syllable words. In all patterns the symbol *C* is considered to be a consonant whether it is a single consonant or two or more consonants pronounced together. In the *CVC* pattern the vowel is pronounced as you say it in the following words:*

REFERENCE WORDS

a as in *hat* and in *flat*
e as in *bed* and in *trench*
i as in *sit* and in *skin*
o as in *hot* and in *shot*
u as in *jump* and in *brush*

GENERALIZATION 4

CVCe Pattern

When the *CVC* pattern is followed by an *e* (*CVCe*), the vowel between the consonants is given the sound that the letter is given when spoken alone—as in reciting the alphabet.

EXAMPLES:

a as in *blame*
e as in *Pete*
i as in *ride*
o as in *stone*
u as in *cube or rude*

GENERALIZATION 5

CVVC Pattern

When two vowels appear together framed by two consonants (*CVVC*), individual teams of vowels usually have the sounds that you give to the teams when you say the words listed below.

* *R* following a vowel puts a word into another pattern.

219

EXAMPLES:

ea	as in	*team*	*ow*	as in	*cow**
oa	as in	*boat*	*oi*	as in	*boil*
ai	as in	*wait*	*oy*	as in	*boy**
ay	as in	*stay**	*au*	as in	*fraud*
ou	as in	*house*	*aw*	as in	*crawl*

GENERALIZATION 6

CVrC Pattern

A vowel followed by *r* usually has a different sound than when it is followed by any other letter. The following words illustrate the most common sounds for each vowel in the *CVrC* pattern.

EXAMPLES:

ar	as in	*car***
er	as in	*term*
ir	as in	*bird*
or	as in	*Ford*
ur	as in	*curl*

GENERALIZATION 8

The Reduced Vowel

When any of the five vowels appears in an unaccented syllable, it may have a sound that is similar to the sound "uh" as heard in the first *a* in *away*. This is known as the *reduced vowel*. Most dictionaries indicate this sound by the symbol ə called the *schwa*.

EXAMPLES:

a	as in	*ago*
e	as in	*open*
i	as in	*sanity*
o	as in	*contain*
u	as in	*focus*

GUIDELINES FOR BREAKING WORDS INTO SYLLABLES (NUMBERS 2, 3, AND 7)

GENERALIZATION 2

A syllable is a part of a word that can be pronounced; it must contain a vowel. Prefixes and suffixes are usually considered separate syllables and do not affect the manner in which a word is divided for pronunciation.

EXAMPLE:

	prefix	*CVC*
inspect	in	spect

* Sometimes a pattern will be incomplete—*CVV* instead of *CVVC*—but the sound of the vowel team is the same.

** Although this pattern often may not have another consonant following *r*, as in *car* and *for*, it remains a *CVrC* pattern. The important thing to remember is that the *r* affects the response given to the vowel. The initial or final consonant may also be omitted in syllables of words of more than one syllable.

EXAMPLE:

	₵VrC	CCr₵
armor	ar	mor

GENERALIZATION 3

When two separately sounded consonants appear between two sounded vowels, words are usually divided between the consonants for the purposes of pronunciation.
EXAMPLE:

CVC *CVC*
mas   cot

GENERALIZATION 7

CV Pattern

When *one* consonant appears between two sounded vowels, the word is usually divided before the consonant for the purposes of pronunciation.
EXAMPLE:

hu man

a. When a word has been separated into syllables for the purposes of pronunciation according to the above generalization, the vowel at the end of a syllable will usually be pronounced as the vowel is pronounced when referred to as a letter.
EXAMPLE:

va   por
fe   tus
vi   brate
mo   sa ic
Cu   ban

b. There are many exceptions to this generalization, but always try it first. If your response to it does not produce a word that sounds right to you, break the word so that the first syllable forms the *CVC* pattern (habit; hab it). Your response to the vowel will then be the usual response to the vowel in that pattern.
EXAMPLE:

panic   pan ic

Consonants

Common Beginning Consonant Teams in English Words

bl	fr	qu	sn	sw
br	gl	sc	sp	th
ch	gr	scr	spl	thr
chr	gn	sh	spr	tr
cl	kn	shr	squ	tw
cr	ph	sk	st	wh
dr	pl	sl	str	wr
fl	pr	sm		

Listed below are a few consonants or pairs of consonants that call for some unexpected responses. You probably know them and respond to them with ease in words you already know.

1. *wr* Listen to yourself as you pronounce the word *wrong*. You are responding to *wr* as if it were *r*.
2. *ph* Say this sentence to yourself. "Will you phone me when you get home, Bill?" You probably responded to *ph* as if it were *f*.
3. *g* Say *gentlemen*, *ginger*, and *gem*. You are responding to *g* as if it were *j*. This is the most common response in English to *g* before *i* or *e*. In other instances the response is the same as is heard in *garden*. Listen to these two sounds in *gigantic*.
4. *c* Now say, "This pretty Christmas ornament is only twenty cents." Of course you pronounced the *c* in *cents* the same as the *s*. *C* before *i*, *e*, or *y* is pronounced like *s*. In other situations *c* is pronounced like *k*. Listen to yourself make two responses to *c* as you pronounce these two words that have been broken into syllables:

      (a) concert   con   cert
      (b) concentric   con   cen   tric

5. *th* Say *then* and *think*. Can you hear the slight difference in the two responses to *th*?
6. *qu* Say the word *quick*. *Q* in English is always followed by *u* and calls for a response as if the spelling were *kw*.
7. *sc* *Sc* is sometimes pronounced like *s* and sometimes like *sk*. You have made these responses many times in the common words *science* and *scandal*.
8. *ch* and *sh* Some students have difficulty hearing the difference between *ch* and *sh*. *Ch* is heard twice in the word *church*. A good example of *sh* is heard in the words *shut* and *show*. Sometimes *ch* is pronounced like *k*, as you pronounced it in the word *Christmas* in number 4 above, or like *sh*, as in *chef*.
9. *kn*, *gn*, and *pn* are each pronounced like *n*. Listen to yourself say *knee*, *gnaw*, and *pneumonia*.